D1527878

Economic Restructuring of the American Midwest

Economic Restructuring of the American Midwest

Proceedings of the Midwest Economic Restructuring
Conference of the Federal Reserve Bank of Cleveland

edited by

Richard D. Bingham

and

Randall W. Eberts

KLUWER ACADEMIC PUBLISHERS
Boston/Dordrecht/London

Distributors for North America:
Kluwer Academic Publishers
101 Philip Drive
Assinippi Park
Norwell, Massachusetts 02061 USA

Distributors for all other countries:
Kluwer Academic Publishers Group
Distribution Centre
Post Office Box 322
3300 AH Dordrecht, THE NETHERLANDS

Library of Congress Cataloging-in-Publication Data

Midwest Economic Restructuring Conference (1988 : Cleveland, Ohio)
    Economic restructuring of the American Midwest : proceedings of
the Midwest Economic Restructuring Conference of the Federal
Reserve Bank of Cleveland / edited by Richard D. Bingham
and Randall W. Eberts.
      p.   cm.
   Conference held Oct. 1988 in Cleveland, Ohio.
   Includes bibliographical references.
   ISBN 0-7923-9066-0
   1. Middle West — Economic policy — Case studies —
   Congresses.
   I. Bingham, Richard D.   II. Eberts, Randall W.   III. Federal
Reserve Bank of Cleveland.   IV. Title.
HC107.A14M514   1988
338.977 — dc20   89-26940
                                      CIP

Printed in the United States of America.

Contents

Contributing Authors

David R. Allardice
Vice President
Federal Reserve Bank of Chicago
Chicago, Illinois   60604

Richard D. Bingham
Professor of Public Administration and Urban Studies
Urban Center
Cleveland State University
Cleveland, Ohio   44115

John P. Blair
Professor of Economics
Wright State University
Dayton, Ohio   45431

Terry F. Buss
Professor of Urban Studies
University of Akron
Akron, Ohio   44325

Randall W. Eberts
Assistant Vice President and Economist
Federal Reserve Bank of Cleveland
Cleveland, Ohio   44101

Rudy Fichtenbaum
Associate Professor of Economics
Wright State University
Dayton, Ohio   45431

Joan Fitzgerald
Assistant Professor
City and Regional Planning
Ohio State University
Columbus, Ohio   43210

David Gemmel
Research Associate
St. Elizabeth Hospital Medical Center
Youngstown, Ohio   44505

W. Richard Goe
Center for Economic Development
School of Urban and Public Affairs
Carnegie Mellon University
Pittsburgh, Pennsylvania   15213

Edward W. Hill
Associate Professor of Urban Studies and Public Administration
Maxine Goodman Levin College of Urban Affairs
Cleveland State University
Cleveland, Ohio   44115

Robert Kraushaar
Director
Bureau of Economic and Demographic Information of the New York State
Department of
Economic Development
Buffalo, New York   14202

James R. Paetsch
Program Analyst
Wisconsin Legislative Audit Bureau
Madison, Wisconsin   53703

David C. Perry
Department of Urban Studies and Public Service
Cleveland State University
Cleveland, Ohio   44115

James L. Shanahan
Director
The Center for Urban Studies
University of Akron
Akron, Ohio   44325

Kenneth P. Voytek
Center for Local Economic Competitiveness
Michigan Department of Commerce
Detroit, Michigan   48201

Michael Wasylenko
Associate Director
Metropolitan Studies Program
Maxwell School of Syracuse University
Syracuse, New York   13210

Sammis B. White
Director
Urban Research Center
University of Wisconsin — Milwaukee
Milwaukee, Wisconsin   53201

Wim Wiewel
Director
Center for Urban Economic Development
School of Urban Planning and Policy
University of Illinois at Chicago
Chicago, Illinois   60612

Wendy Wintermute
Center for Urban Economic Development
University of Illinois at Chicago
Chicago, Illinois   60612

Harold Wolman
Professor of Political Science
Wayne State University
Detroit, Michigan   48202

This book represents the analyses and conclusions of the individual authors and does not necessarily reflect those of their affiliate institutions.

Economic Restructuring of the American Midwest

1 OVERVIEW

Richard D. Bingham and Randall W. Eberts

As we approach the twenty-first century, the United States' economy is undergoing a fundamental transformation, affecting the nature of jobs and work. This transformation has long been recognized in both the economic literature (Fuchs, 1965) and in the popular press (Bell, 1973).

In 1959, the goods-producing sector of the economy accounted for 40 percent of employment. By 1984, it had dropped to 28 percent (although actual employment increased from 27.1 million to 29.6 million). The non-goods-producing sector, on the other hand, increased its share of employment from 60 percent to 72 percent over the same period, providing 37 million new jobs (Waite, 1988). We are now at the point where services, broadly defined as all activities outside of goods and commodities production, account for about 75 percent of U.S. employment.

But the economic transformation was more than just a simple movement from manufacturing to services. Significant restructuring was taking place within manufacturing industries as well. For example, Kutscher (1988) shows that between 1969 and 1984, the number of durable goods industries with negative output and employment trends almost equalled the number of durable goods industries with positive trends.

Most areas of the country were handling this transition fairly well —

at least through 1979. But the 1980 to 1982 recessions did not hit all areas of the country equally.[1] While Texas was experiencing a boom, Michigan's unemployment rate rose from 7.8 percent to 15.5 percent, and earnings of its residents declined by 23.2 percent in real terms during the period (Wolman and Voytek, 1989, p. 1).

By 1986, it became apparent that the traditional postrecession recovery had not occurred everywhere. For example, manufacturing employment in Cleveland never returned to its prerecession levels. A fundamental restructuring had occurred. These changes were most apparent in some of the regional economies of the Midwest, although they have been only vaguely understood.

1. Purpose of the Book

The purpose of this book is to document this fundamental restructuring in the economies of various Midwest regions. Each chapter is a case study of one particular regional economy. The regions, comprised of metropolitan areas, were selected not at random but as representative of the trends taking place in the Midwest.

The reason we elected to analyze regions within states instead of states or larger geographic areas was that regional economies within states are known to be very different from one another. Thus the study of larger areas may mask a great deal of the activity and the shifting that is occurring within local economies. This has been clearly true in Pennsylvania. Jacobson (1988) shows that the Pennsylvania economy is really two economies: the thriving economy of the East and the declining economy of the West. This knowledge led us to develop this book, which focuses on representative regional economies.

The book consists of a unique effort by a group of researchers throughout the Midwest to utilize similar detailed databases to analyze their regional economies and to follow a similar format in developing their chapters. Thus it is easy for the reader to follow the description provided and to understand better the variations in the regional economies of the areas studied.

The unique database made available for this project came from employment and payroll records from each enterprise or firm operating in the various economic regions. The database covers 1979 through 1986. The data are derived from state administrative records, specifically ES202 reports.

ES202 records are part of the Bureau of Labor Statistics (BLS) program to enumerate employment and payroll by industry for each U.S. county. (ES202 is the name of a form sent to the BLS.) This program breaks down employment and payroll of enterprises into Standard Industrial Classification (SIC) county cells and assigns the SIC and location codes to all firms. This level of detail provides an excellent opportunity to analyze the underlying structural changes that are obscured by looking at more aggregated numbers.

The Bureau of Labor Statistics uses ES202 data furnished by the states to publish annual descriptions of the number of reporting units, employment, and payroll by industry and county. These Bureau of Labor Statistics data have become increasingly popular for analysis when compared to other data sources. For example, Dun and Bradstreet data have been widely used for micro-level analysis of employment and structural change; however, recent studies have called into question their coverage and accuracy (Howland, 1988).

ES202 has become increasingly attractive as coverage has expanded over the years to include virtually all employers. A problem in attempting to work with the BLS published reports, however, is that the level of ES202 reported by the BLS is only taken down to the industry group. This is done to preserve the confidentiality of the reports. In other works, in some cases, a listing of the number of employees in a BLS area by industry would cover only one firm, so the employment and payroll of that firm would be known to all who are interested. While the BLS does not make ES202 data available at the industry level, many states, under certain conditions that will preserve confidentiality, will do so.

For this project, most of the authors were able to obtain ES202 data from 1979 through 1986 for their regions from their state offices. This rich data set allowed for a detailed analysis of industries and gave researchers an opportunity to view the restructuring of the economy over time through a nearly complete business cycle. It allowed them to distinguish between industry restructuring and industrial recovery.

Authors did not analyze all employment within their regions, only manufacturing and service-producing industries. Those economic activities not covered are agriculture, forestry, fishing, hunting and trapping, mining, and construction. For major metropolitan areas, agricultural activities and mining do not contribute substantially to employment. Construction was not included because it is not necessarily part of the restructuring, but rather may be a symptom of the restructuring within a local economy. Our concern is strictly with manufacturing and services.

2. Organization of the Chapters

Each of the individual studies that follows contains, first, a background or introduction that briefly describes the metropolitan area in terms of its 1980 census characteristics, such as population and socioeconomic status. The section then describes the employment position of the major industrial divisions as of 1979 and the changes through 1986. In addition, many of the chapters present location quotients for both 1979 and 1986 to give the reader a basic overview of the relative concentration of industries within these regions and the changes in concentration over time.

Location quotients provide a simple way to look at the structure of a regional economy. They measure the concentration of industries by relating an industry's share in total regional employment to its share of total national employment. By expressing this relationship in a ratio, a quotient exceeding 1 indicates that a region's employment share in the industry is greater than the national share, which can be interpreted to mean that the region specializes in that industry.

As an example, we take the case of the hospital industry in Cleveland. In 1985, total employment in the Cleveland PMSA and in the nation was 762,293 and 81,119,257, respectively. Total hospital employment in Cleveland and the nation was 39,023 and 2,943,749. Thus, hospital share of Cleveland's employment was 0.051 (39,023/762,293), and hospital share of national employment was 0.036 (2,943,749/81,119,257). The location quotient is the ratio of these two percentages and is equal to 1.42 (0.051/ 0.036). The location quotient for Cleveland's hospital industry was substantially greater than 1, indicating that in 1985, Cleveland had a significant specialization in this industry.

The location quotient is a fairly simple tool, but it is quite useful. We know that it was not merely the Midwest that restructured between 1979 and 1986; the nation as a whole underwent industrial restructuring. Changes in the regional location quotients, however, allow us to see how each of the regional economies under study here restructured *relative* to the national economy.

Another section of each chapter classifies manufacturing industries by major industry groups into four categories according to their growth/decline pattern in employment from 1979 through 1986. The categories of growth and decline are: (1) continuous decline over the entire period; (2) decline until about 1983 or 1984, then level performance or recovery; (3) relatively little change during the period; and (4) growth industries, that is, industries that have grown during the entire period. Given the fact that a significant amount of change has occurred within the various regions, discussion has been limited to industries having 500 or more employees at the end of the period.

The chapters also identify what are termed the "hidden trend-breakers." A hidden trend-breaker is an industry or industry group that goes against the overall trend of the major industrial group. Employment in miscellaneous plastic products in Akron, Ohio, provides an example. Miscellaneous Plastic Products (SIC 307) is one component of the major group Rubber and Miscellaneous Plastic Products (SIC 30). In the chapter "Akron, Ohio: Regional Economy at the Turning Point," James Shanahan and Richard Goe report that Rubber and Miscellaneous Plastic Products lost 10,876 jobs in Akron between 1979 and 1986. But they also report 842 new jobs over the period in Miscellaneous Plastic Products. Miscellaneous Plastic Products thus broke the employment trend of its major group. Identifying such trend-breakers assists significantly in understanding restructuring. It also points up the importance of analyzing the regional economies in a high level of detail.

The chapters then compare average earnings of the four categories identified in the second section above. The question all authors seek to answer is: Are manufacturing earnings in growing industries as "good" as those in declining industries? Average earnings are simply the total payroll reported by all of the firms within an industry in the region divided by total employees in the industry.

Next begins the discussion of services. We have classified services by slightly modifying a typology developed by Browning and Singelmann (1978). Browning and Singelmann originally described four major categories of services: distributive services, producer services, social services, and personal services. To aid in better understanding the transformation of local economies for our purposes, we have broken down distributive services into two components: (1) transportation and (2) wholesale and retail. Service sector analysis thus covers five categories: transportation, wholesale and retail, producer services, social services, and personal services. This classification is shown in table 1–1.

In the service sector section of each chapter, employment change in the same four categories as described for manufacturing will be documented. Again, authors will classify services as (1) continuous decline, (2) decline then level of recovery, (3) little change, and (4) continuous growth. As with manufacturing, service industries with fewer than 500 employees will not be discussed.

Hidden trend-breakers are also indentified within the service sector. Discussion is also limited to service industries with 500 or more employees at the end of the period.

Table 1–1. Operationalization of Expanding Browning and Singelmann
Typology of the Service Sector

Sector	SIC Code
Transportation Services	40-42, 44-47
Wholesale and Retail Services	
Wholesale	50-51
Retail	52-57, 59
Producer Services	
Communication, Electric, Gas, and Sanitary	48-49
Banking	60-62
Insurance	63-64
Real Estate	65-66
Engineering and Architecture	891
Accounting	893
Miscellaneous Business Services	67, 73, 892, 899
Legal Services	81
Social Services	
Medical Services	801-805, 807-809
Hospitals	806
Education	82
Welfare	832
Nonprofit	86
Postal Services	43
Government	91-97
Miscellaneous Social Services	833-839
Personal Services	
Domestic Services	88
Hotels	70
Eating and Drinking	58
Repair	725, 753, 76
Laundry	721
Barber and Beauty Shop	723-724
Entertainment	78-79, 84
Miscellaneous Personal Services	722, 725-729, 751, 752, 754

Source: Browning and Singelmann (1978).

Average earnings of the four categories of service industries are then
compared to answer the question: Are the earnings in growing services
as high as those in declining sectors?

In the next section, the authors examine the relationship between
change in the job structure of manufacturing and change in the job struc-

ture of services. Is the growth in service sector jobs keeping pace with the loss of manufacturing jobs, and are earnings in growing service industries, especially in producer services, as high as the earnings in declining manufacturing sectors?

In addition, many authors will use shift-share analysis to analyze changes in regional growth. In shift-share analysis, growth is divided into three components. The analysis begins by identifying the aggregate national growth rate for all employment. This is the region's "share" of national employment growth. Thus, if the national growth rate for a period was 4 percent, then one would expect the region to "share" this national growth of 4 percent (Houston, 1967; Ashby, 1968).

The remaining growth represents a net "shift" to the region. For given industry groups, this shift can be due to: (1) the compositional mix, or to (2) competitive position. Compositional-mix growth occurs because the region has a favorable distribution of fast-growing industries. (The national growth rates of these industries are higher than the aggregate national growth rate.) The competitive positive growth is from the fact that the region's industries are growing faster than those same industries nationally. Shift-share thus has three effects: a national growth effect, an industry-mix effect, and a competitive effect.

To understand how shift-share is computed and interpreted, we have taken information on health services from Edward Hill's chapter on Cleveland. Actual employment in health services in the Cleveland Metropolitan Statistical Area (MSA) increased by 12,189 between 1979:1 and 1983:1. But, this increase occurred at a time when the national growth rate was negative. The aggregate national growth rate for total private employment over the 1979 to 1983 period was −0.3 percent. Employment in health services in Cleveland for the base year (1979) was 52,852. Thus the employment share of the national growth was −159 (52,852 × −0.003).

But we knew from ES202 data that actual employment in health services had increased. The health services industry nationally was an extremely strong growth industry. To determine how much of the local employment change in health services was due to industry mix in the Cleveland area in shift-share, we subtract the national growth rate (−0.3 percent) from the national growth rate for the industry (20.9 percent), thus preventing double counting, and multiply by employment in the base year. Thus employment change in Cleveland due to industry mix is 11,205 jobs.

The competitive effect is simply the residual. It is national growth, plus industry mix, minus the actual employment changes, or (−159 + 11,205) − 12,189 = −1,143.

Finally, each chapter ends with a theoretical discussion. We are searching for theoretical explanations of what has occurred. All authors have been asked to give some thought to an explanation grounded in regional economic theory that might explain their findings.

Within the broad guidelines thus identified, authors have been encouraged to be innovative. Thus the chapters are structurally similar, but the format is not stifling and repetitive. For example, John Blair and Rudy Fichtenbaum, in describing Dayton, and Edward Hill, in describing Cleveland, have used an interesting scheme for classifying manufacturing and services as declining, cyclical, and noncyclical; stable, cyclical, and noncyclical; and growing, cyclical, and noncyclical. This approach has proven to be an effective way to distinguish between restructuring and the effects of the business cycle. Each chapter, therefore, has its unique points, and the authors' extensive knowledge of their regions provides interesting stories and insights.

Following these case studies is a concluding chapter that attempts to draw together the common elements of the case studies and to provide the editors' explanations for what has occurred. The chapter concludes with some thoughts about the future development of the various regional economies covered in this book.

2 AKRON, OHIO: REGIONAL ECONOMY AT THE TURNING POINT

James L. Shanahan and W. Richard Goe

Throughout most of the twentieth century the city of Akron, Ohio, has been known as the "Rubber Capital of the World," reflecting the dominion of the rubber industry in the region's economy. Primarily linked to the development of the automobile industry, the growth of the rubber industry elevated Akron to a prominent role in the global economy as a manufacturing center for automobile tires and rubber products. Given the centrality of the automobile to the post-World War II economic expansion in the United States, the Akron region enjoyed a relatively prolonged period of economic growth and stability. Beginning in the late 1970s, however, the region's economy entered a period of wrenching structural change.

In a span of approximately four years, all of the Akron region's tire production plants were phased out and shut down. The core of the region's traditional economic base was uprooted, and the effects rippled through the economy, resulting in severe losses of manufacturing jobs. In a pattern corresponding to the nation as a whole, the Akron economy simultaneously enjoyed steady growth in its service sector industries. However, as recently as 1988, the job growth in the service sector had yet to offset fully the net loss of manufacturing jobs.

9

The future outlook for the Akron region is largely one of uncertainty. While new paths for the resurgence of Akron's economy have appeared, the growth of new industries necessary for a full economic recovery is gradual in coming. Only the outlines of an economic resurgence are visible. The purpose of this chapter is to examine the structural change in the Akron regional economy in order to gauge how far it has progressed along the course of economic restructuring needed to ensure economic prosperity in the future.

The chapter is divided into three primary sections. The first section briefly traces the historical development of Akron's economy and examines factors that contributed to the recent structural economic shifts. The second section is a quantitative analysis of the structural shifts in the Akron regional economy during the 1979 to 1986 period. The first part of the analysis focuses on structural shifts in the manufacturing sector and examines which industries have grown, declined, or remained stable. The second part performs a similar analysis for the service sector industries. The question is examined as to whether new service sector jobs are providing adequate replacements for those lost in the manufacturing sector. Finally, the third section of the chapter discusses factors that are shaping the future course of economic development in the Akron region.

1. Economic Restructuring and the Historical Development of the Akron Regional Economy

The severity of the post-1970 structural change in Akron's economy is without historical precedent. Prior to this point, the decline of historically important industries coincided with the growth of other industries. This mitigated any disruptive effects associated with structural economic shifts. Akron was founded in 1825 as a small mercantile port along the newly constructed Ohio Canal. The city was a natural site for milling operations, which developed into the fledgling cereals industry in the mid-1850s.

Akron-based entrepreneurs also played an active role in the growth of the farm machinery industry in the mid-1860s. By the turn of the century, however, the center for both of these industries shifted away from the city. By 1927, remaining branch plants for farm machinery were closed. Akron remained a branch location for the Quaker Oats Company until 1971 when the last cereal plants were closed.

The decline of these early industries was buffered and offset by rapid growth within the rubber industry, which was established in the city in

1870 with the formation of Goodrich, Tew & Company. Between 1870 and the 1970s, the city became the Rubber Capital of the World, home to the "Big Four" tire manufacturers — Goodyear, Firestone, B.F. Goodrich, and General Tire & Rubber.

By the mid-1970s, a combination of changing production technology, labor problems, and shifts in world economic conditions resulted in corporate restructuring strategies that eventually shifted tire production away from Akron and markedly changed the structure of the Akron regional economy.

The extent of this change can be seen in a comparison of location quotients (LQs) across industries between 1979 and 1986. The LQ for Rubber and Miscellaneous Plastics Products (SIC 30) dropped markedly over this time period. Simultaneously, the LQs for 12 of the remaining 16 major groups in manufacturing increased (see appendix table A-1). The LQ for the manufacturing sector as a whole increased slightly between 1979 and 1986. This was attributable to an increase in the importance of durable goods industries in the Akron economy, especially Miscellaneous Manufacturing Industries (SIC 39), Transportation Equipment (SIC 37), and Fabricated Metal Products (SIC 34). Overall, however, the increases in LQs within Akron's manufacturing sector is not a reflection of the growing competitiveness of Akron's firms in these industries. Rather, it is due to the rates of growth in Akron's service sector industries being insufficient to replace the manufacturing losses between 1979 and 1986. As will be seen in the next section, total employment remains lower than the 1979 level.

The LQ for Akron's entire service sector increased only slightly more than that for the manufacturing sector between 1979 and 1986 (see table 2-1). While the LQs of most major groups in the service sector increased, only several gained a larger share in the Akron economy compared to the national share (LQ>1.0). These were: Automotive Dealers and Service Stations (SIC 55); Eating and Drinking Places (SIC 58); and Auto Repair, Services, and Garages (SIC 75). The three major groups with LQs greater than 1.0 in 1979 — Trucking and Warehousing (SIC 42), Amusement and Recreation Services (SIC 79), and Membership Organizations (SIC 86) — all became less important in the Akron economy as their LQs decreased between 1979 and 1986.

The analysis of LQs indicates that while economic restructuring in the Akron region has involved substantial losses of manufacturing jobs, the structure of the regional economy has continued to be largely dominated by manufacturing industries. While increasing in importance in terms of employment, service sector industries continue to play a smaller role in

Table 2-1. Nonagricultural Employment in the Akron Region, 1979 to 1986

	1979	1983	1986	Net Change 1979–1983	Percent Change 1979–1983	Net Change 1979–1986	Percent Change 1979–1986
Construction	10,640	7,711	10,053	(2,929)	−27.5	(587)	−5.5
Manufacturing	94,337	72,189	74,717	(22,148)	−23.5	(19,620)	−20.8
Transportation and Public Utilities	16,121	13,511	13,948	(2,610)	−16.2	(2,173)	−13.5
Wholesale Trade	13,477	13,277	15,204	(200)	−1.5	1,727	12.8
Retail Trade	52,226	50,894	56,347	(1,332)	−2.6	4,121	7.9
Finance, Insurance, and Real Estate	11,299	10,895	12,009	(404)	−3.6	710	6.3
Services	54,471	57,625	61,946	3,154	−5.8	7,475	13.7
Government	48,042	45,502	46,619	(2,540)	−5.3	(1,423)	−3.0
Total	300,613	271,604	290,843	(29,009)	−9.6	(9,770)	−3.3

Akron's economy compared to the aggregate national economy. The following section examines employment shifts over the 1979 to 1986 period in finer detail.

2. Quantitative Indicators of Economic Restructuring

2.1 Employment Trends Overview, 1979 to 1986

Between 1979 and 1986, the Akron regional economy (Medina, Portage, and Summit counties) experienced its worst economic recession in recent history. This recession coincided with the twin recessions in the aggregate national economy. An economic downswing began in 1979 and bottomed out by the end of 1983. A recovery phase subsequently began in 1984. By the end of 1986, employment in the Akron region (excluding agriculture) remained 3.3 percent below the 1979 level (see table 2–1). In 1986, total employment in the Akron region stood at 290,843 jobs, compared to 300,613 in 1979.

Employment in the manufacturing sector declined dramatically during 1979–1986 as a net 19,620 jobs were lost (see table 2–1). Substantial employment losses also occurred in transportation and public utilities, and in government and construction, which lost a combined 4,183 additional jobs. Employment gains were realized in wholesale and retail trade, finance, insurance, and real estate, and services. The largest net employment gain was in services where employment increased by 7,475 jobs. Wholesale and retail trade also provided net gains of 1,727 and 4,121 new jobs, respectively.

Despite the large net growth of jobs in retail trade, this industrial division experienced much greater job losses during the recession compared to other growing divisions. The dislocation of over 20,000 manufacturing jobs and the net loss of 6,578 persons from the Akron region between 1980 and 1983 due to outmigration are among the major reasons why retail activities underwent cyclical decline.

Employment decline during the recession (1979 to 1983) was 29,009 jobs or 9.6 percent of the total employment base in the Akron region. Through 1986, only 19,239 or 66.3 percent of these jobs had been recovered. These replacement jobs were largely in different industries and undoubtedly involved different occupations. Over 22,000 manufacturing jobs were lost in the recession and only 2,500 were recovered. Replacement jobs created since the recession have been concentrated primarily in retail trade (5,453), services (4,321), construction (2,342), and wholesale trade (192).

2.2 Manufacturing Employment Trends, 1979 to 1986

From 1979 to 1986, eight major group (two-digit SIC level) within Akron's manufacturing sector suffered net losses in employment. The major proportion of this decline was concentrated in the region's three largest major groups: Rubber and Miscellaneous Plastic Products (SIC 30), Fabricated Metal Products (SIC 34) and Machinery, Except Electrical (SIC 35). Over 18,000 jobs were lost in these three interlinked major groups (see table 2–2). In 1979, the eight declining major groups accounted for 83.2 percent of all manufacturing employment. By 1986, this figure had declined to 75.5 percent of the manufacturing job base.

In contrast, five major groups in the manufacturing sector created net employment growth for Akron between 1979 and 1986: Transportation Equipment (SIC 37), Printing and Publishing (SIC 27), Paper and Allied Products (SIC 26), Miscellaneous Manufacturing (SIC 39), and Furniture and Fixtures (SIC 25). Collectively, these major groups added 3,441 net new jobs. This raised total employment in these expanding groups to 13,661 or 19 percent of all manufacturing jobs (see table 2–3). The largest growth occurred in transportation equipment, which gained 1,602 new jobs. All five of these expanding major groups experienced growth during the recessionary years. Four of these major groups — transportation equipment, printing and publishing, miscellaneous manufacturing, and furniture and fixtures — underwent steady growth throughout the entire 1979 to 1986 period. However, employment in paper and allied products reached its peak during the recession and declined afterwards.

The nation's recession served to accelerate the pace of decline in many of Akron's traditional industries. The vast majority of the manufacturing jobs lost in declining major groups during the recession were lost permanently. However, a few of these groups have since reversed their downward slide and have partially recovered in terms of employment. Machinery, except electric, fabricated metals, chemicals and petroleum products, and food products all had net job growth during the postrecession period. In contrast, rubber and plastics products, stone, clay, and glass products, and electronic equipment continued to experience further decline.

By and large, Akron's major groups in manufacturing that have shown growth are ones that are declining in the state of Ohio. These include transportation equipment, paper products, furniture, and miscellaneous manufacturing. Only printing and publishing, and instruments and related products, were growing in the state as a whole. Employment in all of Akron's declining major groups in manufacturing also declined at the state

Table 2–2. Akron's Declining Major Groups in Manufacturing, 1979 to 1986

SIC Code	Industry Title	1979	1986	Net Change	Percent Decline
29	Petroleum and Coal Products	710	588	(122)	– 17.2
20	Food and Kindred Products	3,615	3,044	(571)	– 15.8
33	Primary Metal Industries	2,061	1,477	(584)	– 28.3
28	Chemicals and Allied Products	4,103	2,957	(1,146)	– 27.9
32	Stone, Clay, and Glass Products	2,817	1,442	(1,375)	– 48.8
34	Fabricated Metal Products	18,326	14,848	(3,478)	– 19.0
35	Machinery, Except Electrical	14,386	10,475	(3,911)	– 27.2
30	Rubber and Misc. Plastics Products	32,473	21,597	(10,876)	– 33.5
	Total	78,491	56,428	(22,063)	– 28.1
	Percent All Manufacturing	83.2	75.5		

Table 2–3.   Akron's Growing and Stable Major Groups in Manufacturing, 1979 to 1986

SIC Code	Industry Title	1979	1986	Net Change	Percent Increase
Growing					
37	Transportation Equipment	4,547	6,149	1,602	35.2
27	Printing and Publishing	3,110	3,769	659	21.2
26	Paper and Allied Products	1,102	1,618	516	46.8
39	Miscellaneous Manufacturing Industries	1,092	1,453	361	33.1
25	Furniture and Fixtures	369	672	303	82.1
	Total	10,220	13,661	3,441	33.7
	Percent All Manufacturing	10.8	18.3		
Stable					
38	Instruments and Related Products	842	843	1	0.1
24	Lumber and Wood Products	386	367	(19)	−4.9

Note: Figure in parentheses represents a net loss in employment between 1979 and 1986.

Source: Ohio Bureau of Employment Services, Labor Market Information Division, Workers Covered Under Ohio Unemployment Compensation Law (202 Series).

level. Fabricated metals, machinery, except electric, and food products suffered greater decline in the state as a whole compared to the Akron region. Decline in Akron was greater for chemicals, stone, clay and glass products, and, of course, for rubber and plastics products.

2.3 A Closer Look At Manufacturing

Using higher-level SIC definitions of industry reveals even finer detail of performance. As described above, the growing major groups (of 500+ employees in 1986) in manufacturing generated a total of 3,442 net new jobs in the region's manufacturing base between 1979 and 1986. The declining major groups (of 500+ employees in 1979) triggered a net loss of 22,063 jobs. On balance, the region suffered a net loss of 18,621 jobs. Or, stated differently, the six growing major groups only replaced one job for every six lost in the eight declining major groups. However, many of these major groups subsume industries that may be diverse in nature and face

Table 2–4. Akron's Growing Industry Groups in Manufacturing with 500 Plus Jobs, 1979 to 1986

SIC Code	Industry Title	1979	1986	Net Change	Percent Increase
372	Aircraft and Parts	3,305*	5,285	1,980	59.9
307	Miscellaneous Plastics Products	3,257	4,099	842	25.9
275	Commercial Printing	1,195	1,959	764	63.9
264	Misc. Converted Paper Products	558	1,015	457	81.9
359	Misc. Machinery, Except Electrical	2,821	3,157	336	11.9
284	Soap, Cleaners, and Toilet Goods	438	610	172	39.3
347	Metal Services, NEC	295	456	161	54.6
208	Beverages	582	702	120	20.6
371	Motor Vehicles and Equipment	820	864	44	5.4
202	Dairy Products	986	1,016	30	3.0
384	Medical Instruments and Supplies	675	688	13	1.9
	Total	14,932	19,851	4,919	32.9
	Percent All Manufacturing	15.8	26.6		

*1980 employment

varying opportunities and threats relative to markets. It is common, therefore, to find varied rates of job growth or decline across the industry groups (three-digit SICs) subsumed beneath them. It is also not uncommon to find one or more industry groups breaking the larger trend for the major group as a whole. Separating the industry groups into growing and declining categories reveals ten manufacturing industry groups (with

Table 2–5. Akron's Declining Industry Groups in Manufacturing with 500 Plus Jobs, 1979 to 1986

SIC Code	Industry Title	1979	1986	Net Change	Percent Decline
336	Nonferrous Foundries	715	665	(50)	−7.0
327	Concrete, Gypsum, and Plaster Products	1,006	673	(333)	−33.1
345	Screw Machine Products, Bolts, etc.	1,027	663	(364)	−35.4
342	Cutlery, Handtools, and Hardware	915	457	(458)	−50.1
356	General Industrial Machinery	1,343	881	(462)	−34.4
326	Pottery and Related Products	783	297	(486)	−62.1
281	Industrial Inorganic Chemicals	1,282	687	(595)	−46.4
306	Fabricated Rubber Products, NEC	3,890	3,122	(768)	−19.7
349	Misc. Fabricated Metal Products	1,955	1,167	(788)	−40.3
355	Special Industry Machinery	2,820	1,518	(1,302)	−46.2
344	Fabricated Structural Metal Products	8,081	6,548	(1,533)	−19.0
353	Construction and Related Machinery	3,230	990	(2,240)	−69.3
301	Tires and Inner Tubes	24,668	14,020	(10,648)	−43.2
	Total	51,715	31,688	(20,027)	−38.7
	Percent All Manufacturing	54.8	42.4		

Note: Figures in parentheses represent a net loss in employment between 1979 and 1986.

Source: Ohio Bureau of Employment Services, Labor Market Information Division, Workers Covered Under Ohio Unemployment Compensation Law (202 Series)

about 500 or more jobs in 1986) that generated employment gains from 1979 to 1986 (see table 2–4). The largest absolute gain was in Aircraft and Parts (SIC 372). This was followed by Miscellaneous Plastics Products (SIC 307) and Commercial Printing (SIC 275). The largest percentage gain was in Miscellaneous Converted Paper Products (SIC 264), which had a growth rate of 81.9 percent. Combined, these ten industry groups added 4,919 jobs to the region's manufacturing base since 1979. These industries now comprise 27 percent of all manufacturing jobs in the Akron region.

Thirteen industry groups with 500 + jobs in 1979 experienced employment losses (see table 2–5). Combined, these industry groups accounted for the loss of 20,027 jobs. Tires and Tubes (SIC 301) accounted for one-half of these lost jobs. As expected, many of the other large declining industry groups are traditional heavy manufacturing industries that have undergone restructuring and decline at the national level. Losses in Akron are only reflections of national trends because of the dominant role these industries have historically played in the nation's economy. On balance, 15,108 jobs were lost. Growing industry groups have replaced one job for every four lost during the last seven years.

2.3.1 What a Difference a Year Makes.   By the end of 1987, dramatic changes had occurred in the positioning of Akron's expanding industry groups in manufacturing. Employment in miscellaneous plastics products increased by 1,079 jobs (a 26 percent increase in one year), while aircraft and parts cut back employment by 449. The net result was that the number 1 and 2 industry groups for job growth since 1979 switched positions, with uncertainty clouding future job gains in aircraft (that is, defense-driven) businesses in Akron. Finally, miscellaneous machinery, except electric, dropped a net 490 jobs during 1987, reversing the fortunes of this industry group from one of growth to one of decline.

3. Trend-Breakers Within the Manufacturing Sector

Four of the growing industry groups are part of a declining major group in the manufacturing sector and, as such, are trend-breakers for the local economy (see table 2–6). In two cases (beverages from the food sector and soap, cleaners, and toilet goods from the chemicals sector), this net growth is likely accounted for by the expansion of several specific local firms into medium-sized businesses. But the other two trend-breakers do reflect the general strengths of numerous smaller firms as well as the national growth trends in these industries.

Table 2–6.   Trend-breakers: Akron's Growing Industry Groups Within Declining Major Groups, 1979 to 1986

SIC Code	Industry Title	1986	1979	Net Change	Percent Change
20	Food and Kindred Products	3,044	3,615	(571)	−15.8
208	Beverages	702	582	120	20.6
28	Chemicals and Allied Products	2,957	4,103	(1,146)	−27.9
284	Soap, Cleaners, and Toilet Goods	610	438	172	39.3
30	Rubber and Misc. Plastics Products	21,597	32,473	(10,876)	−33.5
307	Miscellaneous Plastics Products	4,099	3,257	842	25.9
35	Machinery, Except Electrical	10,475	14,386	(3,911)	−27.2
359	Misc. Machinery, Except Electrical	3,157	2,821	336	11.9
	Total Two-Digit Industry	38,073	54,577	(16,504)	−30.2
	Total Trend Breakers	8,568	7,098	1,470	20.7
	Percent of Declining Industries	22.5	13.0		

Note: Figures in parentheses represent a net loss in employment between 1979 and 1986.

Source: Ohio Bureau of Employment Services, Labor Market Information Division, Workers Covered Under Ohio Unemployment Compensation Law (202 Series).

3.1 Miscellaneous Plastics (SIC 307)

The largest source of jobs within the Rubber and Miscellaneous Plastics Products sector (SIC 30) is Tires and Tubes (SIC 301), where most of the employment of the (former) big four rubber companies is reported. Since 1979, employment in this industry has declined by 43 percent, resulting in a loss of 10,648 jobs. Most of this loss reflects the aforementioned phasing out of rubber-related production as part of the restructuring of corporate and technical operations. Job loss continues year to year due to further corporate restructuring.

What remains in Akron in the way of rubber and plastics production work is of two types: (1) custom processing of Polymer Compounds and Blends (SIC 286) to be used in (2) the making of Intermediate and Final

Goods (SICs 306 and 307). The former is largely provided by large firms (A. Schulman, and Polysar), while the latter includes numerous small- to-medium-sized firms that fabricate rubber or plastic products. From our other studies, we know that over half of these fabricators have fewer than 20 workers (Dustin et al., 1985; Shanahan and Parry, 1986). Most do not have proprietary products, sell to just one market segment, and are suppliers of simple parts to other manufacturers. Often their customers are larger firms based in this area or auto manufacturers outside the region.

At the national level, the plastic products industry has long ago exceeded rubber products in terms of value-added employment and continues to offer the greatest market potential. Major markets for plastics products are durable-goods manufacturers (from autos to appliances) and the electronic equipment and construction industries. All of these industries exhibit cyclical tendencies. Consequently, the modest reduction in jobs in miscellaneous plastics products would be expected during the recession. On balance, however, the net job gain of 26 percent between 1979 and 1986 is quite respectable. This industry provided over 4,000 jobs in the region in 1986.

3.2 Miscellaneous Industrial and Commercial Machinery and Equipment (SIC 359)

This industry group primarily provides machining and repair services to other metalworking firms or to firms using the equipment. In Akron, the group primarily serves the regional market and functions in a local service capacity. By 1986, employment reached 3,157 and accounted for 30 percent of the jobs in machinery, except electric. The countertrend of growth in this segment is, in part, reflective of the extent to which manufacturers have been refitting used equipment when upgrading production systems. Further, there is also evidence of a trend by equipment manufacturers to outsource job-shop work to these smaller firms. Thus, it is a trend of vertical "disintegration." These trends suggest a shift in employment from manufacturers of new industrial systems to machinery services.

4. How Do Earnings for New Manufacturing Jobs Compare with Those Lost?

The 1986 average annual earnings per worker for growing major groups in manufacturing were $22,490 (above the average for all industry, including government, which was $20,102) (see table 2–7). This varied from

Table 2–7. Average Annual Payroll per Job for Akron's Growing Major Groups in Manufacturing, 1986

SIC Code	Industry Title	Average Annual Payroll per Job
37	Transportation Equipment	—
27	Printing and Publishing	22,535
26	Paper and Allied Products	28,473
39	Miscellaneous Manufacturing Industries	18,245
25	Furniture and Fixtures	20,852
38	Instruments and Related Products	19,424
	Weighted Average	22,490

Table 2–8. Average Annual Payroll per Job for Akron's Declining Major Groups in Manufacturing, 1986

SIC Code	Industry Title	Average Annual Payroll per Job
29	Petroleum and Coal Products	24,304
20	Food and Kindred Products	20,850
33	Primary Metal Industries	22,505
28	Chemicals and Allied Products	27,228
32	Stone, Clay, and Glass Products	22,534
34	Fabricated Metal Products	29,980
35	Machinery, Except Electrical	24,403
30	Rubber and Misc. Plastics Products	32,852
	Weighted Average	28,962

Source: Ohio Bureau of Employment Services, Labor Market Information Division, Workers Covered Under Ohio Unemployment Compensation Law (202 Series).

$18,245 for workers in miscellaneous manufacturing to $28,423 in printing and publishing. While the new manufacturing jobs pay better than the average of all industry, earnings per worker are substantially less than for the declining major groups in manufacturing.

In 1986, the average annual earnings per worker in declining major groups in manufacturing were $28,962. This was $6,472 greater than average earnings in the growing major groups (see table 2–8). The earnings per worker ranged from $20,850 in food products to $32,852 in rubber and plastics products. The $28,962 average is greatly influenced by the large losses in the dominant industries of rubber and plastics products and fabricated metal products in the local employment base. In aggregate, the new jobs in manufacturing contribute less to payrolls than is typical of industries with heavy job losses.

5. Employment Trends Within the Service Sector of the Akron Regional Economy, 1979–1986

Total employment within the service sector of the Akron regional economy expanded by 10.4 percent between 1979 and 1986. Utilizing the schematic of the service sector developed by Browning and Singelmann (1978), the largest proportion of growth was attributable to social services, which accounted for 36.4 percent or 5,198 out of 14,264 new jobs (see table 2–9). The majority of the new jobs in the social services division were in medical services, followed by miscellaneous social services. The overall expansion in social services was somewhat mitigated by the loss of 586 jobs in nonprofit services (membership organizations).

The second largest source of job growth in Akron's service sector occurred in the producer services division, which gained 4,179 new jobs. The vast majority of these jobs (90 percent) were accounted for by miscellaneous business services. The third largest source of job growth occurred in the personal services division, which gained 3,628 new jobs. These job gains were almost entirely attributable to the growth of employment in eating and drinking places. Job growth was also realized in wholesale and retail services, which gained 2,751 new jobs. The major proportion of these new jobs occurred in wholesale trade. The only industrial division in the service sector to incur a net loss of jobs was transportation services, which lost a net 1,492 jobs during 1979 to 1986.

In total, 17 major groups in the service sector experienced steady growth during 1979 to 1986 that was largely uninterrupted by the recession. As previously noted, the largest absolute job gains occurred in Health Services (SIC 80), Eating and Drinking Places (SIC 88), and Business Services (SIC 73) (see table 2–10). Over 3,000 new jobs were created in each of these three industry sectors. Substantial growth was also realized in Social Services (SIC 83), Wholesale Trade–Durable Goods (SIC 50), and Miscellaneous Retail (SIC 59), which gained over 1,000 new jobs. These six major groups generated 77.5 percent of total net job growth in Akron's service sector.

Table 2–9. Employment Trends in Major Sectors of the Service Economy
Within the Akron Region, 1979 to 1986

	1979	1986	% Change 1979–1986
Transportation Services	57,169	58,428	2.2
Transportation	8,987	7,495	−16.6
Wholesale and Retail Services			
Wholesale Trade	13,546	15,060	11.2
Retail Trade	34,636	35,873	3.6
Producer Services	26,429	30,608	15.8
Communication, Electric, Gas, and Sanitary Services	6,083	5,821	−4.3
Banking	5,054	5,066	0.2
Insurance	3,041	3,123	2.7
Real Estate	1,647	1,679	1.9
Engineering and Architecture	1,049	1,006	−4.1
Accounting, Auditing, and Bookkeeping	585	774	32.3
Misc. Business Services	7,993	11,753	47.0
Legal Services	977	1,386	41.9
Social Services	23,848	29,046	21.8
Medical Services	7,659	11,110	45.1
Hospitals	9,907	9,904	−0.0
Education	1,534	2,112	37.7
Welfare	394	1,055	167.8
Nonprofit	2,945	2,359	−19.9
Misc. Social Services	1,409	2,506	77.9
Personal Services	29,908	33,536	12.1
Domestic Services	192	307	59.9
Hotels	1,886	1,724	−8.6
Eating and Drinking	17,469	20,784	19.0
Repair	2,440	2,557	4.8
Laundry	1,217	1,124	−7.6
Barber and Beauty Shop	1,089	1,298	19.2
Entertainment	4,019	3,669	−8.7
Misc. Personal Services	1,596	2,073	29.9
Total	137,354	151,618	10.4

*Adapted from Browing and Singelmann (1978).

Source: Ohio Bureau of Employment Services, Labor Market Information Division, Workers Covered Under Ohio Unemployment Compensation Law (202 Series)

Table 2–10. Akron's Growing Major Groups in the Service Sector, 1979 to 1986

SIC Code	Industry Title	1979	1986	Net Change	Percent Increase
67	Holding and Other Investment Offices	61	534	473	775.4
47	Transportation Services	223	470	247	110.8
45	Transportation by Air	112	223	111	99.1
83	Social Services	2,016	3,754	1,738	86.2
84	Museums, Botanical, Zoological Gardens	56	90	34	60.7
88	Private Households	192	307	115	59.9
81	Legal Services	977	1,386	409	41.9
73	Business Services	7,902	11,187	3,285	41.6
82	Educational Services	1,534	2,112	578	37.7
59	Miscellaneous Retail	4,741	5,924	1,183	25.0
80	Health Services	17,566	21,014	3,448	19.6
58	Eating and Drinking Places	17,469	20,784	3,315	19.0
50	Wholesale Trade–Durable Goods	9,009	10,607	1,598	17.7
64	Insurance Agents, Brokers, and Services	1,017	1,171	154	15.1
72	Personal Services	3,391	3,730	339	10.0
54	Food Stores	9,040	9,694	654	7.2
46	Pipe Lines, Except Natural Gas	0	28	28	—
	Total	75,306	93,015	17,709	23.5

Source: Ohio Bureau of Employment Services, Labor Market Information Division, Workers Covered Under Ohio Unemployment Compensation Law (202 Series).

The largest rates of employment growth occurred in Holding and Other Investment Offices (SIC 67), Transportation Services (SIC 47), Air Transportation (SIC 45), and Social Services. Employment growth in holding and investment offices expanded by 775.4 percent, pushing its employment level beyond 500 jobs. This high growth rate is only partially a function of new job formation. It reflects the reclassification of jobs to a new SIC code. The formation of holding companies has been a common strategy used by Fortune 500 and other large companies for reorganizing their corporate structures. Their headquarters activities become reported as a separate "holding company."

There were five major groups in the service sector that experienced steady decline during 1979 to 1986. The largest job losses were accounted for by Membership Organizations (SIC 86) which, as was previously noted, lost 586 jobs (see table 2–11). The second-largest decline in employment involved Communication Industries (SIC 48), which lost 363 jobs.

The recession had cyclical effects on employment in 17 major groups in the service sector. These effects followed three primary trends: (1) employment decline during the recession followed by substantial net employment growth in the recovery period; (2) decline during the recession followed by moderate recovery (>50 percent) of jobs lost; and (3) decline during the recession, followed by little recovery (<50 percent) of jobs

Table 2–11.   Akron's Declining Major Groups in the Service Sector, 1979 to 1986

SIC Code	Industry Title	1979	1986	Net Change	Percent Decrease
60	Banking	3,625	3,547	(78)	− 2.2
48	Communication	3,243	2,880	(363)	− 11.2
86	Membership Organizations	2,945	2,359	(586)	− 19.9
66	Combined Real Estate, Insurance, etc.	89	27	(62)	− 69.7
78	Motion Pictures	243	60	(183)	− 75.3
	Total	10,145	8,873	(1,272)	− 12.5

Note: Figures in parentheses represent a net loss in employment between 1987 and 1986.

Source: Ohio Bureau of Employment Services, Labor Market Information Division, Workers Covered Under Ohio Unemployment Compensation Law (202 Series).

Table 2–12.   Employment Trends of Major Groups in the Service Sector with Cyclical Change, 1979 to 1986

SIC Code	Industry Title	1979	Low*	1987	Net Change 1979–Low	Net Change 1987–Low	Net Change 1979–1987	% Change 1979–1987
Cyclical Growth								
49	Electric, Gas, and Sanitary Services	2,840	3,008	2,965	168	(43)	125	4.4
Cyclical Decline — Growth								
61	Credit Agencies Other Than Banks	1,429	1,309	1,433	(120)	124	4	0.3
65	Real Estate	1,558	1,417	1,867	(141)	450	309	19.8
57	Furniture and Home Furnishings Stores	1,742	1,429	1,968	(313)	539	226	13.0
75	Auto Repair, Services, and Garages	2,291	2,061	2,818	(230)	757	527	23.0
89	Miscellaneous Services	1,754	1,499	2,123	(255)	624	369	21.0
52	Building Materials and Garden Supplies	2,105	1,813	2,615	(292)	802	510	24.2
Cyclical Decline — Moderate Recovery								
70	Hotel and Other Lodging Places	1,886	1,473	1,777	(413)	304	(109)	−5.8
51	Wholesale Trade–Nondurable Goods	4,537	4,149	4,453	(388)	304	(84)	−1.9

Table 2–12. Employment Trends of Major Groups in the Service Sector with Cyclical Change, 1979 to 1986

SIC Code	Industry Title	1979	Low*	1987	Net Change 1979–Low	Net Change 1987–Low	Net Change 1979–1987	% Change 1979–1987
Cyclical Decline — Moderate Recovery								
63	Insurance Carriers	2,024	—	—	(2,024)	—	—	—
53	General Merchandise Stores	7,346	7,239	7,068	(107)	(171)	(278)	–3.8
55	Automotive Dealers and Service Stations	7,217	6,006	7,085	(1,211)	1,079	(132)	–1.8
76	Miscellaneous Repair Services	977	696	967	(281)	271	(10)	–1.0
Cyclical Decline — Little Recovery								
42	Trucking and Warehousing	8,413	6,039	6,645	(2,374)	606	(1,768)	–21.0
79	Amusement and Recreation Services	3,720	3,498	3,761	(222)	263	41	1.1
41	Local and Interurban Passenger Transit	239	188	255	(51)	67	16	6.7
56	Apparel and Accessory Stores	2,445	1,698	2,050	(747)	352	(395)	–16.2

*Represents lowest employment between 1983 and 1984.

Note: Figures in parentheses represent a net loss in employment between 1979 and 1987.

Source: Ohio Bureau of Employment Services, Labor Market Information Division, Workers Covered Under Ohio Unemployment Compensation Law (202 Series).

lost. Six of the major groups realized job losses during the recession, followed by net employment growth during the recovery. The largest employment gains in this group occurred in Auto Repair, Services, and Garages (SIC 75), which realized 641 new jobs, and Building Materials and Garden Supplies (SIC 52), which gained 559 new jobs (see table 2–12).

Although suffering a net decline in employment, six of the major groups recovered a moderate-to-substantial proportion of jobs lost during the recession. The major groups with the largest number of jobs recovered were Insurance Carriers (SIC 63), which regained 1,952 out of 2,024 jobs lost, and Automotive Dealers and Service Stations (SIC 55), which recovered 971 out of 1,211 jobs lost. Overall, the largest net employment decline in this group was in automotive dealers and service stations, which lost a net 240 jobs.

The postrecession recovery had little effect in stimulating job growth in four of the major groups that lost jobs during the recession. A large employment decline occurred in Trucking and Warehousing (SIC 42), which lost a net 1,831 jobs during 1979 to 1986. Only 543 out of 2,374 jobs lost were recovered in the postrecession period. This accounts for the overall decline in transportation services during 1979 to 1986. A substantial employment decline also occurred in Apparel and Accessory Stores (SIC 56), which lost a net 655 jobs. Only 92 out of 747 jobs lost were recovered in this major group.

6. Trend-Breakers Within the Service Sector

Two of the major groups that experienced net growth during 1979 to 1986 subsumed industry groups that were declining. The first was Wholesale Trade–Durable Goods (SIC 50), which was one of the major growth areas in the Akron region's service sector. In contrast, Motor Vehicles and Auto Equipment (SIC 501) experienced a net loss of 11 jobs (see table 2–13). The second major group was Personal Services (SIC 72), which gained a net 339 new jobs. In contrast, Laundry Cleaning and Garment Services (SIC 721) lost a net 93 jobs.

Two of the major groups that suffered net decline during 1979 to 1986 subsumed a number of industry groups that expanded during the same period. The first was Wholesale Trade–Nondurable Goods (SIC 51), which experienced a slight decline during 1979 to 1986 with a net loss of 84 jobs. In contrast, three of the industry groups subsumed beneath this sector experienced net growth. Paper and Paper Products (SIC 511) gained a net 168 new jobs, Groceries and Related Products (SIC 514) ex-

Table 2–13.   Trend-Breakers: Declining Industries Within Growing Service
Industry Sectors in the Akron Region, 1979 to 1986

SIC Code	Industry Title	1986	1979	Net Change	Percent Change
50	Wholesale Trade–Durable Goods	10,607	9,009	1,598	17.7
501	Motor Vehicles & Auto Equipment	1,723	1,854	(131)	−7.1
72	Personal Services	3,730	3,391	339	10.0
721	Laundry, Cleaning, and Garment Services	1,124	1,217	(93)	−7.6
	Total Two-Digit Industry	14,337	12,400	1,937	15.6
	Total Trend Breakers	2,847	3,071	(224)	−7.3
	Percent of Declining Industries	19.9	24.8		

Table 2–14.   Trend-Breakers: Growing Industries Within Declining Service
Industry Sectors in the Akron Region, 1979 to 1986

SIC Code	Industry Title	1986	1979	Net Change	Percent Change
51	Wholesale Trade– Nondurable Goods	4,453	4,537	(84)	−1.9
511	Paper and Paper Products	503	335	168	50.1
514	Groceries and Related Products	1,438	1,259	179	14.2
519	Miscellaneous Nondurable Goods	617	213	404	189.7
55	Automotive Dealers and Service Stations	6,977	7,217	(240)	−3.3
553	Auto and Home Supply Stores	1,468	1,154	314	27.2
	Total Two-Digit Industry	11,430	11,754	(324)	−2.8
	Total Trend Breakers	4,026	2,961	1,065	36.0
	Percent of Growing Industries	35.2	25.2		

Note: Figures in parentheses represent a net loss in employment between 1979 and 1986.

Source: Ohio Bureau of Employment Services, Labor Market Information Division, Workers Covered Under Ohio Unemployment Compensation Law (202 Series).

panded by a net 179 jobs, and Miscellaneous Nondurable Goods (SIC 519) gained 404 new jobs for a growth rate of 189.7 percent over the 1979 to 1986 period (see table 2–14). The second major group was automotive dealers and service stations in retail trade, which lost a net 240 jobs during 1979 to 1986. In contrast, Auto and Home Supply Stores (SIC 553) gained a net 314 new jobs over the same period. Overall, most industry groups within the service sector tended to follow the trend of the encompassing major group.

7. How Do Wages in Growing Service Industries Compare with Those Undergoing Decline?

The 1986 average annual earnings per worker for the Akron region's 17 growing major groups in the service sector were $14,221 (see table 2–15). There was considerable variation in average earnings within this diverse

Table 2–15.   Average Annual Earnings per Worker in Akron's 17 Growing Major Groups in the Service Sector, 1986

SIC Code	Industry Title	Average Annual Payroll per Worker
80	Health Services	19,355
58	Eating and Drinking Places	5,921
73	Business Services	13,897
83	Social Services	9,681
50	Wholesale Trade–Durable Goods	24,086
59	Miscellaneous Retail	11,760
54	Food Stores	10,951
82	Educational Services	12,071
67	Holding and Other Investment Offices	41,185
75	Auto Repair, Services, and Garages	14,233
81	Legal Services	26,619
72	Personal Services	10,437
52	Building Materials and Garden Supplies	16,400
47	Transportation Services	16,889
64	Insurance Agents, Brokers, and Services	22,141
88	Private Households	8,664
45	Transportation by Air	—
	Weighted Average	14,221

set of groups. Average annual earnings per worker ranged from $5,921 in eating and drinking places to $41,185 in holding and other investment offices. In contrast, the 1986 average annual earnings per worker for the Akron region's 11 declining major groups in the service sector were $18,214 (see table 2–16). There was also considerable variation in earnings wages within this set of major groups. Average annual payroll per worker ranged from $6,036 in motion pictures to $28,840 in communication.

Major groups in the service sector with nominal net employment change during 1979 to 1986 (plus or minus 100 jobs) tended to exhibit higher average annual earnings in 1986. The 1986 average annual earnings per worker in these industries was $18,733, slightly higher than that for the group of declining industries (see table 2–17). Average earnings ranged from $10,260 in museums, botanical and zoological gardens to $31,760 in electric, gas, and sanitary services. Only two of these ten major groups had average earnings below $15,000 in 1986. These additional findings indicate that the majority of the Akron region's higher-wage service industries have either undergone decline or have been relatively stagnant regarding employment growth. Seven of the 11 major groups with average wages greater than $20,000 underwent decline or nominal employment

Table 2–16.   Average Annual Earnings per Worker in Akron's 11 Declining Major Groups in the Service Sector, 1986

SIC Code	Industry Title	Average Annual Payroll per Worker
41	Local and Interurban Passenger Transit	—
76	Miscellaneous Repair Services	17,069
66	Combined Real Estate, Insurance, etc.	21,660
70	Hotel and Other Lodging Places	7,822
78	Motion Pictures	6,036
79	Amusement and Recreation Services	10,334
55	Automotive Dealers and Service Stations	17,888
48	Communication	28,840
86	Membership Organizations	10,835
56	Apparel and Accessory Stores	8,178
42	Trucking and Warehousing	26,476
	Weighted Average	18,214

Source: Ohio Bureau of Employment Services, Labor Market Information Division, Workers Covered Under Ohio Unemployment Compensation Law (202 Series).

Table 2–17.   Average Annual Earnings per Worker for Akron's Ten Major
Groups in the Service Sector Industries with Nominal Employment Change, 1986

SIC Code	Industry Title	Average Annual Payroll per Worker
49	Electric, Gas, and Sanitary Services	31,760
65	Real Estate	16,158
61	Credit Agencies Other Than Banks	15,124
89	Miscellaneous Services	25,255
57	Furniture and Home Furnishings Stores	14,428
84	Museums, Botanical, Zoological Gardens	10,260
63	Insurance Carriers	22,728
53	General Merchandise Stores	10,497
60	Banking	15,391
51	Wholesale Trade–Nondurable Goods	25,998
	Weighted Average	18,733

Source: Ohio Bureau of Employment Services, Labor Market Information Division, workers covered under Ohio Unemployment Compensation Law (202 Series).

change during 1979 to 1986. Only four major groups in the service sector with 1986 average wages greater than $20,000 experienced growth during 1979 to 1986. These findings broadly mirror those for the manufacturing sector in that average earnings in declining and stagnant service sector industries were higher than those with a growing employment base during 1979 to 1986.

8. Do More Jobs in Services (SICs 70–89) Mean Lower Earnings per Job?

Long-term forecasts project that Services (SICs 70–89) will be the largest source of net job growth for the nation as well as for the Akron region. Overall, average earnings in services ranked eighth of ten industrial divisions, including government. An analysis of the major groups in services indicates that all but two of them have payrolls below the service sector average (see tables 2–15, 2–16, and 2–17).

In health and business services (the largest sources of job growth in the services) average annual earnings fall near the middle range of the scale. But within each major group there is a diverse mix of occupational patterns and pay scales. Health services range from a low of $8,925 for

Nursing and Personal Care Facilities (SIC 805) to $41,672 for Offices of Physicians (SIC 801), which obviously reflects doctors' earnings. Hospitals (SIC 806) — characterized by a much broader range of occupations — generated annual earnings per job of $19,112.

In business services (a diverse mix of industries whose only similarity is that they tend to market their services to other businesses), payrolls range from $6,255 for Services to Buildings (SIC 734 — which includes janitorial services) to $25,580 for Advertising (SIC 731). Using this more detailed level of industry analysis, 18 industry groups had average annual earnings of less than $10,000 per worker. These cut across a wide range of groups: Child Day-Care Services (SIC 835), Automobile Parking (SIC 752), Photographic Studios (SIC 722), Beauty Shops (SIC 723), Civic and Social Organizations (SIC 864), and Nursing and Personal Care Facilities, among others. In contrast, three of 22 industry groups paying over $25,000 per worker are from services: Offices of Physicians (SIC 801), Offices of Osteopathic Physicians (SIC 803), and Engineering and Architectural Services (SIC 891). These findings suggest that the majority of new jobs in services are likely to be lower-wage jobs.

8.1 How Does Akron's Economic Performance Compare to the Nation?

The employment data indicate that Akron's economy was severely hit by the nation's recessions. In fact, the consequences of the recessions were more severe for Akron than for most U.S. cities. This downturn has been augmented by a slow recovery in Akron's economy that is yet to be fully complete. While not dealing with casual forces, shift-share analysis can provide insight into what accounts for this lackluster economic performance. A shift-share analysis was conducted for the 1979 to 1983 period to gain insight into why Akron's economic decline during the recession years was so much greater compared to the nation as a whole. The shift-share analysis for this period reveals that Akron's mix of industry (refer to earlier discussion using location quotients) included a larger proportion of major groups that were severely hit by the recessions at the nation level (both cyclical and permanent decline). Moreover, virtually all major groups did not perform as well in Akron's economy compared to the nation as a whole. Major groups in Akron either declined more rapidly or grew less rapidly.

If Akron had mirrored the nation's economy during 1979 to 1983, only 686 private jobs would have been lost instead of 27,578 (see table 2–18).

Table 2–18. Shift Share Analysis for Akron PMSA, 1979 to 1983 and 1983 to 1986

	Employment Change	National Growth Effect	Industry Mix Effect	Share Effect	Competitive Effect
1979–1983					
Total Private Employment	(27,578)	(686)	(4,841)	(5,527)	(22,051)
Manufacturing	(22,148)	(280)	(13,175)	(13,455)	(8,693)
Services	(2,501)	(374)	9,711	9,337	(11,838)
1983–1986					
Total Private Employment	21,328	26,076	(1,704)	24,373	(3,045)
Manufacturing	2,528	9,261	(5,101)	4,160	(1,632)
Services	16,458	15,826	2,296	18,123	(1,665)

However, the performance of the Akron regional economy was not the same as the national economy. Taking this into account, if Akron's particular mix of major groups had experienced the same downturn in growth that occurred in these major groups at the national level, its job loss would have been increased by another 4,841 jobs, for a total loss of 5,527 jobs. Given the disparity between this total and the actual loss of jobs, the overwhelming explanation for Akron's severe employment decline is clearly the region's loss of share in almost every major group.

Surprisingly, Akron's biggest loss of share occurred in the service sector. The Akron economy lost 2,501 jobs in service sector industries. However, based on trends at the national level, the Akron area should have gained 9,337 jobs (see table 2–18). Given the restructuring of the tire and rubber industry, it is not surprising that the Akron economy experienced a 64 percent greater job loss in manufacturing than would be expected based on national performance of the major groups that comprise Akron's manufacturing base. This lackluster economic performance is partially attributable to the loss of jobs in businesses serving export markets. This, coupled with population decline, exacerbated the decline in demand for goods and services by local businesses and consumers during the recession period.

8.2 Why Has Akron's Economic Recovery Been Weaker than the Nation's?

A shift-share analysis was also conducted for the 1983 to 1986 period to gain insight into why Akron's economic growth following the recession has lagged behind the national economy. There are two explanations for Akron's weak economic recovery. First, Akron's industry mix still includes a greater share of the nation's slower-growing or declining major groups. Second, most major groups are growing more slowly in the Akron economy compared to the nation or are still in decline. The shift-share analysis for the 1983 to 1986 period reveals that if the Akron economy had mirrored the national economy, 26,076 new jobs would have been created instead of 21,328. Given Akron's industry mix, however, the increase in private jobs would have been reduced to 24,373 jobs. On net, a slower recovery has cost the local economy 3,045 jobs. For the major industrial divisions, both Akron's manufacturing and service sectors grew slower than the national economy (having adjusted for Akron's particular mix of major groups) during 1983 to 1986. Akron's manufacturing industries grew at only 61 percent of the national rate, while service sector industries grew at 91 percent.

The most severe share losses in manufacturing during 1983 to 1986 were in rubber and plastics products. The Akron economy continued to lose jobs in rubber and plastics products even though this major group was expanding at the national level (growth rate greater than nation's aggregate growth rate). Stone, clay, and glass products was the only other major group in manufacturing in which a decline in share resulted in a loss of more than 500 jobs. The most severe share losses in the service sector during 1983 to 1986 were in business services and in eating and drinking places. Other major groups in the service sector in which a decline in share resulted in a loss of more than 500 jobs included food stores, general merchandise, and electric, gas, and sanitary services.

8.3 Is the Growth of the Service Sector Sufficient To Replace Lost Manufacturing Activity?

During the 1970 to 1987 period, growth in average total employment in the Akron region was only 5 percent. This figure is not unexpected since employment in the manufacturing sector has been downsized by more than one-third during this period. Job growth in the service sector has not been sufficient to replace the loss of manufacturing jobs. Average total employment in 1987 was still 2 percent below the peak year of 1979.

There is good reason to question whether a service job gained is equal to a lost manufacturing job. Our own industrial surveys for the Akron region indicate that there are few part-time jobs in manufacturing (Heil and Voth, 1987; Heil, 1989). While service sector businesses have more part-time jobs, they are not as prevalent as is popularly assumed. Part-time employment tends to cluster in the larger service firms, particularly retail trade (Voth, 1985). However, certain service industries are structured around a pattern of work commitments of less than 40 hours per week: commissioned insurance and real estate agents and personnel services are two major examples that involve thousands of jobs in the Akron region. Fringe benefits (particularly health care and private pension plans) offered to employees with or without cost-sharing varies substantially across industries. A substantial proportion of Akron's labor force does not currently receive these fringe benefits. A recent labor-force survey estimated this proportion to be 40 percent (Leahy and Sommers, 1988). Even in the manufacturing sector, yearly surveys reveal a rising proportion of firms without health insurance for their employees (Heil and Voth, 1987; Heil, 1989).

The differences found in average annual earnings per worker across industries are primarily related to differences in: (1) quantity of work hours per worker, that is, the mix of part-time, full-time, and overtime work; (2) the occupational mix, that is, the structure of unskilled, semi-skilled, and skilled occupations; and (3) wage structures and pay scales. Wages and salaries vary tremendously across different professional, skilled, and unskilled occupations. Some firms pay more than others for the same occupation and level of experience because of collective bargaining, as a means of attracting scarce labor, and/or due to their ability to pass along these higher costs to customers in the form of higher prices.

It is extremely doubtful whether the new jobs in Akron's growing service sector industries provide adequate replacements for those lost in declining manufacturing industries. There is a small tier of jobs in the service sector that are full time, involve professional and skilled occupations, and pay higher wages than the average found in the manufacturing sector (for example, physicians and corporate executives in holding companies). However, the average annual earnings per worker in growing service industries ($14,221) were over $12,000 less than that in declining manufacturing industries ($28,962). Further, out of the six major groups in the service sector that provided the largest net growth of jobs (health services, eating and drinking places, business services, social services, wholesale trade–durable goods, and miscellaneous retail), four had average annual earnings below $15,000 in 1986. These findings suggest that more often than not, new service jobs within the Akron region are providing a lower standard of living than the manufacturing jobs that were lost.

9. Factors Influencing Future Economic Development in the Akron Region

The structural shifts reflected in employment trends over the 1979 to 1986 period suggest that the Akron regional economy is evolving away from a manufacturing production center toward a center for corporate planning and decision-making and services provision. The hemorrhage of job losses in the manufacturing sector abated following the end of the recession in 1983. However, the growth of service sector jobs and new manufacturing enterprises has only stabilized the Akron economy. It has not stimulated a phase of rapid growth such as that resulting from the expansion of the rubber industry during the 1910 to 1920 period. In this respect, the designation of Akron as an emerging service center may be somewhat premature.

The economic future of the Akron region faces many uncertainties. In fact, throughout much of the 1980s, the Akron region has faced economic self-doubt and a general perception of living-through-crisis conditions. In addition to the decline in total employment since 1979, the region has endured a loss of population. The population within the central county of the Akron region (Summit County) declined by an estimated 38,899 persons between 1970 to 1985. While the fringe counties of the region experienced nominal population growth, this did not offset the loss of population from the central county. The net regional population loss was largely attributable to outmigration (Goe, 1989). The exodus of people from the city of Akron and its immediate surrounding area contributed to the perception of crisis and decline.

The major issue facing the future of economic development in the Akron region is determining what course of economic restructuring is needed to stimulate a phase of rapid economic expansion and to realign the region on a trajectory of long-term growth. In the closing years of the 1980s, the general perception of economic crisis has begun to abate somewhat due to the effects of one of the longest (post-1983) economic recoveries in U.S. history. The outlines of a potential resurgence in the Akron economy have appeared. A successful restructuring of the Akron economy will unfold along one or several key dimensions:

- the maintenance of Akron's function as a corporate headquarters location;
- the revitalization of Akron's traditional heavy manufacturing base;
- the maturation of Akron as a center for development and manufacturing of advanced technology;
- the further development of Akron as a key residential and business center in the broader northeast-Ohio region.

9.1 Will Akron Maintain its Function as a Corporate Headquarters Location?

Despite its decline as a production center, the Akron region remains a strong corporate headquarters location involving both administrative and technical operations. The Akron region is currently the home base for four Fortune 500 firms (Goodyear Tire & Rubber, GenCorp, B.F. Goodrich, and A. Schulman), three Fortune Service 500 firms (Roadway Services, Revco D.S., and Ohio Edison) and a number of promising medium-sized manufacturers (for example, Telxon and Myers Industries). The restructuring of the regional economy has had a wide range of effects on the corporate headquarters infrastructure.

A serious threat to the Akron community's sense of security about its major companies occurred with the attempted hostile takeover of Good-year by financier Sir James Goldsmith in November 1986. In order to ward off the takeover attempt, the firm was forced to sell off several sub-sidiaries and to reduce employment further. This was followed in March 1987 by an attempted takeover of GenCorp — the parent holding com-pany of General Tire & Rubber that was formed in 1984. Finally, in June 1987, Firestone announced that it would move its world headquarters to Chicago, which involved approximately 200 jobs. This rapid succession of events heightened the perception of economic crisis by further expos-ing the vulnerability of the Akron community to the unpredictable winds of economic change.

The ongoing restructuring of the tire industry did transform the own-ership status of several of Akron's tire companies. In 1986, B.F. Good-rich's tire operations were merged with those of Uniroyal to form the Uniroyal Goodrich Tire Company. The new company was equally owned by each firm with its headquarters located in Akron. In June 1988, B.F. Goodrich sold its stake in Uniroyal Goodrich to the New York investment firm of Clayton & Dubilier. This marked the retreat of B.F. Goodrich from the tire industry as the firm became more focused in chemicals and aerospace.

Following the takeover attempt, GenCorp sold its General Tire unit to the West German firm Continental AG in November 1987. This marked the retreat of GenCorp from the tire industry as the firm became more focused in aerospace and automotive and industrial plastics. In May 1988, Firestone Tire & Rubber sold its tire operations to the Japanese firm Bridgestone. In both cases, the North American headquarters of these foreign-owned tire operations were kept in Akron. Thus the shifts in own-ership of Akron's tire companies had the overall effect of augmenting the region's corporate headquarters infrastructure.

The restructuring of the tire industry in the latter half of the 1980s resulted in only minor job losses in the Akron regional economy com-pared to the wave of plant closings during 1978 to 1982. A greater short-term impact was the uncertainty created over whether Akron's major manufacturers would remain located within the region. Even though far fewer people are employed today in Akron's tire industry, these firms along with the former tire manufacturers (B.F. Goodrich and GenCorp) remain among the region's largest employers. Further, these firms repre-sent the Akron region's primary links with the larger global economy. In these respects, the maintenance of Akron's function as a corporate head-quarters location is critical. The future status of this function hinges upon several key questions:

- Under new ownership will the administrative and technical operations of Uniroyal Goodrich, General Tire, and Firestone remain in Akron long term?
- Will medium-sized, high-growth firms like Telxon remain in Akron?
- Has the Akron regional economy spawned a sufficient infrastructure of producer services to support corporate operations — both administrative and technical — with corporate customers inside or outside the Akron region?

A high-quality infrastructure of producer services can be critical for maintaining Akron's headquarters base. It can also serve as a pull factor in attracting other headquarters functions to the region. Akron's growth in producer services suggests that this infrastructure is being put into place.

9.2 Will Akron Revitalize its Traditional Manufacturing Base?

The shifts in ownership within Akron's tire industry may have implications for a return to tire manufacturing in the future. Since control over decision-making in three of Akron's major tire firms (excluding Goodyear) is now outside the community, conventional wisdom would suggest only negative scenarios for Akron concerning future locational decisions made by distant owners. However, circumstances may yield a much different outcome. Given their desire to increase their shares of the U.S. market, both Bridgestone and Continental AG have expressed much greater interest in revitalizing and supporting their new tire operations compared to the old Firestone and GenCorp during their final years of ownership.

Both of these firms have made substantial capital investments in upgrading their newly acquired North American tire plants. Firestone/Bridgestone's employment in Akron increased by 3 percent during 1988 (*Akron Beacon Journal*, 1989a). Further, the firm has also begun to manufacture racing and experimental tires in its Akron technical Center (*Akron Beacon Journal*, 1989b). While not highly probable, a return to tire production in the Akron region by these foreign-owned firms should not be entirely ruled out. This will depend upon a wide range of factors, including the cost of developing modern tire plants in Akron and the importance attached to circumventing organized labor in their corporate strategies. If a return to tire production in the Akron region does occur, it will likely remain at a much smaller scale compared to the height of mass production.

9.3 Will Akron Become an Advanced Technology Center?

Given that the research and development (R&D) and technical operations of the tire industry have largely remained in the Akron area, the region continues to function as a center of development in tire technology and rubber products. However, given the evolution in the spatial organization of the tire industry and the decline of Akron as a production center, new innovations in tire technology do not necessarily translate into new manufacturing jobs within the regional economy. If economic development is to occur in the Akron region via the development of advanced technology, sociotechnical arrangements are needed that involve tighter linkages between innovation and production within the regional economy. Plastics and new composite materials such as polymers are areas of advanced technology that can potentially fulfill these requirements.

The Akron region is not extremely well known for its plastics-based businesses. Market applications from plastics technology have played only a minor role in the diversification strategies of the former big four tire companies, and the vast majority of Akron-based firms producing plastics technology have yet to capture dominant market shares. However, a strong sociotechnical infrastructure necessary to support these technologies has been developed, and the potential capacity for economic development is very much in evidence.

One scenario foresees the Akron region as becoming "polymer valley," where innovations in polymers and plastics technology provide the stimulus for a rapid growth phase within the region. The region has considerable R&D capacity in these areas. The University of Akron has developed a nationally prominent program in polymer engineering. Further, the university is also a partner in the Edison Polymer Innovation Corporation (EPIC) — a public/private R&D venture that is funded by Ohio's Thomas Edison Program and a group of private partners. The purpose of the university's participation in EPIC is to develop commercial applications of polymer technology. However, the extent to which new businesses will ultimately be spun off from these ventures within the Akron region remains to be seen. There is currently little evidence of new business formation or business expansion involving new innovations in polymer technology resulting from these programs.

The major success story in plastics technology within the Akron region has been the growth of A. Schulman — a manufacturer of plastic resins. The firm emerged as a Fortune 500 company in 1987 and has replaced Firestone as one of four Fortune 500 manufacturers based in Akron. The Akron region also has a substantial number of small- and medium-sized firms that manufacture polymer technology. The success of the polymer valley scenario may to a considerable extent be dependent upon the growth of these firms.

The majority of polymer manufacturing in the Akron region is carried out by the small- and medium-sized firms. However, most of these firms are suppliers to larger companies, whether it be General Motors, General Electric, or B.F. Goodrich. These supplier firms are not leading industrial trends, rather, they are responding. As a result, future patterns in the markets for new and expanded applications of rubber and plastics-based materials and in technological advances regarding materials and production systems are likely to be determined by larger companies who are major customers of these suppliers.

To a large extent, end-use industries govern the rate of introduction of new materials technology into their products as well as the choice of these materials. In some cases, the materials technology is known and affordable, but its introduction in certain markets has dragged. Such is the case with the use of polymers in building and construction. In most cases (no matter what the end-use), the cost savings of using the new materials is not sufficient to overcome sources of inertia, such as resistance to use of "plastics" or to the cost of retooling the production system. Decisions by General Motors, for example, to delay plant retooling that would permit the introduction of "composite" body and frame parts into additional car lines is an example of how fragile these commitments are — at least in terms of when they are implemented. This limits or delays the growth potential for firms such as Diversitech (a subsidiary of GenCorp) that is attempting to capture the composite body market.

These large firms also have future decisions concerning their own production strategies. Will they produce a larger or smaller percentage of their own finished products? Will they produce more or less of the early stages of production? In effect, "Will they tend toward vertically integrated production systems, producing more of their own needs, or will they accelerate outsourcing?" The recent trend of U.S. finished-goods manufacturers has been toward outsourcing. A continuation of this trend may present opportunities for Akron-based suppliers of polymers and plastics materials, provided the use of such materials becomes more widespread in manufactured products.

The Akron regional economy is well positioned to capture economic growth resulting from advances in plastics and polymer technology. As was seen in the quantitative analysis, Miscellaneous Plastic Products (SIC 307) was the second-largest growing industry group in manufacturing and the most important trend-breaker within the Akron regional economy during 1979 to 1986 (see tables 2–4 and 2–6). Additionally, 1,079 new jobs were created in this industry group during 1986 to 1987. However, it is yet to be seen whether this industry group will become the dominant force needed to stimulate a phase of rapid growth within the Akron region.

9.4 Will the Importance of Akron as a Key Residential and Business Center in the Northeast Ohio Region Increase?

Akron is one of five contiguous urban areas situated in the northeast corner of Ohio, adjacent to Pennsylvania, New York, and West Virginia (Cleveland, Akron, Canton, Youngstown, and Lorain). Population is nearly 3.9 million for the entire region, down from 4.1 million in 1970. The population loss has not been evenly felt by all five urban areas and has involved spatial shifts within the region. Population has dispersed from the urban counties to the adjacent fringe counties. On balance, the regional population has shifted south from Cleveland to the Akron and Canton areas, despite the net population loss in each of these urban areas.

Half of all immigrants to the Akron region between 1975 to 1980 moved from elsewhere in northeast Ohio (primarily Cleveland). This trend has continued throughout the 1980s (Shanahan, 1986). Former Clevelanders are said to be a major share of new home buyers in Akron where driving time to downtown Cleveland is 35 to 40 minutes. As population and businesses moved into the less developed areas that separated the urban centers of Akron, Canton, Cleveland, and Youngstown, the frequency of commuting to work across urban boundaries increased and continues to do so. Commute-to-work data in the 1980 census reveal that fewer Akronites commute outside the region for work than the reverse.

These two pieces of evidence suggest that the Akron economy has outperformed the surrounding urban areas in attracting and holding businesses and population. Businesses and people considering a location in northeast Ohio can choose one of the five urban areas without impairing ready access to most locations in the other four. As an economy that is a satellite of the larger Cleveland area, Akron has several locational advantages:

- 20-minute commuting time as an average for the region;
- alternative to living/working in a bigger city/downtown (Cleveland);
- a good central city public school system that is financially sound;
- two major state universities with strong research and graduate education programs.

The other urban areas in northeast Ohio have also been severely affected by economic restructuring. In a broader sense, the entire region has been subject to restructuring due to its previous high level of dependence on heavy manufacturing. The critical issue is whether Akron can capture a larger proportionate share of population and jobs as the regional economy is restructured.

10. Conclusions

The Akron region has only progressed partway along the course of restructuring needed to ensure future economic growth. The expansion of the region's service sector has largely failed to provide adequate job replacements for those lost in the manufacturing sector. In practically all cases, the average annual earnings in Akron's growing service industries were far below those in declining manufacturing industries. This creates the image that the regional economy has undergone a "hollowing out" process.

Future success in restructuring will depend heavily on the revitalization and expansion of the region's role as a production center — whether it involves the growth of high-tech manufacturing in polymers and plastics or the less likely return to traditional manufacturing in tires. In conclusion, the Akron regional economy is positioned at a turning point. One path on the horizon is the resumption of regional growth and the development of a vibrant, restructured economy. The other is a gradual, downward ratcheting of the regional economy of which the speed will be mitigated by the stabilizing effects of services growth.

3 BUFFALO, NEW YORK: REGION OF NO ILLUSIONS

Robert Kraushaar and David Perry

One of the most popular T-shirts in Buffalo is not one that immediately excites civic boosters at the Chamber of Commerce or the county industrial development agency; it reads "Buffalo: City of No Illusions." The shirt describes, in efficient detail, the painful economic transformation of the Buffalo Standard Metropolitan Statistical Area (SMSA). The last 15 years have not been kind to western New York.

Economic changes found in the cyclical upswings in the national economy and downward shifts in the regional unemployment rate have not fooled the people of Buffalo: these trends are "illusions" when compared to the deeper structural changes that have created a permanent reconstitution of the regional economy. From 1970 to 1980, the western New York region lost almost 95,000 people, or 5 percent of the total population, and another 2.2 percent from 1980 to 1982. Almost 45,000 manufacturing jobs, one-third of the total manufacturing jobs in the metropolitan area, were lost between 1979 and 1986.

Western New York workers have suffered more than workers have on a national scale. Between 1976 and 1984 alone, manufacturing employment losses were from two to 35 times as great as the national average.

Unemployment averaged 9.6 percent from 1981 to 1985, compared to a statewide average of 7.6 percent. These employment contractions were not unique to western New York. New York State, as a whole, lost more than 250,000 manufacturing jobs in the 1980s; its 18 percent job loss was more than double the national average (*Buffalo News*, 1987). The proportional impact was greater because of the region's historical dependency on basic manufacturing and because these jobs were not being replaced at the same rate as elsewhere in the state or nation.

1. Historical Background

For much of its history the city of Buffalo and its metropolitan hinterland has been, in the words of the historian Mark Goldman (1984) an "industrial giant." Goldman called the metropolis a truly "significant" region: economically significant, not so much as a center or starting point for industrial activity, but as a major link or secondary node in the economic network of the nation.

Early in its history, Buffalo, the terminus of the Erie Canal, was the "Gateway to the West" and an important transshipment point between the eastern states and the rest of the continent. As early as 1850, the city was the most successful break-bulk point in the continental network of extraction, boasting the largest flour mills and inland port in the United States.

Between 1860 and the end of the First World War, Buffalo evolved into an industrial giant, producing a sizable share of the nation's steel, railroad cars and engines, and airplanes and autos.

Buffalo's growth starting in the 1870s was increasingly financed by external investment. By the 1930s, the manufacturing structure of the city and region was no longer locally controlled.

The Second World War produced an unprecedented spurt of manufacturing activity, which continued after the war, resulting in the region's becoming even more dependent on its industrial base.

In spite of the postwar growth, however, the Buffalo area entered into a period of economic retrenchment characterized by a long-term, slow decline of growth in sectors of the area's manufacturing base. This decline was buffered by growth in the service sector.

This postwar shift in employment was a characteristic of a dramatic and important transformation that occurred in the region's economic structure. Where, in 1950, four of the top five employment categories of the Buffalo SMSA were in manufacturing and construction sectors, by 1980 four of the top five regional economic sectors were service-related: education, retail trade, financial services, and health services. In 1970, manufacturing still accounted for 42.1 percent of regional employment; in 1986, it accounted for less than 25 percent of the metropolitan employment base. Today, the percentage of the work force in manufacturing is estimated at less than 20 percent.

1.1 Demographic Changes

The decline of the manufacturing base has been accompanied by a substantial decline in the population of the central city of Buffalo and also by a decline in the overall population of the metropolitan area. Between 1970 and 1980, the SMSA lost almost 95,000 people, and it is estimated that the region has lost another 38,000 since 1980. The only other major metropolitan regions to lose population in the 1980s have been Cleveland and Pittsburgh.

Another disturbing feature of this shift in population is the demographic realignment or the "restructuring" of the age of the metropolitan population that we project to be a long-term result of the region's economic restructuring. Using New York State Department of Economic Development projections and breaking them down by age strata, we conclude that the SMSA could likely lose 86,641 persons in the age group 15 to 24 by the year 2000 (New York State, 1985). If this is correct, the metropolitan area will experience a serious shortage of residents who would comprise the future labor force. Almost 60 percent of the population will be over the age of 30, and the median age of the region's population will be about 40. The result is a labor pool that may become a labor "puddle" (Perry, 1987; Sebastian, 1988).

Changes in the economy and the population have also affected the income of people living in the Buffalo SMSA. While per capita income increased in Buffalo between 1970 and 1985 from $8,544 to $10,016, it was still not enough to lift per capita income in the area above the national per capita income figure of $10,132. At the same time, educational achievement in the metropolitan area is not impressive. Sixty-five percent of the adult population of the Buffalo SMSA has graduated from high school as compared to almost 69 percent of the national population. And only about 14.5 percent of the adult population of Buffalo has graduated from college as compared to 17 percent of the national population.

2. Manufacturing Industries

In a study conducted at the beginning of the 1980s, Noyelle and Stanback (1982) described Buffalo as the largest pure manufacturing city in the country. Put another way, the Buffalo economy was a perfect example of a region dedicated to and dependent on a mature industrial base. Doolittle (1985, p. 30) observed that Buffalo, in the early 1980s, ". . . included more than the national share of jobs in slowmoving or declining durable manufacturing industries."

The decline and restructuring of the mature industries of the United States, disproportionately represented as they were in the region's economy, contributed greatly to the long-term economic decline of the Buffalo region. In the period between 1979 and 1986, the Buffalo SMSA lost almost 45,000 manufacturing jobs, a decline of over 30 percent (see table 3–1). The only increase in total manufacturing employment came in 1984, at the end of the recession, and this change was the result of the regional automobile industry (Major Group 37) returning almost 3,000 jobs to its work force. With rare exceptions (see section 3, "Hidden Manufacturing Trend-Breakers"), the manufacturing sectors of the region demonstrated consistent patterns of decline in employment throughout the 1980s. None of the major manufacturing groups could be defined as consistent sectors of growth during this period, in either the durable or nondurable goods categories.

The loss of the manufacturing jobs in the region was the most dramatic indication of the erosion of the historic structure of the region's export base. The location quotient (LQ) for manufacturing dropped from 1.19 to 1.05 between 1979 and 1986. While the region suffered declines in *all* industry employment totals between 1979 and early 1983, increases in select areas of nondurable goods industries, along with recovery in the automobile industry, softened the precipitous losses in durable goods (see table 3–1). The LQs in durable goods show where the lion's share of the losses in the export base were secured. Overall, the durable goods LQ dropped 26 points — from 1.38 to 1.13. Yet while the losses have been greatest here, the durable goods category still remains the area of manufacturing in which Buffalo has an exportive employment base. This is further borne out by the fact that more industries in the nondurable goods category have shown increases in their LQs, and *still* the nondurable goods base of the region has not registered an overall LQ over 1.0 (see table 3–2).

The radical transformation occurring in the *structure* of Buffalo's economic base is made clear in tables 3–3 and 3–4. The decline in the business cycle between 1979 and 1983 is portrayed in the column "national growth effect." When combined with the cyclical change in each industry (or the "mix effect"), it becomes clear that Buffalo suffered a decline at more than twice the national rate. This decline becomes all the more important when it is shown that, during the three-year period of recovery in the business cycle (1983 to 1986), Buffalo continued to lose manufacturing jobs (see table 3–3).

This loss, when combined with the expected cyclical upturn and national changes in various manufacturing sectors, translates into a further state of regional noncompetitiveness. We estimate that the "competitive effect" of these trends amounted to the loss of almost 10,000 jobs in the region during this period of national economic "recovery." In short, at the aggregate level, the 'bleeding' in the manufacturing base of the region has been slowed, but it certainly has not stopped.

Disaggregating this trend, the largest losses occurred in the durable goods industries of the region. Not one durable goods industry showed a competitive pattern in the region between 1979 and 1983. By 1986, only "wood products" and "instruments" had achieved a state of "competitiveness," and these patterns were hardly enough to make up for the continued structural decline of the region's once-vaunted durable goods manufacturing base. While, by 1986, nondurable goods industries in the region, such as apparel, paper products, and petroleum, had started to generate jobs at rates in excess of national patterns, the growth was still not enough to overcome the anemic state of the rest of the region's nondurable goods industries (see table 3–4).

In general, therefore, the business cycle, while reflected in the manufacturing economy of Buffalo, was not strong enough to catapult the region back to a permanent state of manufacturing competitiveness. The long-term "structural" alterations in the global and national manufacturing processes have had a permanent effect on the region; the decline in the region's manufacturing employment was not simply "cyclical."

2.1 Declining Industries

At the heart of the region's industrial base are the metal manufacturing industries, including primary and fabricated metals, electrical and non-electrical machinery, and steel. At the center of the region's economic restructuring is the decline of these very sectors. Perhaps the most important change in the industrial base of Buffalo occurred in the steel industry (Major Group 32). While the industry all but collapsed nationally,

Table 3–1. Employment by Industry Group, 1979 to 1986

U.S. Data	SIC	1979:1	1983:1	1986:1	Change 1979–1983	Change 1983–1986
Total Employment		416,842	372,189	407,876	(44,653)	35,687
Mining					0	0
Construction		17,819	14,657	17,865	(3,162)	3,208
General Contractors	15	3,904	2,981	3,731	(923)	750
Heavy Contractors	16	2,992	2,359	2,449	(633)	90
Special Trade	17	10,923	9,317	11,685	(1,606)	2,368
Manufacturing		145,216	103,673	100,950	(41,543)	(2,723)
Durable Goods		102,477	67,316	64,577	(35,161)	(2,739)
Lumber and Wood Products	24	794	600	771	(194)	171
Furniture and Fixtures	25	1,074	835	932	(239)	97
Stone, Clay, and Glass	32	6,941	4,282	3,603	(2,659)	(679)
Primary Metals	33	21,714	8,394	4,121	(13,320)	(4,273)
Fabricated Metals	34	13,944	9,798	9,925	(4,146)	127
Machinery, Except Electrical	35	13,320	9,862	10,179	(3,458)	317
Electrical and Electronic Mach.	36	11,529	9,260	8,118	(2,269)	(1,142)
Transportation Equipment	37	26,085	17,595	20,360	(8,490)	2,765
Instruments and Related	38	3,778	3,634	3,965	(144)	331
Miscellaneous Industries	39	3,298	3,056	2,603	(242)	(453)
Nondurable Goods		42,739	36,357	36,373	(6,382)	16
Food & Kindred Prods.	20	8,948	8,356	8,226	(592)	(130)
U321	21				0	0
Textile Mill Products	22	1,234	671	513	(563)	(158)
Apparel and Other Textiles	23	2,497	2,274	2,553	(223)	279
Paper and Allied Products	26	4,195	2,968	3,194	(1,227)	226
Printing and Publishing	27	8,977	8,508	9,355	(469)	847

Chemicals and Allied Prods.	28	9,460	7,974	6,910	(1,486)	(1,064)
Petroleum and Coal	29	1,092	396	392	(696)	(4)
Rubber and Misc Products	30	5,873	4,824	5,064	(1,049)	240
Leather Products	31	463	386	166	(77)	(220)
Services						
Transportation		297,471	295,317	331,486	(2,154)	36,169
U440		13,631	11,716	12,940	(1,915)	1,224
	40				0	0
Local Passenger Transit	41	1,983	2,363	2,869	380	506
Trucking and Warehousing	42	9,038	6,882	7,404	(2,156)	552
Water Transport	44	771	532	410	(239)	(122)
Transport by Air	45	983	829	863	(154)	34
Pipelines, Except Natural Gas	46	0	0	0	0	0
Transportation Services	47	856	1,110	1,394	254	284
Wholesale & Retail Trade		84,662	77,748	86,907	(6,914)	9,159
Wholesale Trade		64,350	57,537	61,888	(6,813)	4,351
Durable Goods Wholesale	50	16,785	15,008	16,241	(1,777)	1,233
Nondurable Wholesale	51	8,269	8,528	8,274	259	(254)
General Merchandise	53	15,804	11,730	12,878	(4,074)	1,148
Food Stores	54	16,789	17,582	19,661	793	2,079
Automotive Dealers	55	8,225	6,761	8,777	(1,464)	2,016
Apparel and Accessory	56	5,427	5,243	5,671	(184)	428
Home Furnishings	57	3,379	3,098	3,403	(281)	305
Miscellaneous Retail	59	9,984	9,798	12,002	(186)	2,204
Producer Services		56,387	59,337	68,315	2,950	8,978
Communication	48	5,105	4,745	4,395	(360)	(350)
Electric, Gas, and Sanitary	49	5,725	6,034	6,070	309	36
Banking	60	8,837	8,868	10,272	31	1,404
Credit Agencies, Except Banks	61	1,219	2,134	3,207	915	1,073
Security Brokers	62	399	576	742	177	166

Table 3–1 continued

U.S. Data	SIC	1979:1	1983:1	1986:1	Change 1979–1983	Change 1983–1986
Insurance Carriers	63	4,874	4,331	4,392	(543)	61
Insurance Agents	64	2,617	2,762	3,045	145	283
Real Estate	65	3,028	3,121	3,624	93	503
Holding Companies	67	228	197	280	(31)	83
Business Services	73	15,866	17,496	22,096	1,630	4,600
Legal Services	81	2,543	3,021	3,779	478	758
Miscellaneous Services	89	5,946	6,052	6,413	106	361
Social Services		97,144	100,578	110,391	3,434	9,813
Health Services	80	41,028	45,215	51,867	4,187	6,652
Education Services	82	40,080	38,958	41,074	(1,122)	2,116
Social Services	83	9,014	9,563	11,289	549	1,726
Membership Organizations	86	7,022	6,842	6,161	(180)	(681)
Personal Services		45,647	45,938	52,933	291	6,995
Eating and Drinking Places	58	27,189	27,189	31,530	0	4,341
Hotels and Other Lodging	70	3,308	3,496	4,144	188	648
Personal Services	72	4,366	4,378	5,215	12	837
Auto Repair	75	3,323	3,285	4,034	(38)	749
Miscellaneous Repair	76	1,489	1,348	1,517	(141)	169
Motion Pictures	78	611	535	555	(76)	20
Amusement and Recreation	79	4,655	4,952	5,154	297	202
Museums, Gardens, and Zoos	84	234	266	261	32	(5)
Private Households	88	472	489	523	17	34

Table 3–2. Location Quotients, 1979 to 1986

Industry	SIC	Year : Quarter 1979:1	1986:1	Change
Mining		0.00	0.00	0.00
Construction		0.77	0.80	0.03
General Contractors	15	0.59	0.62	0.03
Heavy Contractors	16	0.67	0.72	0.04
Special Trade	17	0.90	0.92	0.01
Manufacturing		1.19	1.05	−0.14
Durable Goods		1.38	1.13	−0.26
Lumber and Wood Products	24	0.18	0.22	0.04
Furniture and Fixtures	25	0.37	0.37	0.00
Stone, Clay, and Glass	32	1.72	1.24	−0.47
Primary Metals	33	3.04	1.10	−1.95
Fabricated Metals	34	1.40	1.36	−0.04
Machinery, Except Electrical	35	0.92	0.95	0.03
Electrical and Electronic Mach.	36	0.94	0.75	−0.19
Transportation Equipment	37	2.11	1.97	−0.14
Instruments and Related	38	0.95	1.09	0.14
Miscellaneous Industries	39	1.28	1.43	0.15
Nondurable Goods		0.89	0.93	0.04
Food and Kindred Prods.	20	0.91	1.04	0.13
Textile Mill Products	22	0.24	0.14	−0.09
Apparel and Other Textiles	23	0.32	0.45	0.13
Paper and Allied Products	26	1.03	0.93	−0.09
Printing and Publishing	27	1.25	1.27	0.02
Chemicals and Allied Prods.	28	1.46	1.32	−0.14
Petroleum and Coal	29	0.91	0.45	−0.46
Rubber and Misc. Products	30	1.29	1.26	−0.02
Leather Products	31	0.32	0.21	−0.11
Services		1.16	1.21	0.05
Transportation		0.97	0.96	−0.01
Local Passenger Transit	41	1.24	1.93	0.68
Trucking and Warehousing	42	1.19	1.08	−0.10
Water Transport.	44	0.66	0.47	−0.19
Transport by Air	45	0.39	0.31	−0.07
Pipelines, Except Natural Gas	46	0.00	0.00	0.00
Transportation Services	47	0.83	0.99	0.16
Wholesale and Retail Trade		0.97	1.02	0.05
Wholesale Trade		2.15	2.14	−0.01
Durable Goods Wholesale	50	0.95	0.95	−0.00
Nondurable Wholesale	51	0.67	0.70	0.03

Table 3–2 continued

Industry	SIC	Year : Quarter		Change
		1979:1	1986:1	
General Merchandise	53	1.19	1.10	−0.10
Food Stores	54	1.26	1.37	0.11
Automotive Dealers	55	0.75	0.91	0.15
Apparel and Accessory	56	1.00	1.07	0.07
Home Furnishings	57	0.94	0.88	−0.06
Miscellaneous Retail	59	0.92	1.07	0.15
Producer Services		0.88	0.91	0.03
Communication	48	0.68	0.66	−0.02
Electric, Gas, and Sanitary	49	1.24	1.32	0.08
Banking	60	1.03	1.17	0.14
Credit Agencies, Except Banks	61	0.39	0.79	0.41
Security Brokers	62	0.35	0.39	0.04
Insurance Carriers	63	0.74	0.69	−0.05
Insurance Agents	64	1.06	1.07	0.01
Real Estate	65	0.59	0.63	0.04
Holding Companies	67	0.44	0.36	−0.07
Business Services	73	0.98	0.94	−0.04
Legal Services	81	0.98	1.03	0.05
Miscellaneous Services	89	1.10	1.00	−0.10
Social Services		2.22	2.26	0.04
Health Services	80	1.45	1.59	0.15
Education Services	82	6.34	6.82	0.48
Social Services	83	1.76	1.76	−0.01
Membership Organizations	86	1.78	1.65	−0.13
Personal Services		0.97	1.02	0.05
Eating and Drinking Places	58	1.08	1.11	0.02
Hotels and Other Lodging	70	0.57	0.62	0.05
Personal Services	72	0.80	0.93	0.13
Auto Repair	75	0.98	1.07	0.08
Miscellaneous Repair	76	0.92	0.94	0.02
Motion Pictures	78	0.48	0.96	0.47
Amusement and Recreation	79	1.24	1.34	0.10
Museums, Gardens, and Zoos	84	1.34	1.20	−0.14
Private Households	88	0.77	0.48	−0.29

Table 3–3.   Shift-Share Analysis, 1979 to 1983

Industry	SIC	Employment Change	National Growth Effect	Mix Effect	Share Effect	Competitive Effect
Mining		0	0	0	0	0
Construction		(3,162)	(53)	(2,306)	(2,359)	(803)
General Contractors	15	(923)	(12)	(878)	(889)	(34)
Heavy Contractors	16	(633)	(9)	(332)	(341)	(292)
Special Trade	17	(1,606)	(32)	(915)	(947)	(659)
Manufacturing		(41,543)	(432)	(20,280)	(20,712)	(20,831)
Durable Goods		(35,161)	(305)	(18,425)	(18,730)	(16,431)
Lumber and Wood Products	24	(194)	(2)	(163)	(166)	(28)
Furniture and Fixtures	25	(239)	(3)	(157)	(161)	(78)
Stone, Clay, and Glass	32	(2,659)	(21)	(1,527)	(1,547)	(1,112)
Primary Metals	33	(13,320)	(65)	(8,190)	(8,254)	(5,066)
Fabricated Metals	34	(4,146)	(41)	(3,019)	(3,060)	(1,086)
Machinery, Except Electrical	35	(3,458)	(40)	(2,493)	(2,533)	(925)
Electrical and Electronic Mach.	36	(2,269)	(34)	(696)	(730)	(1,539)
Transportation Equipment	37	(8,490)	(78)	(5,119)	(5,196)	(3,294)
Instruments and Related	38	(144)	(11)	90	79	(223)
Miscellaneous Industries	39	(242)	(10)	(607)	(617)	375
Nondurable Goods		(6,382)	(127)	(3,452)	(3,579)	(2,803)
Food and Kindred Prods	20	(592)	(27)	(600)	(626)	34
Textile Mill Products	22	(563)	0	(228)	(228)	(335)
Apparel and Other Textiles	23	(223)	(4)	(358)	(362)	139
Paper and Allied Products	26	(1,227)	(70)	(269)	(276)	(951)
Printing and Publishing	27	(469)	(12)	450	438	(907)
Chemicals and Allied Prods.	28	(1,486)	(27)	(484)	(510)	(976)

Table 3–3 continued

Industry	SIC	Employment Change	National Growth Effect	Mix Effect	Share Effect	Competitive Effect
Petroleum and Coal	29	(696)	(28)	(48)	(76)	(620)
Rubber and Misc. Products	30	(1,049)	(3)	(754)	(757)	(292)
Leather Products	31	(77)	(17)	(84)	(102)	25
Services		(2,154)	(884)	22,950	22,066	(24,220)
Transportation		(1,915)	(41)	(658)	(699)	(1,216)
Local Passenger Transit	41	380	(6)	(49)	(55)	435
Trucking and Warehousing	42	(2,156)	(27)	(1,033)	(1,060)	(1,096)
Water Transport.	44	(239)	(2)	(43)	(45)	(194)
Transport by Air	45	(154)	(3)	22	20	(174)
Pipelines, Except Natural Gas	46	0	0	0	0	0
Transportation Services	47	254	(3)	190	188	66
Wholesale and Retail Trade		(6,914)	(252)	0	(252)	(6,662)
Wholesale Trade		(6,813)	(191)	650	459	(7,272)
Durable Goods Wholesale	50	(1,777)	(50)	(74)	(124)	(1,653)
Nondurable Wholesale	51	259	(25)	257	233	26
General Merchandise	53	(4,074)	(47)	(1,045)	(1,092)	(2,982)
Food Stores	54	793	(50)	1,590	1,540	(747)
Automotive Dealers	55	(1,464)	(24)	(1,076)	(1,101)	(363)
Apparel and Accessory	56	(184)	(16)	44	28	(212)
Home Furnishings	57	(281)	(10)	(176)	(186)	(95)
Miscellaneous Retail	59	(186)	(30)	517	487	(673)
Producer Services		2,950	(168)	8,168	8,000	(5,050)
Communication	48	(360)	(15)	477	462	(822)
Electric, Gas, and Sanitary	49	309	(17)	614	597	(288)

Banking	60	31	(26)	1,136	1,110	(1,079)
Credit Agencies, Except Banks	61	915	(4)	161	157	758
Security Brokers	62	177	(1)	189	188	(11)
Insurance Carriers	63	(543)	(14)	116	101	(644)
Insurance Agents	64	145	(8)	387	380	(235)
Real Estate	65	93	(9)	194	185	(92)
Holding Companies	67	(31)	(1)	67	66	(97)
Business Services	73	1,630	(47)	3,302	3,255	(1,625)
Legal Services	81	478	(8)	813	805	(327)
Miscellaneous Services	89	106	(18)	878	860	(754)
Social Services		3,434	(289)	16,067	15,778	(12,344)
Health Services	80	4,187	(122)	8,714	8,592	(4,405)
Education Services	82	(1,122)	(119)	1,057	938	(2,060)
Social Services	83	549	(27)	1,762	1,735	(1,186)
Membership Organizations	86	(180)	(21)	80	59	(239)
Personal Services		291	(136)	4,131	3,996	(3,705)
Eating and Drinking Places	58	0	(81)	2,811	2,731	(2,731)
Hotels and Other Lodging	70	188	(10)	337	327	(139)
Personal Services	72	12	(13)	189	176	(164)
Auto Repair	75	(38)	(10)	109	100	(138)
Miscellaneous Repair	76	(141)	(4)	(0)	(4)	(137)
Motion Pictures	78	(76)	(2)	(21)	(23)	(53)
Amusement and Recreation	79	297	(14)	610	596	(299)
Museums, Gardens, and Zoos	84	32	(1)	31	30	2
Private Households	88	17	(1)	203	201	(184)

Table 3–4.   Shift-Share Analysis, 1983 to 1986

Industry	SIC	Employment Change	National Growth Effect	Mix Effect	Share Effect	Competitive Effect
Mining		0	0	0	0	0
Construction		3,208	1,880	2,092	3,972	(764)
General Contractors	15	750	382	680	1,062	(312)
Heavy Contractors	16	90	303	(304)	(2)	92
Special Trade	17	2,368	1,195	1,863	3,058	(690)
Manufacturing		(2,723)	13,299	(7,325)	5,974	(8,697)
Durable Goods		(2,739)	8,635	(2,728)	5,908	(8,647)
Lumber and Wood Products	24	171	77	13	90	81
Furniture and Fixtures	25	97	107	31	139	(42)
Stone, Clay, and Glass	32	(679)	549	(292)	258	(937)
Primary Metals	33	(4,273)	1,077	(1,267)	(190)	(4,083)
Fabricated Metals	34	127	1,257	(483)	774	(647)
Machinery, Except Electrical	35	317	1,265	(786)	479	(162)
Electrical and Electronic Mach.	36	(1,142)	1,188	(373)	815	(1,957)
Transportation Equipment	37	2,765	2,257	1,267	3,524	(759)
Instruments and Related	38	331	466	(360)	106	225
Miscellaneous Industries	39	(453)	392	(393)	(1)	(452)
Nondurable Goods		16	4,664	(3,971)	693	(677)
Food and Kindred Prods.	20	(130)	1,072	(1,101)	(29)	(101)
Textile Mill Products	22	(158)	86	(107)	(21)	(137)
Apparel and Other Textiles	23	279	292	(330)	(38)	317
Paper and Allied Products	26	226	381	(287)	94	132
Printing and Publishing	27	847	1,091	(22)	1,070	(223)
Chemicals and Allied Prods.	28	(1,064)	1,023	(1,166)	(143)	(921)

	Code					
Petroleum and Coal	29	(4)	51	(102)	(51)	47
Rubber and Misc Products	30	240	619	160	778	(538)
Leather Products	31	(220)	50	(141)	(92)	(128)
Services		36,169	37,884	5,496	43,380	(7,211)
Transportation		1,224	1,503	371	1,873	(649)
Local Passenger Transit	41	506	303	(61)	242	264
Trucking and Warehousing	42	522	883	288	1,171	(649)
Water Transport.	44	(122)	68	(112)	(44)	(78)
Transport by Air	45	34	106	76	183	(149)
Pipelines, Except Natural Gas	46	0	0	0	0	0
Transportation Services	47	284	142	178	321	(37)
Wholesale and Retail Trade		9,159	9,974	0	9,974	(815)
Wholesale Trade		4,351	7,381	(1,413)	5,968	(1,618)
Durable Goods Wholesale	50	1,233	1,925	(78)	1,847	(614)
Nondurable Wholesale	51	(254)	1,094	(440)	654	(908)
General Merchandise	53	1,148	1,505	(399)	1,106	42
Food Stores	54	2,079	2,255	115	2,371	(292)
Automotive Dealers	55	2,016	867	344	1,212	804
Apparel and Accessory	56	428	673	(38)	635	(207)
Home Furnishings	57	305	397	551	949	(644)
Miscellaneous Retail	59	2,204	1,257	89	1,346	858
Producer Services		8,978	7,612	3,266	10,878	(1,900)
Communication	48	(350)	609	(936)	(327)	(23)
Electric, Gas, and Sanitary	49	36	774	(552)	222	(186)
Banking	60	1,404	1,138	(777)	360	1,044
Credit Agencies, Except Banks	61	1,073	274	374	648	425
Security Brokers	62	166	74	95	169	(3)
Insurance Carriers	63	61	556	(201)	355	(294)
Insurance Agents	64	283	354	82	436	(153)

Table 3–4 continued

Industry	SIC	Employment Change	National Growth Effect	Mix Effect	Share Effect	Competitive Effect
Real Estate	65	503	400	258	658	(155)
Holding Companies	67	83	25	37	62	21
Business Services	73	4,600	2,244	4,458	6,702	(2,102)
Legal Services	81	758	388	326	714	44
Miscellaneous Services	89	361	776	354	1,131	(770)
Social Services		9,813	12,902	(2,613)	10,289	(476)
Health Services	80	6,652	5,800	(1,657)	4,143	2,509
Education Services	82	2,116	4,998	(2,282)	2,716	(600)
Social Services	83	1,726	1,227	804	2,030	(304)
Membership Organizations	86	(681)	878	(338)	540	(1,221)
Personal Services		6,995	5,893	1,716	7,609	(614)
Eating and Drinking Places	58	4,341	3,488	1,608	5,096	(755)
Hotels and Other Lodging	70	648	448	279	728	(80)
Personal Services	72	837	562	56	618	219
Auto Repair	75	749	421	402	823	(74)
Miscellaneous Repair	76	169	173	27	199	(30)
Motion Pictures	78	20	69	(311)	(242)	262
Amusement and Recreation	79	202	635	(402)	233	(31)
Museums, Gardens, and Zoos	84	(5)	34	37	71	(76)
Private Households	88	34	63	150	213	(179)

the decline of the industry in western New York was even more precipitous: in the period between 1979 and 1986, more than 80 percent of the jobs in the Buffalo steel industry disappeared. Nationally, the industry has restructured, with production carried out in fewer large, integrated steel mills, and with a proliferation of specialized minimills. Regionally, this pattern has not emerged. The major victim in the decline of the steel industry has been Bethlehem Steel. With the virtual shutdown of the Bethlehem steel complex in Lackawanna, along with the total collapse of other integrated steel plants, the region's steel industry was reduced to two minimills and a skeletal operation at the Bethlehem site.

Not surprisingly, the other regional industries associated with metal production (Major Groups 34, 35, and 36) declined as well, though not on the same scale as the steel industry. On average, these groups lost 25 percent of their respective work forces. The basic activities of these groups, machinery and fabricated metals, are directly tied to the region's historically dominant manufacturing activities of steel and auto. With the virtual desolation of the steel industry and the ongoing transformation of auto production (including the increased use of plastic and other lighter-weight materials), the declines in these central sectors of the area's industrial base can be understood (see, for example, Markusen et al., 1985, on the Chicago experience). This linkage to national and regional trends in autos, for example, can be detected in the modest upturn that occurs in employment in all three sectors after the 1981 to 1983 recession.

2.2 Cyclical Industries

Seven manufacturing sectors in the Buffalo SMSA reflect a sensitivity to recent economic cycles. Together they account for almost 35,000 workers. But this figure is deceiving because employment in one of these sectors, Transportation Equipment (Major Group 37) or auto parts, almost equals employment in the other six sectors (Wood Products [24], Furniture [Major Group 25], Paper Products [Major Group 26], Petroleum [Major Group 29], Rubber [Major Group 30], and Instruments [Major Group 38]) combined. The sensitivity of these industry groups, be they durable or nondurable goods producers, to national market shifts is more than matched by their vulnerability. While each of these sectors showed a tendency to recover, in employment terms, from the 1981 to 1983 recession, none of these sectors has been robust enough to match, much less exceed, their prerecession employment levels.

This trend matches a long-term trend in the overall vulnerability of the region's manufacturing base to cycles in the national economy. Since the Second World War, the manufacturing base of the regional economy has constantly ratcheted down — in no case has a recovery in the Buffalo manufacturing sector been enough to replace all the jobs lost during a recession. The combination of the absolute losses in the major employment categories discussed in the previous section, coupled with the absolute losses incurred in the manufacturing sectors experiencing some manner of cyclical recovery, portend another dramatic "ratcheting" down of the Buffalo-area manufacturing base.

The backbone of the limited cyclical recovery in the Buffalo manufacturing economy is the auto industry. The industry is home to three important constellations of plants producing components for the major automobile producers: General Motor's Harrison Radiator Corporation and Chevrolet-Pontiac-Canada Corporation and the Woodlawn Plant of the Ford Motor Corporation. The Harrison Radiator Corporation is a combine of four plants employing over 8,200 employees. The plant is the world's largest manufacturer of temperature cooling systems and, while it is a subsidiary of GM, it has intercorporate linkages with Ford, thereby supplying Ford with radiators and temperature-control equipment. The Chevrolet-Pontiac-Canada Group employs 4,600 and is a large producer of automobile engines. The largest Ford plant is the Woodlawn Plant. The plant employs 3,300 workers and is one of the major metal stamping plants in the domestic Ford network. Together these three plants account for almost 80 percent of all employment in the transportation equipment sector and 45.8 percent of the nearly 35,000 workers in all seven of the region's "cyclical sectors."

The auto industry has been incredibly sensitive to shifts in world and national economic conditions. The essential "recovery" of the industry in the past few years has been in large part a result of the restructuring of the industry. Part of this restructuring allowed for a partial return of the employment base lost in the late 1970s and early 1980s, but another part of the restructuring has meant the permanent loss of jobs. Even with "full recovery," most observers believe that as much as 26 percent of the hourly auto workers in the plants will not ever be returned to the production process. This is in part a product of internal restructuring of the production process (Hadeshian and Perry, 1988; Cole, 1984) and part the movement of large amounts of the production process offshore. Both patterns have been at work in Buffalo. General Motors and Ford both have laid off substantial numbers of workers and closed down forges and other primary production units. The SMSA is also the home of the Trico Corporation, one of the world's foremost producers of windshield wiper blades. However, the lion's share of workers and blades can now be found along the Texas-Mexico border.

2.3 Industries with Little Change

Three industrial groups in Buffalo have been relatively stable during the 1980s. By *stable*, we mean industries that have experienced small year-to-year changes amounting to minor fluctuations in employment. However, seemingly stable employment can mask internal turbulence and change.

The largest stable sector is the Printing and Publishing industry (Major Group 27). Its decline in 1983 can be attributed to the demise of Buffalo's second newspaper. If not for the loss of those jobs, printing could almost be considered a "growth" industry. This points up a difficulty in using employment as a measure of stability. Printing and publishing are really restructuring in most metropolitan areas, consolidating employment while adding capital equipment, and increasing sales and production.

3. Hidden Manufacturing Trend-Breakers

With the generally dismal performance of the manufacturing sectors during the late 1970s and 1980s, any trend-breakers would certainly be welcome. However, there are few regional industries that differ widely from the overall patterns of the more generally described manufacturing sectors. More precisely, the only two sectors that can truly be called positive trend-breakers are both in the Electrical Machinery sector (Major Group 36). Carbon and Graphite Products (Industry 3622) and Communications Equipment (Industry 3662) both exhibited consistent and significant growth over the period 1979 to 1986. This growth is all the more impressive given the fact that the region's largest electrical machinery producer, Westinghouse, closed during this period.

The growth of the communications equipment sector offers an interesting case in the perils of industrial takeovers and the broader arena of industrial restructuring (Kraushaar and Feldman, 1989). The primary reason for the sector's growth has been the success of the sophisticated Sierra Research Corporation, which makes communication devices for the military and for airplanes. The company originated in the Buffalo region and has experienced rapid growth. The irony is that, in 1983, it sold itself to LTV Corporation in an effort to secure more capital needed for expansion. LTV is now in the process of bankruptcy, a casualty of the transformation of the steel industry. By most accounts, LTV is blamed with limiting the phenomenal growth of Sierra.

There were also two negative trend-breakers, both in Major Group 35 (Machinery). While the Compressor Industry (SIC 3563) is restructuring nationwide, it is in the process of employment decline in western New York. Dominated by a few large, traditional firms, the regional compressor sector lost almost 1,000 workers in the 1980s through cutbacks and closures. Industry 3564 (Blowers and Fans) in the Buffalo SMSA essentially contains one large establishment — Buffalo Forge — and several very small firms. Its parent company through much of the 1980s, Ampco-Pittsburgh, has used the plant as a "cash cow," draining capital and reducing employment.

4. Average Earnings in Manufacturing

Historically, the manufacturing wage structure in Buffalo has been higher than the national metropolitan average. Since their peak in 1980, however, average earnings for the area's skilled and unskilled manufacturing workers, compared to the rest of the country, have dropped significantly and are now much closer to the nation as a whole. Even with layoffs of lower-paid workers with less seniority and national collective bargaining agreements, workers in primary metals industries, for example, averaged between 5 percent and 10 percent less salary in 1984 when compared to 1979 (using 1979 dollars) (Doolittle, 1985, pp. 33–35). These declines in earnings are still overshadowed, however, by high earnings in the manufacturing industries we have characterized as "declining" or "cyclical." Average earnings for the more than 40,000 workers in the region's declining industries were in excess of $29,150; the almost 45,000 workers in those industries we defined as cyclical had average earnings of over $30,500. This latter figure is in large part explained by the dominance of the auto industry employees in the cyclical industrial category. In 1986, the auto industry employed over 20,000 workers, who ranked among the highest-paid in Buffalo. When we exclude auto workers, the average earnings of all workers in the declining industries are substantially higher than those paid to workers in all other industrial groups. Concentrating for a moment on the almost 20,000 workers in the region's stable industries, it is apparent that stability does not equate with high earnings. The annual earnings of workers in the stable industries are less than $22,000.

Another result of these trends is a dramatic decrease in the total manufacturing payroll of the region — a product of the highest earnings being paid to industrial workers in sectors suffering the largest absolute declines in jobs.

5. The Service Sector

As elsewhere in the United States, service sector employment has grown in the Buffalo SMSA (see table 3–1). In the period 1979 to 1986, service employment grew by over 34,000 workers. This contrasts sharply with manufacturing employment, which declined by approximately 45,000 during the same period (see above). While the service sector declined overall during the recession of the early 1980s, it has exhibited consistent growth since then.

This shift in the region's once overwhelming dependency on manufacturing to a more diverse (if not more financially secure for workers) economic base with employment more evenly spread across service categories, as well as manufacturing groups, has yielded some important improvements in the service industries' ability to "export" their employment (see table 3–2). Overall, the service sector's LQ went from 1.16 to 1.21 during the 1979 to 1986 time period. Of the five service industry groups, only transportation showed a drop in LQ during this period, and transportation was never a strong industrial group to begin with. The other four groups (wholesale and retail trade, producer services, social services, and personal services) all showed increases in employment and LQs. Three of these groups, personal services, social services, and wholesale and retail trade, all exhibited LQs over 1.0 — evidencing the region's apparent coming of age, so to speak, as a more active center of service employment. Producer services, on the other hand, while exhibiting some signs of growth, remained dramatically below the national norm for export base strength.

In the face of this change in the economic base of the region, the question now becomes: has the shift to services increased Buffalo's "competitiveness"? We know that the competitive position of the region's manufacturing base has continued to slip, but has this pattern been avoided in the ostensibly growing service base (see tables 3–3 and 3–4)? In general, the answer to these questions is "no." In fact, during the cyclical downturn between 1979 and 1983, the region was *less* competitive in its job-generating capacity in the services industries in general than it was in the manufacturing sector.

Further, between 1983 and 1986, the over 36,000 jobs added to the region's service economy, while significant, were still not enough to supply the region with an overall competitive position. In fact, the region registered a negative "competitive effect" in *all* five of the service categories during this period.

At the individual sector level, the ongoing dynamics of the region's competitive decline is shown, most dramatically, in the area of educational services. In location-quotient terms, the education sector is a "growth industry," registering an LQ of over 6.0 — making the industry far and away the most affirmatively active in the region. At the same time, its contemporary state of competitiveness, as measured in terms of its competitive effect, is highly negative for the entire 1979 to 1986 time period. This means that the Buffalo area, even at its most specialized service-based best, is not growing at the national rate. At its best, the region, as stated earlier, is suffering from a long-term case of economic anemia; it is growing at a decreasing rate relative to the changes in the larger national and international economies.

The basic trend-breakers in the services were, for the most part, those that exhibited substantial decline in the face of overall sectorial growth or postrecessionary recovery.

5.1 Transportation

Transportation is one of the least important segments of the Buffalo economy. Employing less than 13,000 workers in 1986, a decline of almost 700 workers from its 1979 total, it represents 4 percent of the total service sector job base. Of the five major groups of transportation industries represented in the region, only local passenger transit and transportation services grew. Although precise data are not available, much of this growth seems to be related to tourism activities (Reeves, 1988).

Two transportation sectors, including Water Transportation (Major Group 44) and Air Transportation (Major Group 45), have declined over the past seven years. The decline in water transportation is directly linked to the decline in importance and traffic of the Buffalo Port. The decline in air transportation reflects the changing nature of the airline industry since deregulation and the decline in the number of airlines offering service to smaller metropolitan areas.

The major employer in transportation is trucking and warehousing. The firms in this sector have been exceedingly sensitive to the business cycle with losses in employment suffered at the trough of the cycle never made up by gains at the end of the cycle. Again, this is an example of a regional industry's is losing more than it gains while experiencing the vicissitudes of the business cycle.

5.2 Wholesale and Retail Trade

Wholesale and retail trade represents more than one-quarter of all service employment and, in some ways, can be seen as one of the most active service sector groups in the Buffalo region. Firms in this service sector added over 2,200 new workers during the 1979 to 1986 time period, with employment rising from 84,662 to almost 87,000. On balance, the wholesale groups seem far less dynamic than the retail industries in the Buffalo region.

Of the nine major wholesale and retail groups, only two, "General Merchandise" and "Durable Goods, Wholesale," lost employment during the period. The others, while exhibiting a sensitivity to the business downturn of the early 1980s, all added employees. Employment in the Building Materials sector (Major Group 52) and Home Furnishings sector (Major Group 57), for example, are linked to changes in the construction industry, another industry very susceptible to the cyclical swings in the economy.

Major Group 53 (General Merchandise Stores) offers an interesting case study of the effects of decline and restructuring. Buffalo used to be dominated by locally owned and operated department stores. With the recessions of the 1970s and early 1980s, and the resultant loss of buying power in the region, several of these stores were forced to close. The downtown retail area went from five major department stores in 1981 to one in 1987. Major local and national department stores have spread out to the suburbs, anchoring seven large shopping plazas in the SMSA. The major sources of new employment in this category have come in the form of nationally owned and operated discount chains such as KMart, TJ Maxx, etc.

The other two cyclical sectors have been Major Group 54 (Food Stores) and Major Group 59 (Miscellaneous Retail Operations). In the case of food stores, there has been significant activity in Buffalo in the development of both "mom-and-pop" stores and new, larger supermarkets.

Stores in between have been squeezed and many have closed. The overall effect has been a consistent increase in employment.

5.3 Producer Services

Between 1979 and 1986, producer services increased by over 22 percent or 12,000 employees which, with the exception of a slight drop in employment in 1982, at the heart of the recession, was the result of a consistent pattern of growth. Producer services were less affected by the recession than the rest of the service sector and have, over the time period 1979 to 1986, increased their share of service employment overall.

It should be noted, however, that the growth and location of these services within the region has been uneven. A recent study of the Buffalo SMSA (Harrington and Lombard, 1987) found that producer services that have contributed to the region's export base are concentrated in the central-city-core-county area, while producer services more directly linked to the manufacturing sector are found in smaller outlying nodes and in the county of Niagara and the city of Niagara Falls. The former services are, according to Harrington and Lombard (1987), more "growth oriented," while the latter services are more likely to exhibit decline in employment in recessionary economic times.

Several producer service sectors exhibited strong growth, including Major Group 61 (Nondepository Credit Institutions), Legal Services (Major Group 81), and Miscellaneous Services (Major Group 89). It should be noted that this growth was consistent with national growth patterns during the same period and that, as of 1985, each represented approximately the national average in western New York.

Several key sectors of the region's producer services exhibited cyclical trends in employment. The two largest sectors, Banking (Major Group 60) and Business Services, including Advertising and Computer-Related Services (Major Group 73), declined in 1981. Banking continued to decline in 1982 and both sectors grew consistently after 1982. A significant difference between cyclical producer service industries and cyclical manufacturing industries is that all the producer service sectors grew at a very pronounced rate after the recession, with employment, by 1986, significantly higher than in 1979. In manufacturing, all the industrial sectors found new, and lower, levels of employment. In short, where manufacturing "ratcheted down" with the last recession and recovery, the recovery in producer services was more than enough to "ratchet up" the employment level of the entire group.

There were four producer service sectors that acted contrary to the dominant trends of growth and cyclical upswings in most of the producer services. The only two with significant employment are Major Group 48 (Communications) and Major Group 63 (Insurance Carriers).

Finally, the only service sector to remain relatively stable with little change over the time period was Major Group 49 (Electric, Gas, and Sanitary Services). Given the declining population in the region, this makes sense. Utility companies have certain fixed capacity that requires certain levels of service and maintenance. While adding little new demand during the 1980s, it would have been very unusual for the region's utility companies to reduce their capacity.

5.4 Social Services

Social services represent the largest employment grouping in the service sector. Over 110,000 people are employed in social services, over one-third of the metropolitan area's total service employment. As a group, social services have been essentially cyclical, declining until 1984 and adding employees since then. Any changes in employment have been slight, with the general result being that social services gained less than 2,000 total new workers since 1979. Social services, as a percentage of total service employment, have declined since the recession.

In spite of the overall stability in social services, six sectors did exhibit significant growth. Buffalo is a major regional center for health services and, correspondingly, this major group exhibited strong growth. Other social services increasing in employment include Major Group 83 (Social Services) and Major Group 92 (Services Relating to Law and Justice), which includes correctional facilities.

The largest cyclical social service has been Major Group 82 (Educational Services) which, though relatively stable, did dip slightly during the recession. Major Group 96 (Administration of Economic Programs) dipped in 1981 at the start of the recession.

Six social service sectors declined during 1979 and 1986. The most significant decline was in Government Services (Major Group 91), which lost approximately 4,500 workers. This is the reverse of Stanback and Noyelle's (1982) analysis, which showed government services growing substantially during the period 1959 to 1976. The second largest group to decline was Major Group 86 (Membership Services). Buffalo has always had more than its share of religious organizations, but the decline matches closely the national trend (Harrington and Lombard, 1987).

5.5 Personal Services

Personal services account for almost 16 percent of total services. While most personal services exhibited some cyclical behavior in the last seven years, their overall growth has been strong, adding over 7,200 jobs to their overall total. No major sector has declined or remained basically stable over the entire time period. Personal services have increased as a percentage of total services since 1979.

The main growth in personal services in Buffalo was in Eating and Drinking Establishments (Major Group 58), which grew by 4,341 during the period 1979 to 1986. Hotels and Other Lodgings (Major Group 70), Personal Services (Major Group 72), and Amusement and Recreation (Major Group 79) also exhibited consistent growth.

The number of movie theaters has increased significantly during the 1980s, with most of the growth in the suburbs. Even so, the total employment in Major Group 78 (Motion Pictures), while cyclical in nature, declined overall.

6. Average Earnings in Services

The service sectors exhibiting little change had the highest average earnings, followed by those showing constant growth. This is tempered, however, by the large percentage of service employment in Buffalo affected by cyclical patterns and their extremely low earnings.

In a comparison of all five service sectors — transportation, wholesale and retail, producer, social, and personal — clear differences emerge. Personal services pay extremely low earnings overall. Producer services, as might be expected, pay the highest. Finally, if present trends continue, manufacturing employment, with its higher average earnings, will continue to decline while services grow. Thus, the overall average earnings of the region will continue to fall both in real dollars and in comparison to the rest of the country, continuing a trend since 1981 (Doolittle, 1985).

7. Theories of Change and Implications on Findings

"Despite the importance of large manufacturing firms, Buffalo seems to have been singularly unsuccessful in moving its economy toward the development of corporate headquarters activities and supporting services, as did most of the metropolitan economies studied here or certain of its neighboring cities, such as Albany and Rochester" (Stanback and Noyelle, 1982, p. 102; also Noyelle and Stanback, 1983).

The economic history of the Buffalo region in many ways mirrors the history of the nation. For most of its history, the region was the beneficiary of economic restructuring. Buffalo, at its inception, was the product of frontier mercantilism, and its initial move to economic prominence was directly the result of its central location in the extraction network of the nation's mercantile economy. As the nation developed as a center of manufacturing, so did Buffalo. Just as Buffalo had been a central cog in mercantilism, so too did the metropolitan area become highly integrated into the mass production order of the economically restructured nation state. Hence, through two definitive epochs of U.S. capitalism, Buffalo prospered.

However, soon after the Second World War, the region began to feel the effects of a structure of production that would, at first slowly albeit continuously, start to disintegrate as the spatial center of manufacturing shifted to other parts of the world. In this latest round of national economic restructuring, Buffalo would be less a beneficiary and more a "victim" of economic change (Perry, 1987). The large concentration of jobs and economic activity in heavy manufacturing would no longer appear as a "competitive advantage" — rather it would be more like an albatross.

With every recession or economic downturn, the manufacturing base of the region ratcheted down until, in the 1980s, those deriving their incomes from manufacturing were less than one-fifth the work force (where at one time they had been over one-half). What was once an "advantage" was viewed by many as a "liability." The region was not positioned to respond to changes in the world economy the way it had in previous periods. Even in its present state of "recovery," the region is exhibiting the least successful patterns of economic change. With few exceptions, the manufacturing base of the region is continuing to decline. Many of its once highly competitive sectors are barely competitive any more. Where there has been manufacturing resurgence, it has occurred in some of the most sensitive and economically vulnerable sectors — not firm footing upon which to rebuild the industrial base.

The service sector, rather than being the "flagship" of a new economic epoch for the Buffalo SMSA, has really been, at best, no more than an economic life raft. In fact, the increases in services have been far less dramatic than national increases and have not produced an overwhelming competitive economic advantage for Buffalo. The result has been, as Noyelle and Stanback (1982, p. 120) conclude, ". . . a heavy competition for low-end service jobs in a failing manufacturing-oriented economy."

Ironically these trends point to the importance of manufacturing as an integral part of the region's economic future. In the face of the dramatic rise in employment in the service sector and the longterm failure of much of the manufacturing sector, it has become both popular and politique to assert that regional renaissance is a distinctly "postindustrial" service sector phenomenon. In Buffalo, however, manufacturing continues to matter (Cohen and Zysman, 1987; U.S. Congress, 1988; and Shapira, 1988).

Two general trends bear this out. First, as manufacturing has declined, the patterns of consistent growth in sectors of the region's service economy that are closely linked to manufacturing have all but disappeared. When manufacturing activity has increased ever so slightly, we have seen concomitant signs of growth in Buffalo's producer services and business service sectors.

Second, service sectors that have exhibited consistent growth in Buffalo are the least well linked to manufacturing, that is, they grew in spite of the decline in manufacturing. While this trend may appear, at first blush, to be quite healthy, it should be pointed out that these sectors also recorded the lowest levels of earnings, less security, and fewer opportunities for advancement. This pattern of consistent growth in economic sectors supplying the lowest earnings has driven this once "high wage" area's overall average earnings below the national average (Doolittle, 1985).

The illusion of Buffalo's transforming itself into a producer service region replete with high-power and high-paying jobs has not materialized. Buffalo is metamorphosing from a high-wage manufacturing town to a low-wage service town. Hence, it is small wonder the T-shirt advocating no illusions is a best seller. The economic structure of Buffalo is still set on a course of long-term decline. Growth has not meant a return to regional competitiveness or a return to high earnings. Growth is still an illusion.

Acknowledgments

The authors wish to thank Edward Hill, Neil Shelley, and Riao Babhur for their assistance.

4 CHICAGO, ILLINOIS: REAPING THE BENEFITS OF SIZE AND DIVERSITY

David Allardice, Wim Wiewel, and Wendy Wintermute

The most striking characteristic of the economy of the Chicago region is its enormous size and diversity. Total employment is over 3 million, and there are over 100,000 workers in each of the major industrial divisions, with the exception of agriculture and mining. Within each of these divisions, there are firms in almost every conceivable type of industry. Indeed, with one exception (mining), Chicago has more firms in every industrial division (one-digit) than any other Great Lakes metro area city (see table 4–1).

Diversity has clear economic benefits. It cushions the shocks of growth and decline in specific sectors as demand for their products changes or as price and competitiveness are affected by changes elsewhere. In exchange for this relatively greater stability, the economy does not always reap the rewards of very rapid growth that can occur in a specialized economy. In the Midwest, Detroit and Chicago have long been the classic examples of a highly specialized versus a diversified economy.

Sheer size accentuates the advantages of diversity. Because of the large number of firms and workers in Chicago's industries, there are many specific sectors in which the region can benefit from agglomeration economies. The presence of a large, trained labor force, plus wholesalers and suppliers, technicians, and consumers, makes Chicago an attractive lo-

Table 4–1. Number of Establishments by Industrial Division For Ten Great Lakes Metro Areas — 1986

Industry	Chicago	Akron	Buffalo	Cleveland	Dayton
Agriculture	1,501	178	187	583	212
Mining	144	51	24	69	37
Construction	11,517	1,119	1,827	3,111	1,569
Manufacturing	13,514	1,157	1,271	4,174	1,568
Transportation and Utilities	5,618	430	657	1,300	519
Wholesale Trade	15,443	1,036	1,804	4,126	1,361
Retail Trade	37,052	3,765	5,807	10,709	5,090
Fire	16,336	1,051	1,593	3,922	1,559
Services	53,892	4,781	6,775	14,806	6,450
Nonclassified	10,640	897	1,556	2,450	1,203
Total	165,657	14,465	21,501	45,250	19,568

Industry	Detroit	Milwaukee	Pittsburgh	Syracuse	Youngstown
Agriculture	935	321	414	140	98
Mining	98	41	233	18	38
Construction	6,779	2,645	4,112	1,326	828
Manufacturing	7,896	2,936	2,399	733	600
Transportation and Utilities	2,615	1,178	1,546	489	363
Wholesale Trade	7,139	2,878	3,624	1,349	660
Retail Trade	19,951	8,023	12,358	3,824	2,963
Fire	6,851	3,003	4,037	1,112	815
Services	31,090	10,915	15,961	4,330	3,523
Unclassified	5,497	2,268	2,963	1,185	691
Total	91,356	34,208	47,647	14,506	10,579

cation for any number of specific industries. Size also makes it possible for an industry to weather changes without disappearing altogether. As certain products become obsolete, there are likely to remain the workers and local expertise to identify and exploit new niches. Each industry or industrial sector of a large enough size has a certain infrastructure of people, institutions, and relationships that makes it more adaptable to change compared to smaller industries (Thompson, 1965; Satterthwaite, 1988; and Giese and Testa, 1988).

The combined effect of diversity and size is particularly noticeable in Chicago's rich infrastructure of business services. Traditional export-base theory considered services a residual, the result of the relative health of the basic sector, which was generally conceived of as manufacturing. Although this linkage continues to be important, as we will show, the relationship has become significantly attenuated and should perhaps be considered in reverse. Wilbur Thompson suggested this 20 years ago when he noted that in ". . . the very long run it may well be the local service sector which is enduring (basic) and the manufacturing plant which is transitory" (1968, p. 44).

In this view, the size and diversity of Chicago's economy has encouraged the development of a varied and sophisticated business services sector. The presence of so many services further enhances Chicago's attraction as a business location, and also increases the likelihood of local entrepreneurship and business expansion.

The importance of this large business services sector is heightened further by the fact that many of these services are themselves export industries. Although accurate data are hard to come by, it is clear that Chicago's financial, legal, accounting, and consulting services export their services to the Midwest, the nation, and indeed the world.

In this chapter, we will show how the size and diversity of Chicago's economy enabled it to generate sufficient innovation and growth to compensate for the large employment losses that occurred in the 1980s, especially in manufacturing. The analysis is based on County Business Patterns data, which are derived from Social Security records and which include all private-sector employment. Such employment data are a reasonable measure of the health of the economy as a whole, although they do not include information on the income generated by the employment, nor do they differentiate between full-time and part-time jobs. Thus, these data do not allow us to draw conclusions regarding the economic well-being of Chicago workers.

Measuring the viability of particular sectors through changes in employment has other limitations. It may well be that some industries that show employment declines are faring very well and applying new labor-saving technologies. Their increased output and value-added may still lead to job creation in Chicago, through the purchase of business services or other inputs. Thus, employment numbers on a specific industry, or sector, alone are not really sufficient to draw conclusions about the ultimate economic health or impact of any individual industry. Hence, the analysis will emphasize broad patterns, rather than fine-grained detail.

1. Chicago Overview

Although this analysis covers the period 1979 to 1986, a brief retrospection is in order, since 1979 actually represents the peak of a period of national expansion that began in 1976. During the period 1976 to 1986, the Chicago area added a total of about 365,400 jobs, a growth of about 14 percent. However, the aggregate data hide the fact that over this period more than 144,000 manufacturing jobs were lost, a decline of 17 percent. On the other hand, all major nonmanufacturing sectors added jobs during this period. The large and diverse local service sector added 282,300 jobs, an increase of 50 percent. Once the dominant sector of the Chicago area economy, by 1986 manufacturing had slipped to second place behind the service sector (see table 4–2).

Table 4–2.   Chicago's Changing Employment Base

Sector	Employment 1976	Employment 1979	Employment 1986	Percentage Employment Growth: 1979–1986 Chicago	U.S.
Total Employment*	2,646,300	3,021,700	3,011,700	−1	12
Agricultural Services	4,800	5,900	8,800	48	46
Mining	3,700	4,500	4,700	5	−11
Construction	110,400	135,600	125,300	−8	1
Manufacturing	865,000	934,700	721,000	−23	−11
Transportation	171,600	176,600	174,100	−1	6
Wholesale Trade	210,800	238,700	253,800	6	10
Retail Trade	496,700	562,600	572,700	2	16
Finance	218,400	251,600	283,700	13	23
Services	564,800	698,600	847,100	21	36
Unclassified	2,800	12,800	22,000	72	88

*Note: Numbers may not sum due to roundings.

Even this level of aggregation is misleading, however. There were many exceptions to the general rule of manufacturing decline and non-manufacturing growth when individual industries are examined. The following sections discuss these changes in manufacturing and services in more detail.

2. Trends in Manufacturing

Between 1976 and 1979, the Chicago area manufacturing base grew by about 8 percent, trailing a national growth rate of slightly over 13 percent in manufacturing. Durable goods manufacturing posted a particularly strong showing, increasing its already dominant share of the area's manufacturing base from 57.7 percent to 59.3 percent. Nondurable manufacturing employment actually declined by 0.7 percent.

2.1 Recession

The back-to-back recessions of the early 1980s decimated the manufacturing base in the Chicago area. Between 1979 and 1983, 229,000 manufacturing jobs were lost, and manufacturing employment declined by almost one-fourth. At the same time, national manufacturing employment declined by about 15 percent.

Table 4–3 illustrates manufacturing sector performance over the period 1979 to 1983. Several points are noteworthy. First, not one sector had a positive growth rate during this period. Second, every major sector in the region declined at rates in excess of their national counterparts. More importantly, the largest declines were centered in the durable manufacturing sector. During this period, the three largest manufacturing sectors (electrical equipment, nonelectrical equipment, and fabricated metals — all durables) lost a combined 96,000 jobs, amounting to a loss of 27 percent of their total employment in 1979, and accounting for 42 percent of all manufacturing losses between 1979 and 1983.

Nevertheless, examining the performance of industries at a four-digit level reveals a total of 78 industries with local employment of at least 500 that had growth rates surpassing the national average for manufacturing over this period. Of these 78 sectors, 46 were in durable goods and 32 were nondurables. Furthermore, of the top 25 growth sectors in manufacturing, all but three had growth rates surpassing that of their national counterparts. However, the shortfalls included the critical areas of radio and television communications and commercial printing and lithography, along with x-ray apparatus and tubes (see table 4–4).

Table 4–3.   Chicago Metro Area Manufacturing Employment, 1979 to 1983

	Employment		Percentage Change: 1979–1983	
	1979	1983	Chicago	U.S.
Total Manufacturing*	934,700	705,600	− 24	− 15
Durable Manufacturing	554,800	381,600	− 31	− 16
24 Lumber	8,100	6,200	− 23	− 22
25 Furniture	19,100	14,100	− 26	− 15
32 Stone, Clay, and Glass	20,200	12,700	− 37	− 38
33 Primary Metal	56,400	29,800	− 47	− 38
34 Fabricated Metal	108,000	79,600	− 26	− 21
35 Nonelectrical Mach.	121,400	80,500	− 34	− 21
36 Electrical Equip.	124,900	92,200	− 26	− 5
37 Transportation Equip.	32,900	19,700	− 40	− 22
38 Instruments	36,200	26,900	− 26	− 4
39 Misc. Mfg.	27,600	19,900	− 28	− 20
Nondurable Manufacturing	291,100	250,700	− 14	− 7
20 Food Products	61,800	55,900	− 10	− 8
21 Tobacco	400	400	− 3	− 7
22 Textiles	2,900	1,500	− 48	− 19
23 Apparel	14,900	11,100	− 25	− 16
26 Paper	30,600	25,100	− 18	− 9
27 Printing and Publishing	81,300	75,000	− 8	3
28 Chemical Products	50,200	44,200	− 12	− 7
29 Petroleum Products	6,400	4,200	− 35	− 6
30 Rubber Products	38,400	31,400	− 18	− 18
31 Leather Products	4,200	2,000	− 54	− 22
Auxiliary	99,000	97,300	− 2	− 7

*Note: Sums may not add due to rounding and data disclosure limits.

Table 4–4.   Top 25 Manufacturing Growth Sectors in Chicago, 1979–1983, Four-digit Level of Data

SIC	Sector	Emp. 1979	Growth Rates		Location Quotient
			Chicago	U.S.	
2754	Commercial Printing, Gravure	1,464	137	11	1.7
2753	Engraving and Plate Printing	653	116	10	1.4

Table 4–4 continued

SIC	Sector	Emp. 1979	Growth Rates		Location Quotient
			Chicago	U.S.	
3573	Electronic Computing Equip.	683	72	31	0.1
3523	Farm Machinery and Equip.	1,735	70	−43	0.3
2011	Meat Packing Plants	1,462	59	−16	0.2
3841	Surgical and Medical Instrument	1,621	57	9	0.7
3496	Fabricated Wire, Misc.	2,385	43	−7	1.6
3646	Commercial Lighting Fixtures	1,918	43	1	2.5
2655	Fiber Cans and Drums	595	42	−22	0.8
3399	Primary Metal Products, NEC	586	39	−54	0.8
3693	X-ray Apparatus and Tubes	758	36	37	0.6
3317	Steel Pipe and Tubes	1,345	30	−33	1.0
2079	Shortening and Cooking Oils	825	29	−9	1.5
3631	Household Cooking Equipment	1,379	27	−6	1.4
2844	Toilet Preparations	3,506	24	6	1.6
2891	Adhesives and Sealants Equipment	1,660	22	5	2.2
3662	Radio and TV Communication Eqt.	12,795	19	22	0.8
2899	Chemical Preparations, Nec.	2,522	18	1	1.6
3823	Process Control Instrument	2,432	15	5	1.3
2641	Paper Coating and Glazing	3,260	14	−2	1.8
3555	Printing Trades Machinery	1,953	14	−7	1.7
2752	Comm Printing, Lithographic	16,282	13	21	1.6
3713	Truck and Bus Bodies	683	11	−40	0.4
3449	Metal Work, Misc.	606	10	6	0.8
3944	Games, Toys, Children Vehicles	2,615	9	−17	1.4

What these data show is that even during a general period of economic restructuring and downturn there are sectors of the economy that show growth. The difficult aspect from a public policy point of view is the ability to identify these sectors in advance as opposed to after the fact.

2.2 Recovery

Between 1983 and 1986, the Chicago area recovered a total of 15,300 manufacturing jobs (see table 4–5). This represents a growth of 2.2 percent

Table 4–5.   Chicago Metro Area Manufacturing Employment, 1983 to 1986

	Employment		Percentage Change: 1983–1986	
	1983	1986	Chicago	U.S.
Total Manufacturing*	705,640	720,925	2	5
Durable Manufacturing	381,700	399,400	5	5
24 Lumber	6,200	6,900	10	11
12 Furniture	14,100	21,500	52	15
32 Stone, Clay, and Glass	12,700	15,600	23	7
33 Primary Metal	29,800	28,200	−5	−2
34 Fabricated Metal	79,600	82,700	4	8
35 Nonelectrical Mach.	80,500	86,400	7	2
36 Electrical Equip.	92,200	91,600	−1	8
37 Transportation Equip.	19,700	20,400	3	16
38 Instruments	26,900	28,400	6	2
39 Misc. Mfg.	19,900	17,800	−11	3
Nondurable Manufacturing	250,700	245,900	−2	0
20 Food Products	55,900	52,800	−6	−1
21 Tobacco	400	400	0	−13
22 Textiles	1,500	1.900	27	−5
23 Apparel	11,000	11,200	1	−4
26 Paper	25,000	25,400	1	5
27 Printing and Publishing	75,000	77,600	4	13
28 Chemical Products	44,200	37,700	−15	−3
29 Petroleum Products	4,200	3,900	−5	−12
30 Rubber Products	31,400	33,000	5	16
31 Leather Products	1,900	1,800	−5	−25
Auxiliary	97,258	103,374	6	8

*Note: Sums may not add due to rounding and data disclosure limits.

Table 4–6. Top 25 Manufacturing Growth Sectors in Chicago, 1983–1986, Four-digit Level of Data

			Growth Rates		Location
SIC	Sector	Emp. 1983	Chicago	U.S.	Quotient
3632	Household Refrig. and Freezers	750	133	33	2.0
3822	Environment Controls	1,870	107	7	3.6
3398	Metal Heat Treating	995	96	24	2.8
3537	Industrial Trucks and Tractors	1,260	82	6	2.8
2434	Wood Kitchen Cabinets	522	74	26	0.4
3561	Pumps and Pumping Equipment	1,259	72	–4	1.1
3273	Ready-Mixed Concrete	892	71	16	0.5
3432	Plumbing Fitting and Brass Goods	1,206	70	5	3.6
3542	Machine Tools, Metal Forming	2,371	66	8	6.1
3272	Concrete Products, Nec.	831	64	26	0.6
2033	Canned Fruits and Vegetables	572	61	–5	0.5
2865	Cyclic Crudes and Intermediates	820	58	9	1.6
3448	Prefabricated Metal Bldgs.	550	53	15	1.0
3549	Metalworking Machinery, nec.	1,249	52	17	2.6
3531	Construction Machinery	6,144	50	–5	3.1
2038	Frozen Specialties	1,686	50	17	1.5
2869	Industrial Organic Chemicals	874	47	–13	0.4
3728	Aircraft Equipment, nec.	560	46	21	0.1
3644	Noncurrent-carrying Wiring Devices	3,083	45	10	4.9
3466	Crown and Closures	1,271	42	–13	7.9
3569	General Industrial Mach., NEC	2,950	41	16	1.8
2335	Womens Dresses	1,428	40	–14	0.5
3563	Air and Gas Compressors	1,395	39	–4	2.1
3953	Marketing Devices	525	35	3	2.5
2789	Bookbinding	2,100	34	19	2.6

over the period, slightly less than half the national rate of 5.0 percent. These data also reveal a strong performance in the durable manufacturing sector relative to the nondurable sector. The durable manufacturing sector as a whole grew by 4.6 percent or 18,000 jobs, compared to a 2 percent decline or loss of 4,800 jobs for nondurables. From 1983 to 1986, only three of Chicago's durable goods manufacturing sectors (primary metals, electrical equipment, and miscellaneous manufacturing) lost employment. Driven by a growth in capital spending and exports, four sectors (furniture; nonelectrical machinery; stone, clay, and glass; and instruments) showed strong local growth, outperforming their national counterparts.

During the same period, the major losses in nondurables were in chemicals and food products, which lost a total of 9,600 jobs. Only two minor nondurable sectors (textiles and leather products) outperformed their national counterparts. However, because the recovery became more consumer-driven after 1986, nondurables are likely to have improved their performance.

A more detailed examination at the four-digit level reveals that 82 industries outperformed the national average manufacturing growth rate between 1983 and 1986. Of these, 62 were in the durable goods sector, 19 were in nondurable goods. Of the top 25 performing manufacturing sectors over the current recovery period, the top 10 come from the durable goods sector (see table 4–6). Moreover, 11 of the 25 had less than 1,000 employees in 1983 and only one had more than 5,000. This finding suggests that Chicago's industrial base, in spite of declines in some sectors, has nevertheless provided the industrial infrastructure, the "seedbed," that has nourished the growth of newer and smaller industries.

Furthermore, 18 of the top 25 sectors had location quotients greater than 1.0 and 13 had quotients greater than 2.0. This indicates that Chicago-area growth was concentrated in those sectors in which the region has a high concentration. During the current recovery, the Chicago area appears to be building on its traditional strengths in durable manufacturing, supporting the growth of newer industries with its existing industrial infrastructure even as some older industries decline.

3. High-Technology Industries

Many metropolitan areas in the United States have targeted high-technology industries as a possible growth area to offset declining sectors. However, high-technology industries have had little positive effect on the

Chicago economy, and Chicago's high-tech industries perform significantly worse than their national counterparts. Chicago's high-tech industries are concentrated in older manufacturing sectors that have experienced significant job losses. In fact, since 1979, 63 high-tech industries lost a total of 80,000 jobs, not nearly enough to offset the gain of 41,000 jobs in the 24 high-tech industries that grew. Most of these losses occurred before 1982, while most of the gains occurred after 1982. Nevertheless, many high-tech industries continued to lose jobs even as recently as the period between 1985 to 1986.

Six of the 15 largest high-tech industries lost jobs between 1979 to 1986, and gains just barely exceeded losses, by 1,137 jobs, or less than 1 percent, for the period (see table 4–7). However, this overall picture masks two very different time trends. Only four of these industries scored gains during the recessionary period of 1979 to 1982. Perhaps more alarming is that the six industries that show a net job loss for the period actually continued losing jobs after 1982.

In spite of losses within their respective manufacturing sectors, a number of individual high-tech manufacturing industries gained jobs. Environmental controls, surgical and medical instruments, and process control instruments all posted employment gains (see table 4–8).

Radio and TV communications equipment, now the second largest high-tech industry in Chicago with 19,900 jobs, added 7,105 jobs. The industry posted the second highest absolute gain in employment, after data processing, though it ranks only tenth in percentage growth. The only other industries displaying significant growth are in the chemical sector, especially toilet preparations.

High-tech industries not located within manufacturing sectors have fared uniformly better. The largest and also one of the fastest-growing high-tech industries in Chicago is a business service industry, data-processing services. In many ways, of course, this industry is not high-tech at all; although its rise is intertwined with the growth in computer usage, the actual work involved is relatively low-skilled and noninnovative. At the same time, its first-place rank gives only a partial view of its importance: many other data-processing jobs are in other industries (especially finance and insurance). The total number of data-processing jobs in Chicago is approximately 21,000.

Two other nonmanufacturing high-tech industries are among the 15 largest local high-tech industries. These include research and development (R&D) laboratories, and computer programming and software. Computer-related services not elsewhere classified and commercial testing laboratories rank 18 and 19, respectively. Together, these five non-

Table 4–7. Largest High-Tech Industries in Chicago, 1986, Compared with 1982 and 1979

SIC	Industry	Jobs			Percentage Change		
		1986	1982	1979	1979–1986	1982–1986	1979–1982
7374	Data Processing Services	21,092	10,396	9,471	122.7	112.9	9.8
3662	Radio and TV Communication	19,900	12,204	12,795	55.5	60.1	-4.6
3661	Telephone and Telegraph	16,289	23,296	29,908	-45.5	-23.4	-22.1
3679	Electronic Comps.	10,830	9,285	10,006	8.2	15.4	-7.2
7391	Research Devel. Labs	9,608	3,784	5,208	84.5	111.8	-27.3
3531	Construction Mach.	9,217	18,729	22,064	-58.2	-43.1	-15.1
7372	Computer Programming and Software	8,385	5,019	2,341	258.2	143.8	114.4
2834	Pharmaceuticals	8,367	8,446	11,683	-28.4	-0.7	-27.7
3544	Special Dies, Tools, Jigs Fixtures	8,282	7,952	8,356	-0.9	3.9	-4.8
3579	Office Machines	5,263	5,743	6,018	-12.5	-8.0	-4.6
2844	Toilet Preparations	4,916	4,874	3,506	40.2	1.2	39.0
3613	Switchgears and Switchboards	4,418	5,296	5,380	-17.9	-16.3	-1.6
3569	General Ind. Mach.	4,155	2,947	3,566	16.5	33.9	-17.4
3542	Machine Tools, Metal Forming Types	3,933	4,282	5,216	-24.6	-6.7	-17.9
3822	Envirn. Controls	3,870	1,925	1,870	107.0	104.0	2.9
	Totals	138,525	124,178	137,388	0.8	10.4	-9.6

Table 4–8. Fastest Growing Chicago High-Tech Industries, Compared to United States, 1979–1986

| Rank | SIC | Industry | Chicago 1979–1986 | | U.S. 1979–1986 | |
			% Growth	Jobs 1986	% Growth	Rank
1	7372	Computer Programming and Software	258	8,385	200	1
2	3674	Semiconductors and Related Devices	238	880	35	10
3	7374	Data Processing Services	123	21,092	49	6
4	3574	Calculating and Accounting Machines	114	375	29	13
5	3822	Environmental Controls	107	3,870	−21	
6	7379	Computer Related Services, NEC	102	2,910	38	2
7	7391	Research Development Laboratories	84	9,608	64	5
8	3841	Surgical and Medical Instruments	65	2,682	7	
9	2869	Industrial Organic Chemicals, NEC	57	1,287	−7	
10	3662	Radio and Communication Equipment	56	19,900	41	7
11	3549	Metal Working Machinery, NEC	53	1,896	−11	
12	3534	Elevators and Moving Stairways	48	365	8	23
13	2844	Toilet Preparations	40	4,916	7	24
14	2813	Industrial Gases	36	357	−8	
15	3823	Process Control Instruments	34	3,267	16	20

manufacturing industries accounted for almost 45,000 jobs in 1986, more than double the number in 1979.

Four of the five nonmanufacturing high-tech industries, along with the manufacture of semiconductors and related devices, had a growth rate of 129 percent between 1979 and 1986; their growth accounts for more than half of all the jobs added by high-tech industries during this period.

The picture that emerges from these data is a dual one. Nonmanufacturing high-tech shows all the promise and performance that its popular image would lead one to expect. On the other hand, the manufacturing high-tech industries show significant decline, especially among several of the largest ones, where high-tech mirrors the performance of manufacturing industries generally.

The only bright lights in manufacturing high-tech are several instrumentation industries and radio and TV communication equipment. What is interesting about this growth pattern is that their industries (SICs 36 and 38) also contain individual industries that had significant declines. This suggests that, to some extent, growth industries are spawned within older and declining industries. This is clearly compatible with a vision of industries maturing, dying, and having new ones emerge from the old ones (see Markusen, 1989). The new industries draw on the same skills, industrial infrastructure, and agglomeration economies as the old. Unfortunately, this new growth is by no means sufficient to offset the immense losses suffered in the older industries.

High-tech fared worse in Chicago than nationwide, but for the United States as a whole, high-tech has not been a net new-job generator during the period. The nationally dominant high-tech growth industries are computer- and space-related. A third important area is that of electronic equipment. As Markusen and associates (1986) pointed out, all of these are in fact strongly related to the defense buildup during the 1980s. Markusen and McCurdy (1989) also show that Chicago has done very poorly in obtaining its share of defense-related contracts. Most of the defense-related industries are either absent or very small in Chicago. Thus, it is not surprising that Chicago houses only seven of the 15 fastest-growing high-tech industries in the United States.

Chicago does have a high-tech industry, but it is clearly no panacea. Its single largest high-tech industry, with the greatest number of jobs added, contains largely low-skilled jobs. Almost half of its 15 largest high-tech industries continued to suffer job losses even during the economic recovery. On the other hand, it shows some strengths, and to some extent these occur in areas in which Chicago has traditionally been strongly represented. Thus, this suggests that the seedbed hypothesis, in which old industries provide the fertile breeding ground for new ones, would be worth further investigation.

4. Services

Nowhere is the size and diversity of the Chicago economy more apparent than in its service sector. In Chicago, the term *services* covers a very large and very disparate collection of industries, ranging from barber shops to wholesalers to railroads. Not surprisingly, then, the performance records of service industries in Chicago during the early to mid-1980s are widely disparate. Even within groups of similar services, performance rates are quite varied. Key factors associated with service industry performance appear to be: (1) the local performance of the primary industrial market for the service; (2) changes in the nature of final consumer demand; and (3) the presence or absence of regulation. The first relationship is the most straightforward: businesses that serve faltering industries fare less well than those that serve growing sectors. Changes in consumer priorities and tastes are more idiosyncratic and tend to be inferred in retrospect. The impact of regulations appears to have benefitted some local industries and disadvantaged others. Once again, the size and diversity of Chicago's economy has enabled it to better withstand the differential impact of these factors on local industries. Local disadvantage in one sector is counterbalanced by local advantages in others.

4.1 Definitions

This analysis begins by defining five major service categories. Wholesale and retail trade sectors are the link between the producer and the ultimate consumer. Transportation services, in addition to carrying goods and services, provide a direct service to the travel consumer. Other services catering to the needs of producers include communications, finance, insurance and real estate, utilities, legal services, and other business services. Consumer services include amusement and recreational services, museums and zoos, lodging places, eating and drinking establishments, a variety of repair services, and personal services. Social services encompass the nongovernmental components of the health-care industry, the education industry, membership organizations and associations, and other social services.

4.2 Wholesale and Retail Trade

Linked more closely than the other sectors to the local manufacturing base, the up and down performance of this group of services is no surprise. Eight of the nine major wholesale/retail groups lost employment during the recession of the early 1980s. Five of these bounced back and, by 1986, employed as many or more workers as in 1979. The other three groups lost up to one-quarter of their job base during the earlier period, showed signs of recovery since 1983, but were unable to fully recoup their losses, posting net declines in employment. Only one group posted continuous gains (see table 4–9).

In wholesale trade, the relative performance of dealers in durable versus nondurable goods confirms the link with related manufacturers.

Table 4–9. Wholesale and Retail Trade, Percentage Changes in Employment, Chicago Metro Area, 1979–1986

| | Percentage Change in Employment | | | |
	1979–1983	1983–1986	1979–1986	1986 Emp.
Decline and Full Recovery				
Wholesale Trade				
50 Wholesale/ Durables	− 11.58	+ 17.51	+ 3.91	150,717
Retail Trade				
52 Bldg. Materials	− 0.77	+ 94.11	+ 92.61	25,508
56 Apparel and Access.	− 6.85	+ 14.65	+ 6.80	43,769
57 Furniture	− 4.09	+ 24.89	+ 19.78	22,290
59 Misc. Retail	− 11.28	+ 13.31	+ 0.53	82,243
Decline and Weak Recovery				
Wholesale Trade				
51 Wholesale/ Nondurable	− 6.45	+ 4.40	− 2.33	88,379
Retail Trade				
53 Gen. Merch	− 23.25	+ 6.58	− 18.21	63,507
55 Car Dealers/Gas Stations	− 24.34	21.15	− 8.34	48,561
Continuous Growth				
Retail Trade				
54 Food Stores	+ 3.73	+ 12.08	+ 16.26	79,188

Wholesalers dealing in durable goods proved both more volatile (larger losses in the earlier period, larger gains in the latter) and, in the end, more successful (up 4 percent in employment) than nondurable wholesalers (which lost 2 percent of its jobs over the period). While wholesale trade performed much better overall than manufacturing, in both durable and nondurable goods, the better performance of durable goods repeated.

Major retail trade groups also presented variations on the theme of decline and recovery during the period. The declines in the early 1980s ranged from nearly a quarter of the job base for car dealers, gas stations, and general merchandise stores to less than 1 percent for building materials. Similarly, gains in the last two years ranged from 94 percent in building materials to a feeble 7 percent recovery for general merchandise stores. The major factor in explaining these differences appears to be, not surprisingly, changes in consumer priorities and tastes.

The big loser in retail was the general merchandise store (down 18 percent), whose decline appears to reflect both the ravages of the recession and a trend toward increased retail specialization or "niche" marketing. The problems confronting auto-related retailers (down 8 percent) bear witness to consumer sensitivity to price and perceptions of quality. The strong recoveries, with net job gains, posted by building materials (up 92 percent) and furniture and home furnishings (up 20 percent) appear to echo the local boom in construction as well as an early rebound in consumer spending.

Only one group, retail food stores, posted consistent gains throughout the period (up 16 percent). However, a relatively high proportion of these jobs are part time.

Even these groupings fail to capture the heterogeneous mix and disparate performances of individual wholesale-retail industries. In many cases, the trend-breakers outnumbered the industries that followed the general pattern of decline and more-or-less recovery.

A number of industries that failed to fully recover are closely linked to declining manufacturing industries. For example, the pummeling suffered by Midwestern steel industries is reflected also in the loss of employment by metal service centers. Similarly, the combination of increased international competition and the recession resulted in an unrecovered loss of employment in production, wholesale and retail sales of automobiles, auto parts and supplies, and auto services. Wholesalers supplying construction, mining or farm machinery posted continuous declines. Wholesalers in industrial supplies and in transportation equipment and supplies posted net job losses, in spite of some recovery since 1983.

In contrast, wholesalers posting consistent gains were marketing to commercial or service sector business purchases or to expanding consumer expenditures. For example, wholesalers of commercial machinery and equipment, professional equipment and supplies, and service establishment equipment did very well. Paper wholesalers did well, particularly stationery suppliers and personal service paper suppliers. Wholesalers and retailers in electrical parts and equipment, especially consumer-oriented sales of radios and TVs, posted continuous gains.

4.3 Transportation Services

Chicago has long been a transportation hub, first for water and rail transportation, later claiming dominance in air transportation, as well as boasting a highly developed local passenger transit system. Transportation industries operate, however, in a context of relatively high regulation. Both Chicago's initial advantage in transportation and changes in regulation appear to have influenced local performance in recent years.

Local transportation service industries included two winners and three losers in the 1980s (see table 4–10). Four of the five transportation groups lost jobs during the early 1980s and recovered jobs since 1983. However, air travel made a rather spectacular recovery (up 35 percent) from a rather modest decline (down 7 percent) for a net gain of 26 percent in employment. Trucking and warehousing, on the other hand, lost almost one-

Table 4–10. Transportation Services, Percentage Changes in Employment, Chicago Metro Area, 1979–1986

| | Percentage Change in Employment | | | |
	1979–1983	1983–1986	1979–1986	1986 Emp.
Decline and Full Recovery				
45 Air Transp.	− 7.10	+ 35.38	+ 25.77	33,150
Decline and Weak Recovery				
41 Local Passenger Transit	− 14.49	+ 9.05	− 6.75	11,231
42 Trucking and Warehousing	− 24.01	+ 5.23	− 20.03	44,610
44 Water Transp.	− 15.98	13.04	− 5.02	1,534
Continuous Growth				
47 Trans. Services	+ 4.74	+ 29.01	+ 35.12	17,144

quarter of its job base in the early 1980s and regained only 5 percent since 1983, for a net loss of 20 percent. Water transportation and local passenger transportation also lost significant employment in the early 1980s, but both staged successful recoveries, posting net losses of 5 percent and 7 percent, respectively. Transportation services, which include freight forwarding and passenger and cargo travel arrangements, gained employment throughout the 1980s.

One explanation for the differential performance of Chicago's transportation services may be that trucking and wholesaling are more oriented toward serving manufacturers and consequently shared their precipitous decline during the recession. Air transportation and transportation services, on the other hand, cater to a broader market of businesses and personal consumers. There is also some indication that both the local gains in air transportation and the losses in trucking reflect the impact of deregulation, which has bolstered the competitive position of the major airlines based at Chicago's two airports, but which has loosened the hold of major firms over the trucking industry and increased competition.

In every category of transportation services, high performers included high-priced or specialty services, including limousine service, ambulance service, nonlocal transportation charters, marinas, oil spill cleanup, and fur storage.

4.4 Producer Services

The relatively strong performance posted by producer services confirms other reports citing Chicago's strength in business services. Among the 12 major producer services groups, all but one posted net employment gains over the 1979 to 1986 period (see table 4–11). The communications industry was the only one of these industries to lose employment continuously over the seven-year period, all of which was accounted for by a 23 percent decline in the area's telephone industry. This local decline reflects a national trend, which shows a decline in communications employment from its peak in 1981. No doubt deregulation is the key factor, suggesting that whatever its other effects, it has resulted in a net decline in industry employment.

Three major groups lost jobs in the early 1980s, but gained in 1983 to 1986. In the case of insurance carriers, the gains were not sufficient to recoup losses, resulting in a net job loss of 3 percent, although insurance remains a major local employer. Real estate bounced back strongly, with a net gain of nearly 10 percent. Miscellaneous business services, which

Table 4–11.   Producer Services, Percentage Changes in Employment, Chicago Metro Area, 1979–1986

	Percentage Change in Employment			
	1979–1983	1983–1986	1979–1986	1986 Emp.
Decline				
48 Communication	− 4.04	− 10.68	− 14.28	36,503
Decline and Recovery				
63 Insurance Carriers	− 10.57	+ 8.47	− 2.99	71,218
65 Real Estate	− 9.74	+ 21.36	+ 9.53	47,671
89 Misc. Services	− 4.31	+ 25.45	+ 20.05	49,781
Growth				
49 Elec. Gas, and Sanitary	+ 5.01	+ 0.16	+ 5.18	24,578
60 Banking	+ 4.85	+ 0.30	+ 5.17	66,504
61 Credit Agencies	+ 2.53	+ 25.73	+ 28.92	32,848
62 Security, Commodity Brokers	+ 46.50	+ 18.00	+ 72.87	27,619
64 Insurance Agents, Brokers	+ 1.06	+ 14.72	+ 15.94	24,007
67 Holding, Investments	+ 17.00	+ 28.32	+ 50.13	10,104
73 Business Services	+ 14.82	+ 23.27	+ 41.54	218,033
81 Legal Services	+ 24.23	+ 24.28	+ 54.39	33,247

includes engineering and architectural services, accounting, auditing and bookkeeping, and noncommercial educational, scientific, and research organizations, also posted a strong recovery, with a net gain of 20 percent.

The remaining eight major groups posted consistent growth throughout the period. By far the largest of these were business services, which grew by 42 percent, for a 1986 employment total of 218,033. However, business services are themselves a rather diverse grouping of industries with varied performance, as we shall see. Three major groups — electric, gas, and sanitary services; banking; and security and commodity brokers — actually increased faster during the early 1980s, tapering off significantly in 1983 to 1986. All of these winners paralleled national trends, although in every case national growth outpaced local growth by as much as two to one.

Business services are the largest and most heterogeneous of the major producer services groups and provided many internal exceptions to their general rule of continuous growth. Of 24 industries in this group, only nine enjoyed continuous growth. Another nine declined in the early 1980s and rebounded. Three grew during the early 1980s and have slipped only recently. Only three posted absolute declines.

Among the other business service "winners" were two building maintenance industries, window cleaning (+307 percent) and disinfecting and exterminating services (+13 percent), and several types of personnel supply agencies, including management, consulting, and public relations (+58 percent), detective agencies (+46 percent), and employment agencies (+14 percent). These industries appear to fit the description of services once provided for "in-house," but increasingly likely to be "contracted out" to independent service firms.

Other major producer services groups also aggregated diverse performances. The pattern of decline and recovery for insurance carriers, for example, actually reflects strong growth in accident and health insurance (+142 percent), hospital and medical plans (+4 percent), and fire and marine casualty insurance (+8 percent), on the one hand, and net losses in life insurance (−12 percent), surety insurance (−58 percent), title insurance (−19 percent), and pension, health, and welfare funds (−80 percent). These shifts in consumer "preference" in insurance have been linked to high inflation rates (which have diminished the appeal of whole-life insurance, for example) and increasing demands and costs for health insurance. At any rate, Chicago's diversity in the insurance industry has, again, enabled it to offset declines in one area with growth in another.

4.5 Consumer Services

With a population of nearly 7.5 million and effective buying income in excess of $22,000 per capita, the Chicago area provides one of the strongest consumer markets in the country. In spite of the recession, consumer services as a group made a strong showing. Seven of the eight major groups posted net gains, with all seven losing ground during the early 1980s, but more than recovering those losses between 1983 and 1986. Amusement and recreation, on the other hand, lost 41 percent of its jobs during the recession and was able to recoup only 4 percent in later years (see table 4–12).

However, consumer services include a varied array of industries with similarly diverse growth trends. The principal explanation for most of these trends would seem to derive from priorities and shifts in consumer spending.

Table 4–12. Consumer Services, Percentage Changes in Employment, Chicago Metro Area, 1979–1986

	Percentage Change in Employment			
	1979–1983	1983–1986	1979–1986	1986 Emp.
Decline				
79 Amusement, Recreation	− 41.04	+ 3.68	− 38.87	23,231
Decline and Recovery				
58 Eating and Drinking Places	− 0.78	+ 11.90	+ 11.03	172,473
70 Hotels, Lodging	− 8.55	+ 16.66	+ 6.68	35,110
72 Personal Services	− 0.54	+ 15.00	+ 14.37	37,591
75 Auto Repair, Services	− 11.42	+ 30.12	+ 15.26	23,763
76 Misc. Repair	− 9.27	+ 21.63	+ 10.35	12,541
78 Motion Pictures	− 19.82	+ 52.49	+ 22.26	7,118
84 Museums, Zoos	− 54.25	+ 238.32	+ 54.79	3,955

For example, while eating and drinking places posted impressive gains throughout the period, the growth was entirely in eating places, which added 14,152 jobs (up 10 percent) during the period. Documented increases in consumer expenditures for out-of-home meals is related, many argue, to the increase in working women. The continuous decline in drinking places (down 28 percent) is provocative but, to our knowledge, unexplained.

Amusement and recreation services, in total, lost nearly 15,000 jobs between 1979 and 1986. In fact, almost all the net job loss was accounted for by a net loss of 14,130 jobs (down 81 percent) in theatrical producers and services. (Recent anecdotal evidence suggests that this trend may be reversing.) Professional sports clubs and promoters, on the other hand, more than doubled its employment base with continuous growth totalling 108 percent.

The motion picture industry rebounded strongly after the recession, although the most dramatic gains were in TV movie production (up 82 percent) and distribution (up 341 percent).

Personal services comprise yet another diverse category. While the overall pattern was net growth, five industries posted net job losses. Of these, the largest was commercial laundries, which lost jobs throughout the seven-year period, totalling almost two-thirds (63 percent) of the 1979 job base. The exception within this industry was diaper services, which more than doubled employment (up 120 percent) — the result, perhaps, of a baby boomlet and ecologically concerned parents?

4.6 Social Services

Perhaps dependent more on demographics trends than on economic shifts, the four social service industry groups all posted employment gains, although two overcame modest losses during the 1980s, while two showed consistent gains throughout the period. Again, differences were evident within each major group (see table 4–13).

Caught in the crunch between rapidly rising costs, increased emphasis on efficiencies and cost-containment, staff, capital, and patient shortages, the health-care industry in Chicago, as elsewhere, is shifting its emphasis from general hospital care to a diversity of specialized and outpatient options. Though growing modestly throughout the recession, hospitals cut back on staff since 1983, as evidenced by a number of hospital closings. Allied health services (blood banks, visiting nurse associations, medical photography and art) and outpatient facilities, on the other hand, posted large and continuous gains, totalling 195 percent and 95 percent, respectively, over the seven-year period. Employment in offices of all types of medical practitioners increased briskly, as did employment in medical (but not dental) labs. Nursing homes continued to grow (up 24 percent), spurred on by demographic trends, changing public policies, and familial patterns of care.

Table 4–13. Social Services, Percentage Changes in Employment, Chicago Metro Area, 1979–1986

	Percentage Change in Employment			
	1979–1983	1983–1986	1979–1986	1986 Emp.
Decline and Full Recovery				
83 Social Services	− 1.93	+ 29.96	+ 27.45	37,382
86 Membership Orgs.	− 3.02	+ 11.76	+ 8.38	59,077
Growth				
80 Health Services	+ 14.52	+ 4.95	+ 20.18	223,840
82 Educational Services	+ 3.06	+ 9.17	+ 12.51	68,268

The general pattern of decline and recovery for membership organizations actually masks quite different experiences. The largest of the membership organizations, religious organizations, actually grew throughout the period, with a total gain of 40 percent, bringing 1986 employment up to 26,727. Chicago, which claims the highest concentration of religious schools and institutions outside the Vatican, has targeted religious headquarters for attraction efforts, succeeding, to date, with the new Lutheran Church headquarters.

Professional organizations, similarly, grew throughout the 1980s, adding 31 percent gains over the seven-year period, reflecting also Chicago's success in attracting business headquarters. Business associations did trim staff during the recession but more than recouped losses since 1983, for a total gain of 7 percent. Labor unions took a beating, cutting staff nearly in half (down 49 percent), with most losses occurring in the early 1980s, but continuing into the latter period.

4.7 Recap

The Chicago experience supports the contention that local service industries are dependent on the health of other industries that contract for their services, on population trends and tastes, and on shifts in regulation. In any case, there are clear implications for public policy. The argument that manufacturers increasingly contract out for services that formerly were provided in-house, accounting for significant shifts in classification of workers, though not in work performed, is compelling, but to date we have seen no satisfactory study of the question, perhaps because the data are not available. If this argument is true, then even a "postindustrial" Chicago cannot afford to neglect its industries.

The notion that consumer priorities and "tastes" can be influenced by public policies is nowhere more evident than in the shifts in the health-care sector. Cost-containment policies pursued by public and private sector insurers and providers have forced a shift from expensive hospital care to less expensive outpatient facilities. The growing realization that in-home and preventive care may not only be cheaper but also better for us and plays no small part in the realignment of priorities in health care.

Although government regulation in such industries as transportation and public utilities is the most obvious example of public policies affecting the performance of service industries, it is by no means the only impact. Public and private decisions about investments, taxes, income and benefits, and international relations all combine to create implicit policies affecting industries, workers, nonworkers, and their families.

5. Conclusion

What does the performance of Chicago's economy ultimately mean regarding the health of the area and its likely future? Does the fact that Chicago growth rates consistently lag behind the nation indicate serious underlying problems? The true measure of an area's well-being is not found in the analysis presented here; that would require an assessment of the changes in real income of area households and in local purchasing power compared to other regions. However, the present analysis does suggest that Chicago is becoming more like the nation as a whole which, for Chicago, means a decline in its relative position.

This is brought out very clearly by a shift-share analysis. Chicago's meager gain of 10,800 jobs between 1979 and 1986 consists of losses in all but one of the manufacturing sectors and gains in all but one of the service sectors. The industry-mix effect overall, as well as for manufacturing and services individually, was slightly positive. In other words, Chicago's particular mix of industries included somewhat more industries with high growth, and somewhat fewer with low growth compared to the nation as a whole. The competitive-share effect for Chicago, though, is negative for every significant industrial sector, with the exception of furniture and manufacturing auxiliary services (see table 4–14). Chicago would have created 363,600 more jobs if its industries had grown at national growth rates. Although a mature area such as Chicago does not necessarily need to keep pace with growth in the nation, and though there are many individual industries that outperformed their U.S. counterpart, this widespread lag is quite disturbing.

Furthermore, the restructuring that has taken place during the period is likely to have negated the advantage that Chicago would have enjoyed during the years since 1986, when Midwestern manufacturing was finally rebounding. Thus, Chicago appears to have suffered the disadvantages of a concentration in manufacturing on the downside of the business cycle, but did not reap the benefits on the upswing, because by that time the area economy had significantly restructured. Indeed, restructuring in Chicago occurred at a more rapid rate than in the nation from 1976 to 1983, and at a slower pace after that. Chicago's economy is now more similar in structure to that of the nation as a whole than it historically has been and, in that sense, its overall performance should be similar to that of the national economy.

Our analysis does not provide an answer to the question of why Chicago is lagging behind the national growth rate across the board. One analysis suggests, contrary to our hypothesis, that Chicago has actually done quite poorly in performing its "seedbed function." In their analysis

Table 4–14. Components of Change in the Chicago Economy, 1979–1986

Sectors	Change in Chicago Employment	Micro Nation Growth Effect	Industry Mix Effect	Competitive Share Effect	Total Differential
Agriculture	2,848	5,247	−2,529	−131	−2,399
Mining	228	−4,118	3,638	709	4,346
Construction	−10,247	2,014	−554	−11,657	−12,212
Durable Mfg.					
Lumber	−1,267	−4,223	3,113	−154	2,959
Furniture	2,318	−559	38	2,834	2,872
Stone, Clay, Glass	−4,504	−4,414	1,073	−1,166	−93
Primary Metal	−28,258	−19,438	−2,798	−6,036	−8,834
Fabricated Metal	−25,323	−9,883	−5,414	−10,048	−15,462
Nonelec. Mach.	−35,013	−19,344	−4,208	−11,408	−15,616
Elec. Equip.	−33,296	2,273	1,297	−36,858	−35,561
Transp. Equip.	−12,542	−7,767	4,612	−9,378	−4,766
Instruments	−7,834	−593	−248	−6,996	−7,244
Misc. Mfg.	−9,819	−3,250	−1,613	−4,948	−6,561

Nondurable Mfg					
Food Products	−9,016	−5,474	58	−3,587	−3,529
Tobacco	−10	−453	380	63	443
Textiles	−967	−8,137	7,475	−307	7,168
Apparel	−3,631	−10,162	7,370	−847	6,523
Paper	−5,136	−1,413	−211	−3,514	−3,725
Printing and Publishing	−3,650	8,104	4,868	−16,584	−11,716
Chemical Prods.	−12,487	−3,667	−1,246	−7,579	−8,825
Petroleum Prods.	−2,482	−1,062	−35	−1,386	−1,421
Rubber Products	−5,306	−1,610	−271	−3,414	−36,865
Leather Products	−2,382	−4,022	−2,267	−629	−1,638
Auxiliary	6,116	81	69	5,933	6,002
Transp., Utils.	−2,564	11,392	−619	−13,425	−14,043
Trade, Wholesale	15,163	21,873	2,938	−9,547	−6,609
Trade, Retail	10,085	97,436	−8,244	−79,332	−87,576
Fire	32,018	49,130	9,923	−26,926	−17,003
Services	8,501	247,675	6,552	−105,490	−98,938

of high-technology industry in Chicago, Markusen and McCurdy (1989) argue that Chicago's relative decline is strongly related to its inability to move into new industries related to defense. This, in turn, they ascribe to several historical factors. One set of these is related to the degree of unionization and long-standing bias toward coastal locations for defense installations and industries. Another set, however, relates to a Midwestern corporate orientation toward producer goods and consumer durables, as well as a history of sufficient market dominance to make changes unnecessary. It is not clear whether the absence of a successful seedbed function extends to nonhigh-tech industries as well, or whether the current relative deemphasizing of defense as a national priority will enable Midwestern industries to regain a competitive edge. Clearly, more detailed analysis of the shifting pattern of growth and decline within specific industries is needed to determine in which industries, and under what conditions, the seedbed function occurs successfully.

In addition to the national economy and patterns of defense spending, the other major factor likely to influence Chicago's economic future is the continuing internationalization process. In the global economy, cities on the East and West coasts have a more strategic location than Chicago does for access to Europe, Asia, and Latin America. On the other hand, America's largest trading partner is Canada, and here Chicago has both strong economic ties as well as the potential of a trade advantage in its well-developed business services sector. Also, Chicago might be able to profit from its role as an access center to the Midwest for all foreign businesses, as well as a source of expertise for Midwestern companies seeking to do business abroad. Its business services, transportation, and wholesale trade sectors might benefit from this specialization.

In sum, then, Chicago definitely lost ground when compared to the nation during the past ten years, as it underwent massive restructuring in a shift of employment from manufacturing to services. However, it did not suffer the devastation, and is probably better positioned for the future, than most other Midwestern cities. The main reason for this is the enduring size and diversity of Chicago's economy, which allows local firms and workers to respond quickly to and accommodate shifts in industrial demand, consumer tastes, or other factors affecting individual industries. Although the pace of restructuring has slowed, this flexibility is likely to continue to be of crucial importance for the region's future.

5 CLEVELAND, OHIO: MANUFACTURING MATTERS, SERVICES ARE STRENGTHENED, BUT EARNINGS ERODE

Edward W. Hill

A period of unrivaled industrial entrepreneurism from 1870 to the late 1920s laid the economic foundation for old-order Cleveland. Steel, iron ore, coal, shipping, and oil built the city, and it evolved into a durable goods economy that included automotive production, lighting, electrical motors, and chemicals, paint, and coatings.

Things began to change in the mid 1970s. By 1979 — a watershed year — the secular erosion of the area's durable goods base became evident as the city and its surrounding area began an abrupt economic restructuring.

The shift from the old to the new order is traced in this chapter. The result of economic restructuring is disentangled from the influence of the 1979 to 1986 business cycle, and the impact that restructuring has had on the the region's economy is outlined. There are four noticeable results from the change in economic order.

- The economy is more diversified in 1986 than it was in 1979. Durable goods manufacturing plays a greatly reduced role in the regional economy but remains critical to the wealth of the community.
- Business services are key to generating new jobs. The vitality of busi-

ness service employment results from a combination of the growth in the number of regional offices; from local manufacturers moving into distribution and marketing activities, thereby requiring more inputs from the business service sector; and from manufacturing activities having higher indirect employment multipliers than in previous decades.

• The regional economy is less cyclically sensitive than it was before 1979. One-third of its employment base, however, remains susceptible to cyclical fluctuations.

• Earnings generated in this new economy have become more unequal. Unionized manufacturing jobs have been lost, and there has been an increase in the number of jobs providing either high or low earnings in the service sector, resulting in an absolute decline in the number of jobs in the middle of the earnings distribution.

The movement from cyclical peak to trough resulted in the loss of 13 percent of the jobs that were present in 1979. The Cleveland Primary Metropolitan Statistical Area (PMSA), consisting of Cuyahoga, Geauga, Lake, and Medina Counties, lost 117,000 jobs from the third quarter of 1979 (1979:3) to the first quarter of 1983 (1983:1). It took nearly six years to regain the jobs lost in the 1979 recession. But the new jobs are in very different industries, causing significant changes in the distribution of earnings.

Manufacturing employment dropped by more than 28 percent from 1979:1 to 1987:1. Losses continued through the second quarter of 1988, when a small gain was realized — the first increase in manufacturing employment in this region since late in 1978. The 1979 to 1983 recession was so severe that the entire service sector, defined as transportation services, wholesale and retail services, producer services, social services, and personal services, declined by nearly 20,000 jobs. The recovery of service sector employment became noticeable in 1983.

The abruptness of the economic transition in the Cleveland PMSA is starkly displayed in figure 5–1. The actual time trend in total private employment from 1979:2 to 1987:2 is graphed using a solid line. The fitted values of the trend are shown by the dashed line.[1] The severity of the recession from 1979 to 1983 is clearly indicated by the distance between the solid and dotted lines in the figure. The recession bottomed out in the first quarter of 1983, but the recovery was not fully established until the third quarter of that year.

From 1979 to 1987, the rate of growth of employment in the region has been more sensitive to the level and rate of growth of local earnings than

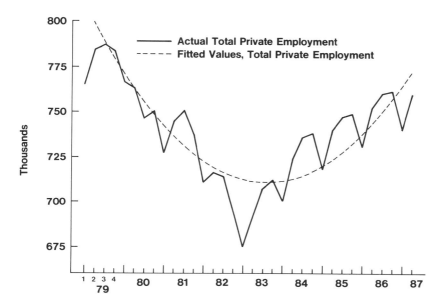

Figure 5-1. Private employment.

to the performance of the national economy. In the short run, the relationship between average real national earnings and employment in Cleveland is highly inelastic.[2] A 1 percent change in national average earnings results in a 0.05 percent change in local employment for a five-quarter period. However, the initial impact is negative, -0.11 in the first half-year. This implies that economic growth occurs elsewhere in the nation, then gradually filters into Cleveland after a lag from one-half to a full year. Employment in the region is also inelastic with regard to regional average earnings, 0.12 after a year. The largest impact occurs two and three quarters after an increase in earnings is registered. These results imply that when the national economy turns down it will take Cleveland with it, but if Cleveland does not have a base of competitive, well-paying jobs, it will not benefit from national economic well-being.

The economic restructuring of Cleveland that began in the late 1970s is paradoxical. Cleveland is a command and control center of modern manufacturing capital. Yet, the largest complex of manufacturing employment in the region is composed of the Big Three automakers and their suppliers. Decisions in this complex are not made in the region. The durable goods industry is much less diversified than it was before the economy was restructured. Before 1979, this sector was evenly balanced between automobiles, steel, and machine tools, plus significant employment in paints, chemicals, and oil.

Today, the economy is more diversified, but the durable goods sector is much more dependent on the fortunes of the domestic automotive industry. Ironically, as local durable goods manufacturing employment is more dependent on automobile production, locally headquartered manufacturers are less dependent on supplying the automotive industry. They used automotive technology, and retained earnings from supplying automotive assemblers in the 1950s and 1960s, to diversify into electronics and aircraft parts production.

1. Is There a New-Order Cleveland?

Did a new economic base emerge in Cleveland's PMSA during the 1979 to 1986 business cycle? The region clearly remains a manufacturing center. Even though manufacturing's location quotient (LQ) dropped from 1.24 in 1979 to 1.19 in 1986 (see table 5–1), it appears that Cleveland has retained a strong specialization in durable-goods manufacturing, which

Table 5–1. Location Quotients, 1979:1 to 1986:1

		Year : Quarter		
Industry	SIC	1979:1	1986:1	Change
Mining		0.11	0.15	0.04
Construction		0.69	0.56	−0.12
General Contractors	15	0.54	0.47	−0.07
Heavy Contractors	16	0.58	0.33	−0.25
Special Trade	17	0.82	0.68	−0.14
Manufacturing		1.24	1.19	−0.05
Durable Goods		1.52	1.40	−0.11
Lumber and Wood Products	24	0.13	0.20	0.07
Furniture and Fixtures	25	0.53	0.47	−0.06
Stone, Clay, and Glass	32	0.77	0.68	−0.09
Primary Metals*	33	2.35	3.46	1.11
Fabricated Metals	34	2.52	2.48	−0.04
Machinery, Except Electrical	35	1.89	1.62	−0.27

Table 5–1 continued

Industry	SIC	Year : Quarter		
		1979:1	1986:1	Change
Electrical and Electronic Mach.	36	1.19	1.02	−0.17
Transportation Equipment	37	1.47	1.07	−0.40
Instruments and Related	38	0.80	1.19	0.39
Miscellaneous Industries	39	0.70	0.90	0.20
Nondurable Goods		0.79	0.88	0.10
Food and Kindred Products	20	0.50	0.46	−0.04
Textile Mill Products	22	0.10	0.11	0.01
Apparel and Other Textiles	23	0.44	0.45	0.01
Paper and Allied Products*	26	0.55	0.60	0.04
Printing and Publishing	27	1.13	1.22	0.08
Chemicals and Allied Prods.	28	1.40	1.51	0.11
Petroleum and Coal	29	1.99	2.78	0.79
Rubber and Misc. Products	30	1.55	1.64	0.09
Leather Products	31	0.03	0.03	−0.00
Services		0.96	1.00	0.04
Transportation		0.94	0.86	−0.08
Local Passenger Transit	41	0.53	0.57	0.03
Trucking and Warehousing	42	0.98	0.90	−0.07
Water Transportation	44	1.51	1.14	−0.37
Transport by Air	45	0.88	0.79	−0.09
Pipelines, Except Natural Gas	46	0.24	0.46	0.22
Transportation Services	47	0.88	0.98	0.09
Wholesale and Retail Trade		1.01	1.02	0.01
Wholesale Trade		1.17	1.19	0.02
Durable Goods Wholesale	50	1.44	1.41	−0.03
Nondurable Wholesale	51	0.78	0.88	0.10
General Merchandise	53	1.09	0.95	−0.14
Food Stores	54	0.96	0.95	−0.02
Automotive Dealers	55	0.79	0.89	0.09
Apparel and Accessory	56	0.89	0.87	−0.02
Home Furnishings*	57	0.75	0.73	−0.02
Miscellaneous Retail	59	0.89	1.02	0.13
Producer Services		0.93	0.97	0.04
Communication	48	0.92	0.92	0.00
Electric, Gas, and Sanitary	49	0.73	0.94	0.21
Banking	60	0.82	0.82	−0.01
Credit Agencies, Except Banks	61	1.21	1.11	−0.10
Security Brokers	62	0.81	0.74	−0.07
Insurance Carriers	63	0.92	0.94	0.02
Insurance Agents	64	0.74	0.76	0.02

Table 5–1 continued

		Year : Quarter		
Industry	*SIC*	*1979:1*	*1986:1*	*Change*
Real Estate	65	0.86	0.86	0.00
Holding Companies	67	0.61	0.02	−0.58
Business Services	73	1.05	1.13	0.08
Legal Services	81	0.99	1.08	0.08
Miscellaneous Services	89	0.99	0.97	−0.01
Social Services		0.99	1.15	0.16
Health Services	80	1.02	1.21	0.19
Education Services	82	0.93	1.21	0.28
Social Services	83	0.81	0.92	0.11
Membership Organizations	86	1.16	0.99	−0.17
Personal Services		0.87	0.91	0.04
Eating and Drinking Places	58	0.89	0.92	0.04
Hotels and Other Lodging	70	0.64	0.55	−0.09
Personal Services	72	0.99	1.10	0.11
Auto Repair	75	1.02	1.16	0.14
Miscellaneous Repair	76	1.13	0.93	−0.20
Motion Pictures	78	0.50	0.99	0.49
Amusement and Recreation	79	0.76	0.91	0.15
Museums, Gardens, and Zoos	84	1.81	1.80	−0.01
Private Households	88	0.73	0.58	−0.15

Source: ES202, except for *; *from County Business Patterns.

had a LQ of 1.40 at the end of the time period studied, yet nearly 62,000 jobs were lost in this industrial division. At the same time, services have strengthened to the point that its proportion of employment is at the national average. Social services and wholesale and retail trade are now part of the region's economic base; they were not in 1979. Specific major groups of employment in producer services are also basic to the region's economy. The largest proportional changes in producer services are in electric, gas, and sanitary services, business services, and legal services.

2. Manufacturing

The Cleveland region led the nation in manufacturing employment losses and lagged in gains. The 1979 to 1987 data on regional manufacturing employment are drawn in figure 5–2 with a solid line; the fitted values from a time-trend regression equation are represented by dashes.[3] Manufacturing employment rebounded from 1983:1 to 1984:4, but continued erosion set in after that point in time. (Employment declines reversed once again in 1988.) The regression model indicates that the true turning point was not reached until the third quarter of 1986. The rate of decline in manufacturing employment has slowed considerably, indicating that restructuring was largely completed from 1983 to 1984.

The relative strength of manufacturing rests on a few major groups in durable goods production. Even though employment decreased markedly in some of these groups, it did so at a slower rate than in the same industries nationally. A good example is primary metals. The LQ was 2.35 in 1979, which increased to 3.46 in 1986 despite major layoffs in the late 1970s and early 1980s. The industry lost nearly 7,500 jobs from 1979 to 1986, but the combined competitive effect over that time period was 4,700 (see tables 5–2 and 5–3). Forty-eight percent of the employment that re-

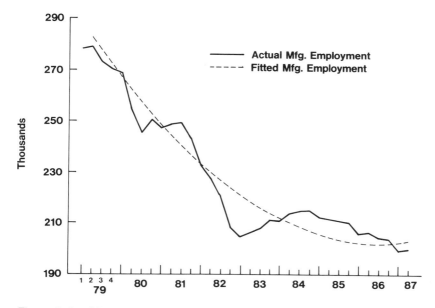

Figure 5–2.   Manufacturing employment.

Table 5-2. Shift-Share Analysis, 1979 to 1983

Industry	SIC	Employment Change	National Growth Effect	Mix Effect	Competitive Effect
Mining		65	(3)	47	22
Construction		(8,317)	(87)	(3,789)	(4,441)
General Contractors	15	(2,803)	(19)	(1,467)	(1,316)
Heavy Contractors	16	(2,003)	(14)	(520)	(1,469)
Special Trade	17	(3,511)	(54)	(1,513)	(1,945)
Manufacturing		(73,550)	(827)	(38,882)	(33,841)
Durable Goods		(65,825)	(612)	(37,044)	(28,169)
Lumber and Wood Products	24	(231)	(3)	(215)	(13)
Furniture and Fixtures	25	(780)	(9)	(421)	(350)
Stone, Clay, and Glass	32	(2,325)	(17)	(1,248)	(1,060)
Primary Metals*	33	(9,734)	(91)	(11,604)	1,964
Fabricated Metals	34	(15,204)	(137)	(9,991)	(5,075)
Machinery, Except Electrical	35	(19,669)	(149)	(9,387)	(10,132)
Electrical and Electronic Mach.	36	(4,393)	(80)	(1,614)	(2,696)
Transportation Equipment	37	(13,281)	(99)	(6,556)	(6,625)
Instruments and Related	38	(144)	(17)	140	(266)
Miscellaneous Industries	39	(65)	(10)	(605)	550
Nondurable Goods		(8,215)	(206)	(5,605)	(2,404)
Food and Kindred Products	20	(1,451)	(27)	(604)	(821)
Textile Mill Products	22	(72)	(3)	(184)	116
Apparel and Other Textiles	23	(1,243)	(19)	(895)	(329)
Paper and Allied Products*	26	(757)	(12)	(266)	(479)
Printing and Publishing	27	(246)	(44)	747	(949)
Chemicals and Allied Prods.	28	(2,007)	(50)	(852)	(1,106)

Industry	No.				
Petroleum and Coal	29	235	(13)	(192)	440
Rubber and Misc. Products	30	(2,647)	(39)	(1,667)	(942)
Leather Products	31	(28)	(0)	(14)	(14)
Services					
Transportation		(8,918)	(1,337)	34,723	(42,304)
Local Passenger Transit	41	(6,544)	(72)	(1,172)	(5,300)
		(242)	(5)	(39)	(199)
Trucking and Warehousing	42	(3,993)	(41)	(1,560)	(2,392)
Water Transportation	44	(1,961)	(10)	(177)	(1,774)
Transport by Air	45	(578)	(12)	94	(660)
Pipelines, Except Natural Gas	46	(10)	(0)	3	(13)
Transportation Services	47	240	(5)	372	(127)
Wholesale and Retail Trade		(19,268)	(481)	0	(18,787)
Wholesale Trade		(6,813)	(191)	650	(7,272)
Durable Goods Wholesale	50	(6,345)	(139)	(207)	(5,999)
Nondurable Wholesale	51	(468)	(52)	547	(962)
General Merchandise	53	(5,893)	(79)	(1,752)	(4,062)
Food Stores	54	(1,497)	(70)	2,224	(3,652)
Automotive Dealers	55	(2,553)	(47)	(2,078)	(427)
Apparel and Accessory	56	(1,823)	(26)	72	(1,869)
Home Furnishings*	57	(745)	(15)	(259)	(471)
Miscellaneous Retail	59	56	(53)	919	(811)
Producer Services		4,604	(325)	15,843	(10,914)
Communication	48	770	(38)	1,181	(373)
Electric, Gas, and Sanitary	49	542	(18)	665	(104)
Banking	60	513	(39)	1,674	(1,122)
Credit Agencies, Except Banks	61	199	(21)	931	(711)
Security Brokers	62	324	(5)	811	(482)
Insurance Carriers	63	(660)	(33)	264	(892)
Insurance Agents	64	263	(10)	497	(224)

Table 5–2 continued

Industry	SIC	Employment Change	National Growth Effect	Mix Effect	Competitive Effect
Real Estate	65	351	(24)	519	(145)
Holding Companies	67	454	(2)	170	285
Business Services	73	489	(92)	6,468	(5,887)
Legal Services	81	1,275	(14)	1,509	(220)
Miscellaneous Services	89	84	(29)	1,443	(1,330)
Social Services		13,272	(237)	13,174	335
Health Services	80	12,189	(157)	11,225	1,120
Education Services	82	1,364	(32)	284	1,112
Social Services	83	1,267	(23)	1,493	(203)
Membership Organizations	86	(1,548)	(25)	96	(1,619)
Personal Services		(982)	(223)	6,786	(7,545)
Eating and Drinking Places	58	285	(121)	4,215	(3,809)
Hotels and Other Lodging	70	(37)	(20)	689	(706)
Personal Services	72	(82)	(30)	430	(483)
Auto Repair	75	(502)	(19)	208	(692)
Miscellaneous Repair	76	(1,171)	(10)	(0)	(1,161)
Motion Pictures	78	(563)	(3)	(39)	(520)
Amusement and Recreation	79	832	(16)	688	160
Museums, Gardens, and Zoos	84	121	(2)	77	46
Private Households	88	135	(2)	351	(213)

Source: ES202, except for*; *from County Business Patterns.

Table 5–3. Shift-Share Analysis, 1983 to 1986

Industry	SIC	Employment Change	National Growth Effect	Mix Effect	Competitive Effect
Mining		(6)	150	(279)	123
Construction		1,501	2,689	2,991	(4,179)
General Contractors	15	1,321	477	849	(5)
Heavy Contractors	16	(680)	344	(346)	(678)
Special Trade	17	860	1,867	2,910	(3,917)
Manufacturing		1,009	26,280	(14,475)	(10,797)
Durable Goods		4,006	17,986	(5,681)	(8,299)
Lumber and Wood Products	24	405	104	17	284
Furniture and Fixtures	25	42	269	79	(306)
Stone, Clay, and Glass	32	167	430	(228)	(35)
Primary Metals*	33	2,261	2,699	(3,175)	2,737
Fabricated Metals	34	1,542	3,969	(1,527)	(901)
Machinery, Except Electrical	35	611	3,911	(2,430)	(870)
Electrical and Electronic Mach.	36	(2,518)	2,874	(902)	(4,489)
Transportation Equipment	37	(265)	2,582	1,449	(4,296)
Instruments and Related	38	2,046	735	(567)	1,878
Miscellaneous Industries	39	(286)	414	(414)	(285)
Nondurable Goods		545	7,849	(6,682)	(622)
Food and Kindred Products	20	(1,065)	969	(996)	(1,039)
Textile Mill Products	22	(209)	119	(148)	(180)
Apparel and Other Textiles	23	(418)	641	(724)	(334)

Table 5–3 continued

Industry	SIC	Employment Change	National Growth Effect	Mix Effect	Competitive Effect
Paper and Allied Products*	26	273	436	(328)	166
Printing and Publishing	27	1,346	1,880	(38)	(496)
Chemicals and Allied Prods.	28	(498)	1,880	(2,143)	(235)
Petroleum and Coal	29	(304)	592	(1,190)	294
Rubber and Misc. Prods.	30	1,430	1,326	342	(239)
Leather Products	31	(9)	6	(18)	3
Services		51,519	56,590	8,210	(13,282)
Transportation		3,077	2,273	560	244
Local Passenger Transit	41	193	170	(34)	58
Trucking and Warehousing	42	1,406	1,239	404	(237)
Water Transportation	44	538	160	(262)	640
Transport by Air	45	355	454	326	(425)
Pipelines, Except Natural Gas	46	35	5	(10)	40
Transportation Services	47	550	246	307	(2)
Wholesale and Retail Trade		12,918	18,283	0	(5,366)
Wholesale Trade		4,351	7,381	(1,413)	(1,618)
Durable Goods Wholesale	50	2,922	5,187	(210)	(2,055)
Nondurable Wholesale	51	1,428	2,194	(883)	117
General Merchandise	53	(601)	2,643	(701)	(2,543)
Food Stores	54	2,312	2,820	144	(652)
Automotive Dealers	55	2,042	1,710	679	(347)
Apparel and Accessory	56	1,269	904	(51)	416
Home Furnishings*	57	841	541	751	(452)
Miscellaneous Retail	59	2,704	2,284	161	258

Producer Services		17,254	14,621	6,274	(3,642)
Communication	48	(2,479)	1,720	(2,645)	(1,554)
Electric, Gas, and Sanitary	49	1,041	865	(617)	792
Banking	60	(699)	1,736	(1,186)	(1,249)
Credit Agencies, Except Banks	61	806	930	1,270	(1,394)
Security Brokers	62	501	261	334	(93)
Insurance Carriers	63	199	1,346	(486)	(660)
Insurance Agents	64	259	464	108	(312)
Real Estate	65	393	1,083	697	(1,387)
Holding Companies	67	(1,005)	133	193	(1,331)
Business Services	73	15,868	4,050	8,043	3,775
Legal Services	81	1,088	769	647	(329)
Miscellaneous Services	89	1,281	1,265	577	(562)
Social Services		7,792	11,921	(2,414)	(1,714)
Health Services	80	5,417	8,344	(2,384)	(543)
Education Services	82	899	1,556	(710)	54
Social Services	83	1,712	1,142	748	(179)
Membership organizations	86	(236)	879	(339)	(777)
Personal Services		10,478	9,492	2,764	(1,778)
Eating and Drinking Places	58	6,064	5,266	2,428	(1,629)
Hotel and Other Lodging	70	(201)	863	537	(1,601)
Personal Services	72	1,241	1,264	127	(150)
Auto Repair	75	2,029	747	713	569
Miscellaneous Repair	76	504	282	43	179
Motion Pictures	78	436	76	(345)	705
Amusement and Recreation	79	225	781	(494)	(62)
Museums, Gardens, and Zoos	84	(1)	90	98	(189)
Private Households	88	180	122	292	(234)

Source: ES202, except for *; *from County Business Patterns.

mains in this group is in the Blast Furnace and Steel Mill Industry (SIC 3312) and another third is in the Grey Iron Foundry Industry (SIC 3321).

U.S. Steel closed its Cleveland plant. LTV Steel cut back employment drastically, but its two factories continued to run with bankruptcy court protection, give-backs by its employees, and new-found concern for product quality. LTV runs a flat-rolled production facility and opened a galvanized steel mill in partnership with Sumitomo Metals; the mill's customers are concentrated in the automobile industry. American Steel and Wire is a new firm that reopened the old U.S. Steel plant in July 1986.

The region has also benefited from the evolution of the instruments industry. Its LQ increased from 0.80 to 1.19. The industry is an emerging part of the region's economic base, even though it is a relatively small employer. The competitive effect was negative in the first portion of the cycle and strongly positive during the post-1983 recovery. The 1988 Ohio Industrial Directory lists 515 establishments manufacturing instruments in the Cleveland region. Eleven of the firms employ more than 100 people; they include Techmar — a producer of circuit boards — and Keithley Instruments, Inc. — a manufacturer of laboratory test and calibration equipment. Many of the firms in this industry provide instruments to other manufacturers. Cleveland has developed a specialization in the Process Control Instrument industry (SIC 3823) and in an industry that the SIC calls "Instruments, Measuring, Testing Electrical and Electronic Signals" (SIC 3825).

Four major groups of nondurable goods manufacturers were also part of the region's economic base in 1986: printing and publishing, chemicals and allied products, rubber and miscellaneous products, and petroleum and coal. In all cases, the LQs of these groups increased from 1979 to 1986, and it appears that, with the exception of printing, they are closely connected to national headquarters activity of the direct line of business. All of the industries, with the exception of petroleum, showed declines in their competitive effects over both segments of the business cycle. The weakest performing of these industries was printing and publishing.

The LQ of petroleum and coal increased from 1.99 to 2.78. This reflects British Petroleum's (BP) absorption of Sohio and the movement of BP's North American headquarters from New York into Sohio's corporate headquarters. In addition, major coal operators are headquartered in Cleveland, and coal employment is high due to the presence of the steel mills.

Chemical and allied products are well represented in Cleveland. The LQ increased by 11 points from 1979 to 1986, despite the fact that the industry lost 2,500 jobs. The competitive effect of the shift-share analysis was negative over both parts of the business cycle, indicating that the region's comparative advantage is somewhat tenuous. This may be due to the fact that the chemicals industry in greater Cleveland is not highly diversified, the region appears to be specialized in headquarters employment and manufacturing employment in the paint and coatings segments of the industry.

The look of chemical factories in Cleveland is very different from those located near Niagara Falls. Cleveland's plants are not intensive users of electricity. Instead, PPG's automotive paint group is headquartered in a factory complex in Lakewood, on Cleveland's border. Sherwin Williams' national headquarters and research and development laboratories are in the heart of Cleveland's Public Square. Glidden is headquartered near Public Square and its industrial coatings division is based in the region. Ferro Corporation recently moved into new corporate headquarters and employs 800 in the region. Its coatings, color, and refractories divisions are located in the city of Cleveland, while the Bedford chemicals division has a plant in the suburbs. The rubber and miscellaneous products group in Cleveland has been restructured completely from 1979 to 1986. The LQ stands at 1.64 and the competitive effect shows declines in both parts of the business cycle, but there was actual employment growth from 1983 to 1986 due to the national and industry mix effects. Aggregate data for this major group hide the dynamic nature of the region's firms. They have experienced substantial declines in the rubber business — many corporations divested their rubber operations — and have grown in plastics and polymer production and fabrication.

The Small Business Administration's Small Business Database identifies 140 fast-growing manufacturing establishments in the Cleveland region. Eighteen polymer manufacturers appear on the list, forming the largest cluster. Nearly all of the polymer firms that responded to a survey conducted by the Greater Cleveland Growth Association indicated that transportation access to their customers provided the Cleveland region with a competitive advantage over other potential sites (Flynn, 1989). Little Tykes, a division of Rubbermaid headquartered in Hudson, Ohio, pioneered rotational molding of plastics to manufacture extremely durable children's toys. The firm employes 1,100 in the region. Evenflo Products, manufacturers of infant-care products, employes 200 people in Ravenna. Glastic Company, recently purchased by Japan's Kobe Steel, employs over 200 in the city of Cleveland, producing insulators, fiber optic rods, and various injected molded plastic parts.

The M. A. Hanna Company has intentionally restructured its holdings in reaction to shifts in the regional and national economies. The company is an old-line Cleveland firm that helped to open Michigan's iron pits and the Mesabi Range in Minnesota. Until recently Hanna was heavily invested in iron ore and coal properties. By 1986, the scope of its restructuring was evident. The firm sold its Minnesota and Michigan iron mines, retaining a 28 percent interest in a Canadian iron-ore firm. It has sold all of its eastern coal mines and only retains a 50 percent interest in a Colorado coal property and it has largely moved out of the metals business, selling Hanna Silicon in the process. The bulk of the proceeds from these sales were used to move Hanna solidly into the polymer production businesses; many of its new subsidiaries are located in the Cleveland and Akron PMSAs.

The fabricated metals major group has held its position relative to the nation; the LQ is 2.48, despite massive regional employment losses. Finding optimistic things to say about the performance of this major group in Cleveland is an exercise that would make Pollyanna blush, despite the high LQ. Only two small industries did not decline from 1979 to 1983. These are the Metal Cans Business (SIC 3411), which employed 375 people in 1986, and Hardware Not Elsewhere Classified (SIC 3429), which employed 861. However, the latter industry lost a significant number of jobs from 1983 to 1986. Parts of the fabricated metals industry that lost at least 1,000 positions are: Screw Machine Products (SIC 3451), Bolts, Nuts, Rivets, and Washers (SIC 3452), Automotive Stampings (SIC 3465), Metal Stamping Not Elsewhere Classified (SIC 3469), and Ammunition (SIC 3483).

Three components of the fabricated metals industry have managed to recapture significant portions of their employment losses in the second part of the cycle: Metal Doors, Sash and Trim (SIC 3442) gained nearly 800 employees; Metal Stampings Not Elsewhere Classified (SIC 3469) gained 548 employees; and Metal Services and Polishing (SIC 3471) gained 534 jobs. Overall, employment in the major group increased by 1,500 in the second part of the cycle; all of the growth was attributed to the national effect in the shift-share analysis.

Nonelectrical machinery remains a basic employer but experienced a 27 point drop in its LQ, to 1.62. Nearly 20,000 jobs were lost from 1979 to 1983. The competitive effect remained negative throughout. Industrial Trucks and Tractors (SIC 3537) lost over 90 percent of its 1979 employment base. Construction Machinery (SIC 3531) declined by more than 80 percent. The two segments of the Machine Tools Industry (SICs 3541 and 3542) declined by more than two-thirds.

The electrical and electronic machinery business nearly disappeared. Its LQ went from 1.19 in 1979 to 1.02 in 1986. Nearly half of the jobs lost in the electrical equipment industry were in Electrical Lighting and Wiring (SIC 364). The largest share of the loss was generated by the Electrical Lighting Fixtures Industry (SIC 3645), due to General Electric's closing of its production facilities. Two four-digit electrical equipment industries disappeared for all practical purposes during the business cycle: Radio and Television Communications Equipment (SIC 3662) and Electrical Engine Equipment (SIC 3694).

The story of the transportation equipment business is complicated. The LQ has dropped from 1.47 to 1.07 and the total competitive effect is − 10,921. Yet it remains a dominant force in Cleveland's Consolidated Metropolitan Statistical Area, which consists of the Cleveland, Akron, and Lorain PMSAs. The apparent loss of comparative advantage in the PMSA is largely due to the closure of two facilities on the city of Cleveland's east side: White Motor's truck assembly plant and General Motor's Coit Road factory. Nearly half of the remaining employment in the transportation equipment major group is in the Motor Vehicle Parts and Accessories Industry (SIC 3714), which employs 7,600.

2.1 The Cyclical Sensitivity of Cleveland's Manufacturing Base

Loss of employment is not, in and of itself, a sign of the loss of comparative advantage. American manufacturers have been shedding labor as part of their drive to become globally competitive. Major declines in employment, however, are one sign of trouble. In addition, the question remains as to whether restructuring has lessened the region's traditional exposure to cyclically caused unemployment. Approximately 40 percent of Cleveland's manufacturing employment is in major industrial groups that are sensitive to business-cycle fluctuations (see table 5–4). Unfortunately, 68 percent of manufacturing employment is in industries that have experienced a steady decline in employment through the past business cycle; 30 percent of total manufacturing employment is in the intersection of these two sets — declining and cyclically sensitive industries.

The major industrial groups that were classified as being stable through the cycle and are part of the region's economic base employed 35,218 people, or 18 percent of manufacturing employment. The instruments group was the only part of the base that was a growing employer.

A large portion of Cleveland's manufacturing base is dependent on the success of the American automobile industry. Half of the employment in the transportation equipment group, most of the workers in primary

Table 5–4. Classification of Manufacturing Industries: Employment and Average Quarterly Earnings, 1987:1

Category	SIC	Name	Employment	Average Earnings
Stable Noncyclical	27	Printing and Publishing	15,905	5,754
	29	Petroleum and Coal	4,416	11,254
	39	Miscellaneous Industries	3,080	5,139
Stable Cyclical	30	Rubber and Plastics	11,817	5,273
Declining	20	Food and Kindred	6,806	6,505
	25	Furniture and Fixtures	2,094	6,163
	28	Chemicals	14,212	8,652
	35	Machinery Except Electrical	29,092	6,520
	37	Transportation Equipment	19,557	10,141
Steep Decline	22	Textile Mill Products	727	4,021
	23	Apparel	4,078	3,945
	36	Electrical and Electronic Equipment	18,205	7,167
Cyclical Growing	24	Wood and Lumber Products	1,768	6,379
	38	Instruments and Related	6,878	7,591
Cyclical, Declining Strong Rebound	32	Stone, Clay, and Glass	3,748	6,933
	33	Primary Metal*	23,301	
Weak Rebound	34	Fabricated Metal	31,627	6,656

Sources: ES202, U.S. Department of Labor; *Data for SIC 33, Primary Metals, is from County Business Patterns 1986:1.

metal, and a large fraction of the chemical business are part of the automotive industrial complex. This means that they are vulnerable both to business cycles and to offshore competition. Further research must be conducted to gauge the sensitivity of employment in nonelectrical machinery and fabricated metals to the changing fortunes of domestic automotive plants. As of this date, Cleveland's automotive suppliers have not made large inroads in supplying Japanese-owned automotive factories located in the United States (Florida et al., 1988; and Iannone, 1988).

A distinction is made in table 5–4 between major industrial groups that experienced decline throughout the cycle and those that experienced steep decline. Unfortunately, electrical and electronic machinery fell into the latter category, yet it remains the fifth largest manufacturing employer in the region. This industry, along with fabricated metal and nonelectrical equipment, remain at risk to major employment losses in any future recession. Together they accounted for 78,924 jobs in the first quarter of 1987.

A note of caution must be made about predictions based solely on employment trends. No causal relationships have been examined in this chapter. I do not know with any degree of certainty what caused the loss of employment over the 1979 to 1986 business cycle. These losses may be due to any of a large number of problems: an irreversible loss of comparative advantage, high wages, outmoded capital, adversarial labor-management relations, poor product quality, the collapse of traditional sources of demand, or poor strategic decisions on the part of management. All of these factors have been blamed for the collapse of the manufacturing sector in the Cleveland region. No doubt, all came into play at some time over the past decade, and all have been the subject of public and private initiatives over the past years. The stabilization of employment in these major industrial groups depends on the success of those efforts.

The result of the restructuring of the region's manufacturing base is striking:

- The region is less diversified within durable goods manufacturing than it was in 1979, but it appears to be more competitive.
- Two new major industrial groups have been added to the region's economic base, polymers and instruments.
- Employment in transportation equipment and primary metals is more dependent on domestic automobile demand than ever before.
- Finally, there is reason to be concerned about the fate of the tens of thousands employed in fabricated metals and the two machinery industries.

3. Services

During the first part of the business cycle, from 1979 to 1983, employment in the service sector fell from 450,673 to 430,835 (see table 5–5). Most of the drop in employment was in retail trade, followed by wholesale trade and transportation services (see table 5–6). The loss in employment was probably due to two factors. Retail sales plummeted with the decline in blue-collar incomes. The close connection between transportation and durable goods wholesale trade to the region's manufacturing base accounts for employment losses in those sectors. All five components of the service sector grew during the recovery, accounting for 90 percent of private sector job growth during that period. Nearly one-quarter of the increase was in wholesale trade; retail trade accounted for 16 percent of the increase.

Social services, and some major industrial groups within producer services, became part of the region's economic base between 1979 and 1986. The absolute number employed in social services increased from 1979 to 1983, due to employment growth in the region's hospitals. Employment in producer services dropped a bit during the first part of the cycle, but its relative share of employment within the service sector increased. Business services were the dynamic force within producer services.

In 1979 transportation, and wholesale and retail trade constituted 40.5 percent of the service economy; now it is 37.0 percent. Durable goods wholesale, however, remains a part of the region's economic base with an LQ of 1.41 in 1986, despite the fact that the competitive effect of the shift-share calculation remained negative in both portions of the cycle. There are at least four steel service centers in the region with employment of more than 100 and there are major wholesalers of industrial machinery. The continued strength of wholesale trade may be due to wholesalers of foreign-made goods replacing some domestic manufacturers in the national economy.

Nondurable goods supplanted durable goods as the primary wholesale employer during the recovery. Retail trade was also a substantial employer, gaining 10,407 jobs from 1983 to 1986. I suspect that the dynamic characteristics of these two industries are linked but I cannot verify that suspicion. Yet, when the LQs and shift-share numbers are closely examined, it appears that the region remained underrepresented in retail trade in 1986.

Producer services generated nearly 19,000 new jobs during the recovery, mostly in miscellaneous business services. Miscellaneous business services are composed of Holding and Other Investment Offices (SIC 67),

Table 5–5. Employment in the Service Sectors, Cleveland PMSA, 1979, 1983, 1986

Name of the Sector	SIC	1979	1983	1986
Total Employment for Services		450,673	430,835	495,162
Transportation	40–42, 44–47	24,211	18,254	19,806
Wholesale and Retail Trade		158,582	140,848	166,710
Wholesale	50–51	63,356	56,881	72,336
Retail	52–57, 59	95,226	83,967	94,374
Producer Services		119,473	118,174	136,858
Communications	48–49	21,444	21,337	20,500
Banking	60–62	20,275	21,514	21,717
Insurance	63–64	17,717	14,235	16,751
Real estate	65–66	11,278	11,795	12,681
Engineering and architecture	891	4,008	4,429	5,670
Accounting	893	4,542	4,127	5,516
Misc business services	67, 73, 899	35,139	34,821	46,787
Legal services	81	5,070	5,916	7,236
Social Services		79,015	89,399	100,390
Medical services	801–805, 807–808	19,921	25,070	31,302
Hospitals	806	34,704	38,403	40,154
Education	82	13,518	15,019	13,370
Welfare	832	0	0	0
Nonprofit	86	4,248	9,240	13,462
Postal services	43	NA	NA	NA
Government	91–99	NA	NA	NA
Miscellaneous	833–839	1,624	1,667	2,102

Table 5–5 continued

Name of the Sector	SIC	1979	1983	1986
Personal Services		69,392	64,160	71,671
Domestic	88	0	0	0
Hotels	70	8,828	6,583	7,611
Eating and drinking places	58	42,734	40,885	46,900
Repair	725	0	0	0
Laundry	721	3,870	3,104	2,909
Barber and beauty shops	723–724	3,594	3,624	4,087
Entertainment	78–79	8,194	7,658	7,597
Miscellaneous	725–729	2,172	2,253	2,567

Note: NA = Not available.
Source: County Business Patterns: 1979, 1983, 1986.

Table 5–6. Employment Changes for the Services Sectors

Name of the Sector	SIC	1979	1983	1986
Total Changes		−19,838	64,327	44,489
Transportation	40–42, 44–47	−5,957	1,552	−4,405
Wholesale and Retail Trade		−17,734	25,862	8,128
Wholesale	50–51	−6,475	15,455	8,980
Retail	52–57, 59	−11,259	10,407	−852
Producer Services		−1,299	18,684	17,385
Communications	48–49	−107	−837	−944
Banking	60–62	1,239	203	1,442
Insurance	63–64	−3,482	2,516	−966
Real estate	65–66	517	886	1,403
Engineering and architecture	891	421	1,241	1,662
Accounting	893	−415	1,389	974
Misc business services	67, 73, 899	−318	11,966	11,648
Legal services	81	846	1,320	2,166
Social Services		10,384	10,991	21,375
Medical services	801–805, 807–808	5,149	6,232	11,381
Hospitals	806	3,699	1,751	5,450
Education	82	1,501	−1,649	−148
Welfare	832	0	0	0
Nonprofit	86	−8	4,222	4,214
Postal services	43	NA	NA	NA
Government	91–99	NA	NA	NA
Miscellaneous	833–839	43	435	478

Table 5–6 continued

Name of the Sector	SIC	1979	1983	1986
Personal Services		−5,232	7,511	2,279
Domestic	88	0	0	0
Hotels	70	−2,245	1,028	−1,217
Eating and drinking places	58	−1,849	6,015	4,166
Repair	725	0	0	0
Laundry	721	−766	−195	−961
Barber and beauty shops	723–724	30	463	493
Entertainment	78–79	−536	−61	−597
Miscellaneous	725–729	81	314	395

Note: NA = Not available.
Sources: County Business Patterns: 1979, 1983, 1986.

Business Services (SIC 73), and Services Not Elsewhere Classified (SIC 899). This sector generated nearly 12,000 net new jobs during the recovery. The LQ of business services increased from 1.03 to 1.30 and the competitive effect accounted for a third, or 3,775, of the increase in new positions. The Cleveland region has developed a competitive advantage in this industrial group. Four of the components of producer services grew throughout the cycle: Engineering and Architecture (SIC 891), Legal Services (SIC 81), Real Estate (SICs 65 and 66), and Finance (SICs 60,61,62).

Browning and Singelmann (1978) placed the health-care industries in the social service category. This industry was the leading generator of employment during the first part of the cycle. Two-thirds of employment growth in hospitals took place during this phase. But their contribution to the growth of the local economy was dwarfed by medical services (SICs 801–805, 807, 808), which produced twice as many jobs from 1979 to 1986. Medical services produced 5,149 positions during the first phase and 6,232 in the second. The growth in hospital employment fell during the second part of the cycle, in concert with the federal government's change in the method for reimbursing hospitals for Medicaid and Medicare coverage, replacing customary fee schedules with diagnostic recovery groups.

The component industries of the services sector were classified according to their employment pattern over the cycle (see table 5–7). Distributive services, producer services, and personal services behaved cyclically. Employment declined during the first part of the cycle and grew during the second. Only social services experienced continuous growth, thanks to the performance of the health-care industry.

There was variation in the employment pattern within the major groups that compose the four service sectors. County Business Patterns had employment data on 26 industries within the service sector. Three were in a state of continuous decline; nine were cyclical; ten grew continuously; one was countercyclical. Employment data for three of the component industries were not available.

There are two ways in which to consider earnings in the service sector. What are the average earnings in each of the four sectors? And can they compensate, or offset, the regional macroeconomic and income distributional effects of the loss in earnings from the manufacturing sector? The service sector generates lower earnings than average for the PMSA. This is despite the relatively high earnings in the distribution sector (excepting retail sales), producer services (excepting real estate), and the health-care industry. Large employment gains have been made in low-wage service industries, especially in retail sales and in the entire spectrum of personal services.

Table 5–7. Service Sectors: Categorized As Growing, Declining, or Cyclical

Name of the Sector	(1) Continuous Decline	(2) Cyclical	(3) Stable	(4) Countercyclical	(5) Growth
Transportation		X			
Wholesale and Retail Trade		X			
Wholesale		X			
Retail		X			
Producer Services		X			
Communications	X				
Banking					X
Insurance		X			
Real estate					X
Engineering and architecture					X
Accounting		X			
Misc business services		X			
Legal services					X

Social Services			X	
Medical services				X
Hospitals				X
Education		X		
Welfare*				
Nonprofit	X			
Postal services*				
Governments*				X
Miscellaneous				
Personal Services	X			
Domestic*				
Hotels	X			
Eating and drinking places	X			
Repair				X
Laundry	X			
Barber and beauty shops				X
Entertainment	X			
Miscellaneous				X

*Data suppressed.
Sources: County Business Patterns: 1979, 1983, 1986.

The service sector has a bimodal distribution of earnings while manufacturing, which in some sense the service sector is replacing, is tightly grouped around the middle of the earnings distribution. Bluestone and Harrison (1982), Harrison and Bluestone (1988), and Bradbury (1986) have presented the hypothesis that deindustrialization, or the structural change, of the economy has resulted in a shift in the earnings distribution. They argue that the distribution has become more bimodal. This implies that there are proportionately more jobs at the upper and lower ends of the wage scale and fewer in the middle. The service sector is adding jobs at the extremes of the earnings distribution, and there is hypothesized to be an absolute decline in the number of jobs in the middle. This is the declining-middle hypothesis. Empirical work to date has used national data (Horrigan and Haugen, 1988). If the hypothesis holds, it should be most evident in a local labor market that has historically relied on unionized manufacturing employment, such as Cleveland.

4. The Impact of Restructuring on Earnings

A direct test of the hypothesis that the earnings distribution has changed over time requires inspecting individual and family data on incomes and earnings. Unfortunately, these are not available. Instead, quarterly average earnings data at the two-digit SIC level from the Bureau of Labor Statistic's ES202 records were used to create a "synthetic" earnings distribution.

The earnings distribution was synthesized in two respects. First, the 69 two-digit industries present in the Cleveland PMSA were rank-ordered by their real earnings. This was done for each quarter from 1975:1 through 1987:2. Then each industry's portion of total employment was added to the percent employed in all industries with lower average earnings, creating a cumulative density function of employment based on earnings. Each industry's average earnings were then treated as grouped data in calculating the mean and standard deviation of the earnings distribution. The reported average quarterly earning for the PMSA is a true mean but the standard deviation is synthesized.[4] These parameters were then used to calculate the coefficient of variation and skewness of each quarter's distribution of earnings.

An important transition in the relationship between median and average earnings occurred near the 1983 trough. Low-wage employment became relatively more important after the 1983 trough was reached. Median earnings became greater than average earnings. This implies that during the last recovery, more jobs were added at the far left of the earnings distribution, the low end, than at the far right. This is in contrast to the earlier distributions. The addition of low-wage jobs drags down average earnings.

This point is reinforced when the skewness statistic of the earnings distribution is examined. The earnings distribution would be symmetrical if the skewness statistic equals 0.0; if a positive number indicates that the distribution is skewed to the right — toward high-wage employment. All of the skewness statistics from 1983:1 to 1987:2, with the exception of fourth-quarter calculations, are negative, while those from 1979:1 to 1982:4 are positive. This means that since the 1983 trough the modal job added to Cleveland's economy has paid a relatively low wage. There is nothing in the data to indicate that this is a short-term and, therefore a purely cyclical problem. A secular change in the structure of Cleveland's regional economy has taken place.

A concise picture of change in the earnings distribution is provided by plotting the Gini coefficient (figure 5–3).[5] The Gini coefficient measures the spread of the distribution; larger Gini scores indicate wider distribu-

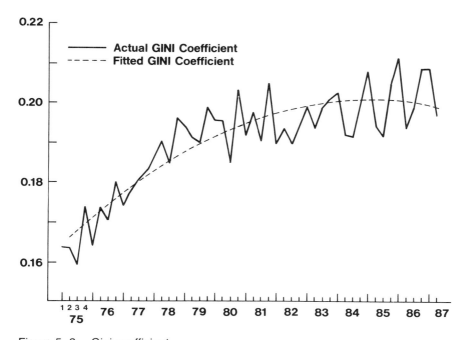

Figure 5–3.   Gini coefficient.

tions. The result is unmistakable. Gini scores have been on an unremitting upward climb since the recovery from the 1975 recession. There are two lines drawn on figure 5–3. The solid line traces the path of the Gini scores from 1975:1 to 1987:2. The dashed line is a plot of the fitted values from a time-trend regression equation. The Gini score was estimated as a function of a time indicator, TIME, and its square. TIME was given a value of one in the first quarter of 1975 and increased by one in each subsequent quarter. The combination of the variables allows us to gauge the rate of change in the Gini score (the estimation corrected for first-order serial correlation):

	GINI =	$B1$	$+B2$(TIME)	$+B3$(TIME**2)	RHO
COEFFICIENT		0.162561	0.001857	-0.000022	0.01466
t-STATISTIC		(55.59)*	(7.18)*	(4.64)*	(0.90)*

Note: $R**2 = 76.3$; Durbin-Watson = 1.99; and an asterisk indicates that the coefficient is statistically different from 0.0 at the 0.01 significance level.

The equation indicates that the Gini scores have increased in a nonlinear fashion, implying that the rate of increase in inequality has tailed-off significantly in recent quarters. The function reached a turning point in the first quarter of 1985, and the Gini scores have shown signs of moderating for the last year-and-a-half of the series.

It appears that the rate of increase in the Gini coefficient was a leading indicator of the structural change in the regional economy. There was a gradual shift in the distribution of earnings throughout the 1976 to 1979 recovery that preceded the widely recognized structural change in this particular part of the rust belt economy. The rate at which inequality is increasing has diminished since 1981, and has shown signs of marginal reversal from 1985 to 1987. This means that the economy is generating a fairly stable distribution of earnings — not a more equal distribution.

Two tests were performed to determine if changes in the Gini coefficient are attributable to shifts in the structure of employment since 1975. The hypothesis could not be tested in a single equation because of the strong negative correlation between the percentage of people employed in the manufacturing sector and in the service sector. I expected to see that decreases in the portion of the working population employed in manufacturing (PCTMFG) would be associated with increases in the Gini coefficient and that increases in the portion employed in the service sector (PCTSERV) would be positively associated with movements in the Gini coefficient. The following equations were estimated:

	GINI =	B1	+ B2(PCTMFG)	RHO
COEFFICIENT		0.2609	-0.00245	0.495
t-STATISTIC		(13.75)*	(3.66)*	(3.94)*

Note: R**2 = 63.9; Durbin-Watson = 2.26.

	GINI =	B1	+ B2(PCTSERV)	RHO
COEFFICIENT		0.1345	0.00278	0.449
t-STATISTIC		(8.27)*	(3.55)*	(3.35)*

*Note: R**2 = 62.0; Durbin-Watson = 2.30.*
Significantly different from 0.0 at the 0.01 significance level.

In each case the expectation was supported by the data.

The earnings distribution has become less tight over time. This by itself tells little about the direction of inequality in earnings. But the skewness statistics inform us that the modal wage has also shifted from the right side of the distribution to the left, from higher quarterly earnings to lower quarterly earnings. We also know that the average and median real quarterly earnings remains substantially below that of the late 1970s. At the same time, the path of the Gini coefficients indicate that the earnings distribution has become wider. These facts, combined, imply that the modal wage in the Cleveland economy has deteriorated significantly, and that jobs have been added to the high end of the distribution but more have been added at the low end. The unmistakable conclusion is that the middle has deteriorated both in absolute and relative terms.

There are three caveats to these findings. First, the results are optimistic. The data are biased in an upward direction because they do not show the impact that nonemployment has had on the income distribution. Second, the synthetic earnings distribution assumes that there is no variance in earnings within a two-digit industry. This will result in underestimating the degree of earnings inequality. Third, these are earnings data, not income data. Income distributions are much more unequal than earnings distributions in the nation as a whole. This is a result of the concentration of unearned income among the top quintile and decile of the population. There is no reason to expect that the relationship between the earnings and income distributions will be any different in Cleveland.

The other way in which economic restructuring may affect Cleveland's labor market is by making the economy less sensitive to swings in the business cycle. In some sense, people may be willing to trade off earnings at any one point in time for higher expected lifetime earnings. This prospect was examined by classifying all two-digit industries according to their variation in employment over both parts of the 1979 to 1986 cycle. Table 5–8 lists the level of employment in the seven sets of industries and their average quarterly earnings in the first quarter of 1987.

Nearly 42 percent of private employment in the Cleveland region is in industries that grew during the business cycle, but the average quarterly earnings for these industries were under $5,000. This is contrasted by the fact that over a third of all private workers were in declining industries, which provide the highest average earnings in the region. One-quarter of private employment is with stable employers. Cyclically sensitive stable employers tend to provide low earnings, $4,150 in 1987:1, while noncyclical stable industries provided $5,317 in average quarterly earnings.

About one-third of private employment in the Cleveland region is exposed to cyclical fluctuations and 51 percent work in stable, or growing noncyclical, industries. The remaining workers are in industries that have been in a steady state of decline. (Most of these industries are manufacturing industries where the rate of decline can be expected to accelerate in coming recessions.) The cyclical sensitivity of employment in the region has lessened due to economic restructuring but it is not inconsequential. Between one-third and one-half of the work force is employed in industries that may feel the effects of cycle. Lower earnings and an increased role of services in Cleveland's economy will not insulate the region from the negative effects of future business cycles.

Table 5–8. Seven Components of the Regional Economy
Cleveland PMSA, 1987:1

Employment Change 1979–1987	Cyclical Behavior	Percent of Private Employment	Average Quarterly Earnings
Decline	Noncyclical	17	$7,518
Decline	Cyclical, weak rebound	14	$6,103
Decline	Cyclical, strong rebound	3	$5,952
Stable	Cyclical	12	$4,201
Stable	Noncyclical	13	$5,317
Growing	Cyclical	4	$4,150
Growing	Noncyclical	38	$4,855

Source: ES202.

5. Outline of a Regional Development Strategy

The economy of Cleveland has been reshaped from 1979 to 1986. It is no longer dominated by durable goods manufacturing, and a number of service industries have joined the region's economic base. Restructuring, however, has also resulted in a more unequal distribution of earnings, and there has been both an increase in the poverty rate, coupled with a decline in the regional unemployment rate (Hill and Bier, 1989, p. 143). The economy is less susceptible to the business cycle than it was before restructuring occurred, but up to a third of all workers are employed by industries that remain vulnerable to recession.

Restructuring has affected the incomes of Cleveland's residents, its neighborhoods, and its prospects. It is clearly better to live in Cleveland today then it was in 1979 or 1983, but the task of developing the economy is far from complete. The two greatest dangers facing this region, outside of a prolonged recession, lie in the realm of local public policy. If local leaders focus myopically on Cleveland's central business district, or on the service industry, development will be retarded and the citizens of the city of Cleveland and its inner-ring suburbs will not share in its benefits. The key to Cleveland's continued economic revitalization lies in spreading the benefits of reindustrialization. A development strategy for the Cleveland region can be based on a simple vision, derived from economic data considered in this chapter.

Cleveland is engaged in a competitive struggle with Pittsburgh, Columbus, and Detroit to become the economic capital of the eastern end of the Great Lakes region. The city is starting with a disadvantage in this competition due to the anemic performance of its financial institutions since the mid-1970s, but it has an unusually strong base in legal services, advertising, and accounting.

The foundation for the new economic order is in place. Two types of headquarters employment will be important to the region's future. The Fortune 500 firms that are already located in the region are a critical part of the region's base. The other employment type depends on attracting regional headquarters and the headquarters of subsidiaries of out-of-region firms to the region. The continued vitality of these two forms of headquarters employment depends on the strength of the central business district and on the amenities that are available in downtown Cleveland. The condition of the airport and quality of telecommunications links are also of central importance to these employers.

The condition of the central business district of Cleveland is of regional concern and the region benefits from the economic activity that it generates, yet it is the city of Cleveland that is being asked to subsidize capital investments that undergird its renewal. This ranges from subsidies to convention hotels, the restoration of its waterfront, the renewal of sports stadiums, and lobbying for downtown housing for upper-income people. The city does not have the resources to continue to fuel the recovery. A way must be devised to have the region share the burden of the physical renewal of the city's and the region's core.

Cleveland has a comparative advantage in regional office employment, and it is extremely competitive with American coastal cities for all but the highest-level corporate activities. This is due to the low cost of living and the large, dependable, and relatively low-cost professional labor force present in the region. The region, however, does not have a clear-cut advantage over other heartland cities. The competitive question that remains is which of the cities in the eastern Great Lakes states will emerge as the region's office capital. Each city will probably share in this activity, but the relative share will depend on the success of public investments made in the core.

The second leg on which the region's economy will grow is by providing business services to three separate manufacturing belts in the eastern basin of the Great Lakes. The first belt is in the city of Cleveland, with approximately 80,000 jobs. The second belt is made up of manufacturers who have moved, or spun off, from the city and who are located in nearby Lake and Lorain counties. The third consists of a belt of fairly large manufacturing operations that span northeast Ohio stretching from Youngstown in the east, to Canton in the south, and to Toledo in the west.

The third leg of a regional development strategy rests with the city of Cleveland. Manufacturing matters greatly to both the city and the region. The city of Cleveland must reinforce its existing manufacturing base if its residents are to benefit from the recovery of this region. There is little prospect that there will be a boom in manufacturing employment in the future; there may even be further declines. However, if the city is to retain the manufacturing employment base it has, its manufacturers must develop a more highly skilled and literate work force. A work force that can work with capital equipment that will become more sophisticated. This means that the city should shift the focus of its development efforts to its manufacturing neighborhoods and leave investments in the central business district to the state and county. A comprehensive manufacturing-based development policy for the city would address manufacturing land use, traffic movement, and workplace literacy.

Manufacturing facilities in the city were established at a time when employees walked to work and factories were intensive users of land. Today, single story operations are required to be competitive. The city must identify its manufacturing districts, ensure that the existing infrastructure can support manufacturing activities and provide the land-use tools required to allow factories to expand and rationalize their layouts. This means using powers of eminent domain to acquire land for plant expansion and employee parking, separating truck from residential traffic — ensuring that trucks can enter industrial areas cheaply and easily.

Manufacturers are also searching for a well-trained and stable labor force. Modern manufacturing is no longer a place where illiterate and semiliterate workers can work and earn a good living. They are being replaced by capital. The modern workplace will be filled with people who can work in teams, be self-managing, and retrain themselves over their work lives. This means that they must have the skills that only the top half of high school graduates had in the 1950s. Unfortunately, Cleveland's public schools have failed to produce a literate work force. Nearly half of all high school entrants drop out; those who graduate, and do not go on to higher education, are not functionally literate. The city must realize that workplace literacy is an economic development issue.

The manufacturing and headquarters bases of the regional economy, and business services that are required to support these activities, will require a deepening of existing higher education resources in the region, focusing on graduate-level education in management, computer sciences, process-oriented engineering, and public administration. Cleveland has for too long relied on Columbus, Ann Arbor, and Boston for its trained managerial leadership.

The current fad of investing in high technology science and in the region's medical complex may yield a corporation or two but it does not play to the comparative advantage of this region. Using Boston as a model for development policy is a mistake and is largely irrelevant. Investments in higher education should complement the emerging service base in the local economy and reinforce its existing manufacturing strengths. It is for this reason that computer sciences and high-technology research should focus on the application of new technologies in old industries. Vastly improved management schools should be available to provide a deep pool of administrative talent to local corporations. And all of the region's management schools should increase their visibility in the region. The political leadership should work in harmony to make Cleveland's professional graduate education complex the best in the region and competitive with the best in the nation.

The last component of regional development will be filled by the market. This is the deepening of the region's retail industry and the provision of local services. There is enough entrepreneurial talent to fill market-generated niches — all the region requires is better incomes for all of its residents.

The Cleveland region experienced significant economic restructuring from 1979 to 1986, which has laid the foundation for a new cycle of growth and development. The problems in manufacturing employment are not yet over, despite the scope of changes manufacturers in the region has experienced over the past ten years. Cleveland is likely to witness significant employment losses in the fabricated metals and the non-electrial machinery industry group during the next recession. The expected losses in these groups does not mean that manufacturing is not critical to the economic success of the new economic order in Cleveland. To the contrary, Cleveland's service sector is dependent on providing and exporting business services to the manufacturing sector of the economy. Manufacturing, in Cleveland's new economic order, is complemented by regional and national headquarters office employment. When the data on the service sector are examined, it is apparent that Cleveland is not a center for financial services, and it is only a minor medical center. Employment in the service sector is dependent on the success of manufacturing in the region.

Cleveland's new economic order also presents significant challenges. New public institutions must be developed to continue the renewal of the city's core, which remains the business center of the region. Extensive efforts must be made to improve the level of literacy in the workplace — especially among manufacturing workers. Finally, the benefits from the new economic order must be spread to those who have suffered the most in the economic transition: those who benefited from the old order, semi-skilled and unskilled blue collar workers and their families.

Acknowledgments

The title of this chapter is borrowed in part, from Cohen and Zysman (1987). Judy Czi Pann provided research assistance for portions of this chapter and was a helpful critic throughout. Conversation with Richard Bingham, John Blair, Randall Eberts, David Perry, and Richart Shatten helped to clarify many of the issues raised in this chapter. Peg Gallagher and her staff in the research department of the Greater Cleveland Growth Association were of help in identifying companies. Funding was received from the Urban University and Academic Excellence Programs of the Ohio Board of Regents and through a University Technical Assistance Grant from the U.S. Department of Commerce, Economic Development Administration.

Notes

1. The hypothesis that the time trend in employment over the period 1979:1 to 1987:2 is nonlinear was tested by regressing employment as a polynomial function of time: PRIVEMP is total private employment in the Cleveland PMSA; TIME is the time trend variable where 1975:1 = 1; TIME**2 is the square of TIME; where: PRIVEMP = $B1 + B2(TIME) + B3(TIME**2)$. The results are:

Variable	Coefficient	t-Statistic
CONSTANT	1,073,978	18.19***
TIME	− 20.522.96	5.81***
TIME**2	290.06	5.79***
RHO	0.430	2.78**

Note: R**2 = 79.2; Durbin-Watson = 1.77.
*$t>Pr(t=0.10)$; ** $t>Pr(t=0.05)$; *** $t>Pr(t=0.01)$.

The inflection point was found by taking the first derivative of the estimating equation with respect to time which yields: $d(PRIVEMP)/dTIME = B2 + 2B3(TIME)$; TIME = $-.5(B2/B3)$. In this case TIME = 35, or 1983:3.

2. The elasticity was estimated by regressing real average national earnings, using a four-quarter lag, and real average regional earnings, with data from the current quarter in addition to a four-period lag, on total private employment. All variables were expressed in natural logarithms. The regression corrected for first-order autocorrelation, where: LNPEMP is the natural logarithm of private employment in the Cleveland PMSA; LNUSPE is the natural logarithm of real average private earnings in the United States; LNCLPE is the natural logarithm of real average private earnings in the Cleveland PMSA.

Variable	Coefficient	Standard Error	t-Statistic
CONSTANT	1.197	0.429	2.79**
LNUSPE(− 1)	− 0.100	0.031	3.16***
LNUSPE(− 2)	− 0.007	0.033	0.24
LNUSPE(− 3)	0.036	0.033	1.07
LNUSPE(− 4)	0.117	0.032	3.58***
LNCLPE	0.023	0.011	2.04*
LNCLPE(− 1)	0.097	0.027	3.64***
LNCLPE(− 2)	0.050	0.026	1.90*
LNCLPE(− 3)	0.019	0.027	0.70
LNCLPE(− 4)	− 0.067	0.027	2.52**
RHO	0.872	0.090	9.68***

Notes: R**2 = 94.1; Durbin-Watson = 1.06.
* $t>Pr(t=0.10)$; ** $t>Pr(t=0.05)$; *** $t>Pr(t=0.01)$.

3. The regression equation used to generate figure 5–2 was estimated in the same manner as the total employment equation in note 1, using quarterly manufacturing employment as the dependent variable. The results of the regression equation are:

Variable	Coefficient	t-Statistic
CONSTANT	415,236	7.19***
TIME	−9,077	2.86***
TIME**2	96.75	2.30**
RHO	0.118	6.59***

Notes: $R**2 = 97.1$; Durbin-Watson $= 1.34$.
* $t > Pr(t = 0.10)$; ** $t > Pr(t = 0.05)$; *** $t > Pr(t = 0.01)$.

4. The synthetic earnings distribution will understate inequality because it assumes that earnings are equal within each two-digit industry. One example is in SIC 80, Health Care. We are forced to assume that all health-care workers from janitors to residents and chief executives are paid an equal wage. This is clearly false. If we assume that the dispersion of earnings remains roughly constant within each industry over time then the movement in the summary measure, the Gini coefficient, is an accurate reflection of the trend in inequality in the region. The same logic holds for median quarterly earnings reported in the chapter. They may be overstated because they are the industry average earnings for the industry which employs the median worker. These are imperfect measures of the regional earnings distribution but they are the only ones available in noncensus years.

5. The Gini coefficient is a summary measure of inequality of income or earnings distributions. The coefficient varies from 0 to 1, where 0 means complete income equality and 1 complete inequality. Therefore, greater inequality is associated with higher Gini scores (Apgar and Brown, 1987, pp. 211–213).

6 DAYTON, OHIO: A DRAMATIC REBOUND

John P. Blair and Rudy Fichtenbaum

The three pillars of Dayton's economy have their foundations in the innovations and inventions of great men.[1] First, Dayton is an automobile town. Charles Kettering's automobile-related inventions led to the founding of Delco Products (acquired by General Motors [GM]) and the establishment of several automobile-related facilities. Currently, GM alone employs 25,000 area employees. However, the area's automobile complex also includes a major Japanese automotive presence, Chrysler's Acustar Division, Navistar (formerly International Harvester), and numerous small manufacturers.

Dayton is also a military town. Wright Patterson Air Force Base with over 35,000 civilian and military employees reflects the legacy of the Wright brothers, who invented the airplane in their Dayton bicycle shop. The Air Force base has attracted numerous defense contractors and ancillary facilities that have further increased military-related employment.

Finally, Dayton is also a corporate headquarters city. It is headquarters for five Fortune 500 companies. Major corporate headquarter activities account for about 15,000 jobs and, just as important, provide a catalyst for other activity. NCR—formerly National Cash Register—the largest of the corporations headquartered in the region, was founded by John Paterson whose business acumen turned a small enterprise into the largest business machine company in the world.

The importance of entrepreneurship and technical innovation remain a part of the region's collective perception of how to revive the economy. Simultaneously, residents are adjusting to the reality that institutions and forces beyond the region are playing an important role in Dayton's destiny. Decisions regarding the federal budget and intragovernmental politics affect the region's military economy. The local newspapers regularly report on Air Force decisions, such as base closures, and speculate on local repercussions. Likewise, decisions made by Wall Street financiers affect the future of corporate headquarters activity in the region. Rumors of takeovers frequently spark concerns about the region's future. The automobile sector continues to be buffeted by internal corporate decisions made in Detroit, by fluctuations in international exchange rates, and by federal policies.

Dayton has experienced several major shocks that preceded the nationwide concern about deindustrialization. The decline of the region's manufacturing base can be traced to the mid-1970s when the NCR Corporation drastically reduced its blue-collar manufacturing employment. The layoffs were attributable to the relocation of production activity to low labor-cost locations and to the conversion from mechanical to electronic business machines. Later, another shock was experienced when a large Frigidaire plant (a GM subsidiary) was shut down. Because Dayton experienced major manufacturing job losses prior to other industrial regions, the Dayton area had an (unwelcome) head start in restructuring.

The purpose of this chapter is to examine the restructuring process in light of the national business cycle. During the 1979 to 1983 recession, the region experienced a 12 percent employment drop, but the decline was uneven among the components of the economy. Many of the sectors that lost employment did not rebound during the recovery, while other sectors appeared to be unaffected by the recession. However, the recovery began in mid-1983, and by 1986 over 150 percent of the jobs lost during the recession had been regained. The asymmetrical response of local sectors to the business cycle provides a framework for understanding Dayton's restructuring.

1. Economic Structure and Structural Change

Location quotients (LQs) are useful for illustrating the extent that a region's employment pattern is similar to the rest of the nation. If all industries in a region had location quotients equal to 1, the region's structure would be identical to the benchmark (in this case, the nation). Table 6–1 shows employment size and location quotients for industrial divisions in 1979 and 1986. Stability of the LQs is the most notable aspect of the comparison. The only change in the rank order of the industrial divisions was the drop in construction employment below that of the transportation sector.

Manufacturing was the most important sector in the Dayton area economy in terms of employment, and it was also the sector with the highest LQ in both 1979 and 1986. In fact, the manufacturing LQ actually increased between 1979 and 1986, indicating that the relative decline in manufacturing in the Dayton region was less than the nationwide decline. The service category had the second highest employment LQ in both 1979 and 1983. The employment gap between services and manufacturing activities declined during the period, indicating that the strength of the service sector absorbed some of the manufacturing job losses.

The nature of the Dayton area's structure becomes more apparent from an examination of the location quotients of major employment groups (two-digit) as shown in table 6–2. High location quotients tend to be in the durable manufacturing activities, while low location quotients are apparent in several manufacturing sectors such as apparel, leather, petroleum, textiles, lumber, chemicals, and furniture. Low location quotients in these categories are typical for many northern urban areas. Like the analysis of the industrial division, the data on major employment groups

Table 6–1. Employment and Location Quotients Industrial Divisions

1979			1986		
Employment (1,000s)	Sector	LQ	Employment (1,000s)	Sector	LQ
123	Manufacturing	1.27	105	Manufacturing	1.30
74	Services	1.04	96	Service	1.08
69	Retail	1.01	72	Retail	.98
17	Wholesale	.72	19	Wholesale	.78
16	Fire	.73	17	Fire	.67
15	Construction	.80	14	Transportation	.67
14	Transportation	.67	11	Construction	.61
.5	Mining	.13	.5	Mining	.13

Source: Country Business Patterns.

Table 6–2.   Major Groups with Largest and Smallest LQ — 1986

Largest		Smallest	
Machinery	2.68*	Apparel	.05*
Transportation Equipment	2.48*	Leather	.15*
Membership Organization	2.07*	Petroleum	.22*
Fabricated Metals	1.66*	Heavy Construction	.24*
Education	1.60	Passenger Transportation	.24*
Misc. Repairs	1.55	Security Brokers	.26*
Credit Agencies	1.40*	Textiles	.29*
Transportation Services	1.38	Lumber	.33*
Personal Services	1.25*	Chemicals	.39
Printing	1.23*	Furniture	.39*

*Among the largest or smallest sectors in 1979.

also indicate a general stability in the structure of the economy. Seven of the ten major employment groups with the largest location quotients in 1986 were also among the top ten in 1979. Similarly, all but one of the sectors with the smallest location were also in the lowest group in 1979. However, the apparent stability masks changes that would be apparent from a more detailed industrial breakdown and obscures changes that have occurred during the business cycle.

In order to examine how employment in detailed sectors behaved during the recession and recovery, a 3-by-3 classification matrix was developed. Industries were classified according to (1) overall performance between March 1979 and March 1986, and (2) cyclical behavior during the March 1979 to March 1983 recession and the subsequent recovery.

Overall performance between 1979 and 1986 was based upon whether the industry was (1) growing, (2) stable, or (3) declining. A growing industry had an employment increase of over 10 percent between 1979 and 1986 (roughly the national average). A stable industry had an employment change of plus or minus 10 percent during the entire time period, and a declining industry had an employment decline of 10 percent or more during the period.

Sectors were also classified according to their cyclical behavior. A sector was either (1) cyclical, (2) acyclical, or (3) countercyclical. Cyclical industries had employment declines during the period March 1979 to March 1983 and had employment growth between March 1983 to March 1986. Thus, they followed the basic pattern of the national business cycle.

Acyclical industries either grew during both periods or declined during both periods. Essentially, the forces for growth or decline were so strong among the acyclical industries that the effects of the national business cycle were overwhelmed. These forces may have been industry-specific, region-specific, or both. Countercyclical industries showed employment increases during the 1979 to 1983 recession and employment declines during the recovery. Figure 6–1 illustrates the classification matrix. Table 6–3 shows the industrial classifications according to major groups (two-digit SIC). Table 6–4 employs the same 3-by-3 matrix to show the performance of the major sectors that will be examined in this report — manufacturing, producer services, social services, personal services, transportation services, and wholesale and retail services. Table 6–4 was derived from industry group employment changes (three-digit SIC).

Notice that the total employment change at the major group (two-digit) level of disaggregation is less than the change shown in Table 6–4 because the employment changes reflect averaging that occurred within a two-digit category. If employment in some industry groups (three-digit level) grew while other industry groups declined, only the net job change is

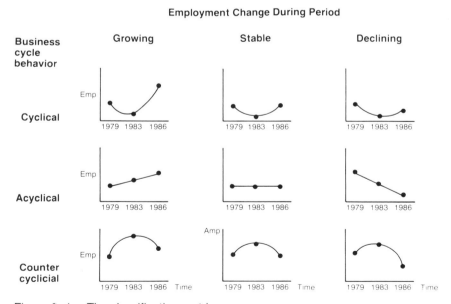

Figure 6–1.   The classification matrix.

Table 6–3. Employment Changes, Two-Digit Classification

SIC	Cyclical	Growing
34	Fabricated Metal Product	
59	Misc. Retail	
67	Holding/Investment	
86	Membership Organizations	
		Total Employment Change = 4,734

	Cyclical	Stable
12	Mining (Coal)	
16	Heavy Construction	
17	Special Trade Contractors	
37	Transp. Equipment	
42	Trucking/Warehousing	
50	Wholesale Trade	
52	Retail/Building/Garden	
54	Food Stores	
55	Auto Dealers/Service Stations	
56	Apparel and Accessories	
57	Furniture	
64	Insurance Brokers/Services	
65	Real Estate	
75	Auto Repair/Services/Garages	
79	Amusement/Recreation	
		Total Employment Change = 993

	Cyclical	Declining
15	Gen. Contracting/Building	
20	Food	
24	Lumber and Wood Products	
26	Paper	
27	Printing/Publishing	
28	Chemicals	
32	Stone/Clay/Glass Products	
35	Machinery (Except Electrical)	
36	Electric and Electronic Eqpt.	
53	Genl. Merchandise Stores	
84	Museums/Botanical/Zoological	
		Total Employment Change = −18,810

Table 6–3 continued

	Acyclical	Growing
7	Agri Services	
45	Air Transportation	
47	Transportation Services	
61	Credit Agencies Other Than Banks	
62	Security, Commodity Brokers/ Services	
73	Business Services	
76	Misc. Repair Services	
80	Health Services	
81	Legal Services	
82	Educational Services	
83	Social Services	
89	Misc. Services	

Total Employment Change = 29,338

	Acyclical	Stable

(No industries fell into this category.)

	Acyclical	Declining
14	Nonmetallic Minerals, Except Fuels	
23	Apparel and Other Textile Products	
30	Rubber/Misc. Plastic Products	
33	Primary Metal Industries	
39	Misc. Manufacturing Industries	
41	Passenger Transit	
60	Banking	
63	Insurance Carriers	
70	Hotels/Lodging Places	
78	Motion Pictures	

Total Employment Change = −14,959

Table 6–3 continued

	Counter-cyclical	Growing
51	Wholesale/Nondurable Goods	
		Total Employment Change = 976

	Counter-cyclical	Stable
25	Furniture/Fixtures	
29	Petroleum/Coal Products	
38	Instruments/Related Products	
72	Personal Services	
		Total Employment Change = 334

	Counter-cyclical	Declining
48	Communication	
49	Electric/Gas/Sanitary Services	
		Total Employment Change = −779

Source: County Business Patterns and authors' calculations.

shown. Thus, the two-digit level hides important changes among industrial subcategories.

Tables 6–3 and 6–4 indicate that most job growth tended to be in the acyclically growing category — activities that grew during the 1979 to 1983 recession as well as during the expansion. For instance, table 6–4 indicates that 30,091 jobs were created in acyclically growing industries or about 70 percent of the region's gross employment gain. The overwhelming portion of the acyclically growing sectors were service-oriented.

The cyclically growing and cyclically stable categories include activities that declined between March 1979 and March 1983 but that expanded during the recovery. These sectors either moderately increased or retained their relative importance with the Dayton economy. Manufacturing firms represent the largest component of the cyclically growing category.

Cyclically declining activity had weak recoveries. Manufacturing also dominated the job losses due to cyclical decline. These activities failed to recoup the losses experienced during the recession. The acyclically declining activities experienced employment declines throughout the 1979 to 1983 and the 1983 to 1986 periods. Unless major changes occur, the

Table 6–4.   Three-Digit Employment Change

Industry	Growth	Stable	Decline
Cyclical			
Manufacturing	4,238	−949	−11,905
Personal Services	1,223	6	−1,566
Social Services	123	0	−906
Producer Services	664	46	−626
Transportation Services	0	−650	−225
Wholesale and Retail	1,928	388	−2,336
Total	8,186	−1,159	−17,564
Acyclical			
Manufacturing	2,233	0	−2,380
Personal Services	9,739	0	−3,090
Social Services	12,318	0	0
Producer Services	1,134	0	−193
Transportation Services	1,941	0	−174
Wholesale and Retail	2,726	0	−3,156
Total	30,091	0	−18,999
Counter-Cyclical			
Manufacturing	488	262	−392
Personal Services	2,325	−25	−76
Social Services	0	−75	−13
Producer Services	37	107	−279
Transportation Services	0	0	0
Wholesale and Retail	1,215	0	87
Total	4,065	−255	−847
Total	42,342	−1,414	−37,410

Source: County Business Patterns.

prospects are that cyclically declining, and especially the acyclically declining, industries will continue to experience employment losses.

2. Manufacturing

This section describes manufacturing job change. Over the entire period, the region lost about 15,000 net manufacturing jobs. At the major group level, only Fabricated Metal Products (SIC 34) and Textile Products (SIC 22) were classified as growth sectors.

While most of the manufacturing declines during the 1979 to 1983 recession can be attributed to gradual erosion rather than to abrupt change or crisis, there were two important plant shutdowns. First, the loss of 1,170 jobs in the Commercial Printing Sector (SIC 275) was due to the closing of Dayton Press, a printer of national publications. The closure was attributed to high costs, including labor costs. However, the facility was also outmoded and a major contract was lost prior to the closure.

The Dayton area has a strong employment agglomeration in printing. It is the corporate headquarters for Mead, which produces paper and a variety of related products; and for Standard Register, a Fortune 500 company that produces business forms; and a major printing research subsidiary of Eastman Kodak is located in one of the area's new research parks. The closing of Dayton Press appears to "explain" the placement of the printing and publishing sector in the cyclically declining category. However, the loss did not appear to seriously damage the printing agglomeration, particularly the advanced imaging activities. The strong recovery is due to the resilience of the advanced technology printing and related activities. Most of the three-digit industries within SIC 27 showed significant rebounds during the 1983 to 1986 period, although the later gains were insufficient to offset the closing of Dayton Press.

A second plant closing, Dayton Tire and Rubber, explains the decline in the Rubber and Miscellaneous Plastics products sector (SIC 30). The reasons for the closure involve both loss of markets and labor-cost concerns. Unlike the printing example, the decline of the rubber-plastics sector appears to have dropped business activity below the critical mass necessary to maintain a viable agglomeration. Thus, Rubber and Miscellaneous Plastics was acyclically declining and failed to evidence a significant rebound. Notice that all of the three-digit industry groups in the Rubber and Plastics (SIC 30) category showed either decline through the recovery or had very weak recoveries. This suggests that the rubber-plastics sector may have fallen below the critical mass necessary to reestablish itself as a major component in the local economy.

The employment declines in the Metal Working sector (SIC 35) accounted for the loss of about 7,000 jobs during the 1979 to 1986 period. Most of the industry groups (three-digit industries) in this category (SICs 351, 352, 353, 355) were acyclical-declining, meaning that employment decline continued through the recovery. However, because some sectors rebounded (SICs 358 and 359), the sector as a whole had a weak rebound.

A previous study by Wright State University's Department of Economics and the Dayton Development Council indicated that part of the problem in the metalworking sector could be attributed to a manpower shortage of skilled machinists. Another reason for the decline in the machine-tool sector is that many firms in the industry have not shifted to prototype production. The region's metalworking capabilities are dominated by firms seeking "long-run" orders. However, the relatively high wage in the area tends to make local firms less competitive in seeking routine contracts. Yet they are not able to compete with the best regions in prototype production. Finally, the machine tool industry has been dominated by small independent firms. At the same time, technological changes such as the use of computer-aided design and computer-aided manufacturing (CAD/CAM) require huge investments that small firms have difficulty providing.

The General Industrial Machinery (SIC 356) sector produces pumps, compressors, and bearings, among other things. This sector is closely allied to the automobile sector. It suffered a dramatic decline during the recession, recording a loss of 2,600 jobs. However, it had a modest comeback during the recovery, due largely to rebound of the automobile sector.

2.1 The Manufacturing Heart — Cars and Trucks

Automobiles and related industries are the heart of the region's manufacturing base. Although this sector experienced major job losses during the 1979 to 1983 recession period, evidence of a strong employment rebound, exurban employment growth on the fringe of the Dayton region, and locational analysis indicate that the automobile sector will remain strong in the Dayton area. The transportation sector (of which automotive is the largest component) is integral to the Dayton region's manufacturing base. It is by far the largest component of the manufacturing base and includes several General Motors divisions, Chrysler, Navistar (formerly International Harvester), major Japanese facilities, and numerous suppliers.

The Transportation sector (SIC 37) lost about 5,000 jobs during the recession. However, it made a strong comeback locally during the 1983 to 1986 period. Overall, the sector showed modest gains, so it was classified in the cyclically stable category. However, important industry groups (three-digit subcategories) grew over the period. Specifically, SIC 371 (Motor Vehicles and Motor Vehicle Equipment) increased from 17,300 to 19,200 during the 1979 to 1986 period (particularly after 1983). Evidence since 1986 indicates that the growth is continuing.

The strength of the recovery indicates that the region has the locational attributes needed to remain a center of automotive production. In addition, several Japanese automotive facilities, including Honda and many of its suppliers, have recently located in the exurban counties around Dayton and Columbus. These facilities are strongly linked to area firms and have contributed to the region's automotive agglomeration, even though many of the facilities are not in the four-county area that is the focus of this study.

> Winger (1989) recognized the growth potential of the automobile sector: "The automobile industry remains as an important component in the economy and appears . . . a positive economic force in the future" (p. 25).

The overall stability of the transportation sector, coupled with the nationwide restructuring of the industry, has led local business leaders to explore the reasons for the strength of the automobile sector. Corporate

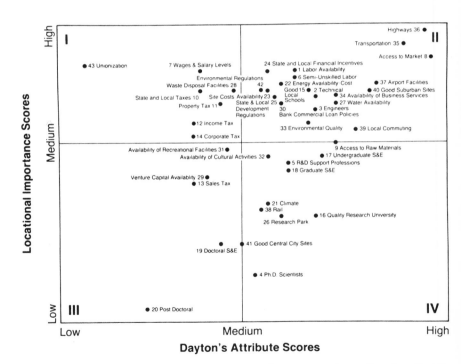

Figure 6–2.   Dayton's auto components manufacturers and suppliers locational matrix.

officers from 17 local companies were asked to rate key locational factors according to (1) the importance of each locational factor and (2) the score of Dayton compared to ". . . other cities in which your establishment might locate." The results are shown in figure 6–2. (Wright State University and the Area Progress Council, 1987).

While considerable space could be devoted to discussing each locational factor that is critical to the automotive sector, some overall summary statements can be made. First, the upper righthand corner of figure 6–2 shows import locational factors for which the Dayton region is rated highly. Factors related to market access, including the ability for intra-industry trade and the technical labor force, were important strengths. Second, "hard cost factors" such as transportation, labor, and other costs are dominant. The questionnaire was completed by local executives, so there may be some bias toward Dayton (that is, automotive firms that did not believe Dayton was a good environment would not be in the area in the first place). Nevertheless, the locational analysis indicated that the region has the locational attributes to remain an important automotive center. Third, locational factors in quadrant II are an important weakness. Cost-related factors, such as taxes and wage levels, are prominent. The excellent labor relations in Japanese facilities are providing a model for American companies to address the unionization factor that was considered a major weakness.

2.2 Advanced Technology

Most local observers view advanced technology as a regional strength. These activities also reflect the heritage of innovation discussed in the introduction. However, when the performance of the specific high-technology industries identified by Markusen, Hall, and Glasmeier (1986) were examined, the Dayton region's high-tech sector did not perform well during the 1979 to 1986 period.

The performance of high-tech industries as defined by Markusen and associates is shown in table 6–5.[2] It indicates that Dayton's advanced technology sector is small and has performed poorly. Over the 1979 to 1986 period, the high-tech sectors declined by nearly 5,000 jobs. Employment losses in electronic equipment and machinery, except electrical, are notable. The decline was particularly severe in the acyclical declining category, indicating that the employment loss was due to more than the national business cycle, since these are "non-bounce-back" industries. In

Table 6–5.   Employment Shifts in High-Tech Industries (Markuson et al.
Classification)

| | Growth Status | | |
	Growth	Stable	Decline
Cyclical	3917	− 442	− 5996
Acyclical	112	0	− 3585
Counter-cyclical	450	− 285	0
Total	4479	− 727	− 9581

Note: Growth defined as employment rate of greater than 10 percent. Stable is defined
as employment rate between a negative 10 percent and a positive 10 percent. Decline is
defined as employment rate of greater than a 10 percent decline.
Source: County Business Patterns.

contrast to the declining industries, the growing three-digit high-tech industries had a total employment change of only 4,479.

In contrast to the evidence based upon the Markusen classification,
the opinion among Dayton observers is that the high-tech sector is strong
and a source of employment growth. (Local observers refer to "advanced
technology" in an effort to indicate that Dayton's strength is in the implementation stage of technology development rather than the pure research
stage.) In fact, the community is proud of its advanced technology base.
Development officials believe Dayton is able to compete with the major
"second tier" high-tech locations in the nation and that it is competitive
with some of the best research sites in the nation in selected areas. There
are several local business groups devoted to strengthening the advanced
technology sector.

Several factors indicate that advanced technology is a strength with
the region:

1.   The Dayton region has the highest percentage of scientists and engineers among Ohio cities according to the Dayton Area Chamber of
Commerce. Wright Paterson Air Force Base is a major research, development and logistic center.
2.   Within the last few years, over a million square feet of office space
has been constructed and occupied by research-oriented consulting
firms. The region has one of the highest rates of patent registration in
the nation.

3. The region is the corporate headquarters of NCR, Mead, Reynolds and Reynolds, and Standard Register. These are Fortune 500 corporations that are strongly computer- and information-oriented. Unfortunately, NCR has transferred most of its R&D activities away from Dayton.
4. Recent studies have examined technologies most applicable to the region. They concluded that the region has strengths in Strategic Defense Initiative (SDI) technologies, manufacturing technologies, materials, artificial intelligence, imaging, and biotechnology-bio-medicine.
5. A survey of executives in over 150 Dayton high-tech industries indicated the locational strengths and weakness of the region according to locational importance. The survey results are summarized in figure 6–3. Clearly, the region has more important strengths (Quandrant II) than weaknesses (Quandrant I).

How can this local observation of Dayton's technological strength be reconciled with the employment changes indicated by the Markusen classification? One explanation is that the Markusen classification failed to include legitimate advanced-tech activities. It is inherently difficult to classify high-technology activities by industry because all industries include some advanced technology activities. As Phillips and Vidal (1970) noted:

> . . . While it would be desirable to analyze recent trends in high technology employment, these jobs are scattered among a variety of two- and three-digit SIC categories and *are not readily identifiable* [Emphasis added].

High-tech classifications should consider both what is produced (product) and how it is produced (process). Furthermore, the Markusen scheme did not include nonmanufacturing employment. Dayton's advanced technology base is dominated by consulting firms that are not within a manufacturing facility. For instance, the BDM Corporation is a major computer research consultant with the Air Force. It is classified as an engineering and architectural firm. The automotive sector (SIC 371) is not considered a high-technology sector event even though one of GM's strategic goals is the establishment of "a high-technology culture" (UAW-GM Human Resources Center, 1989, ch. 9, p. 9).

In spite of the success of the region's advanced technology sector, the fact that many local research firms depend upon the federal budget and upon bureaucratic decisions places many activities at risk to forces beyond regional control.

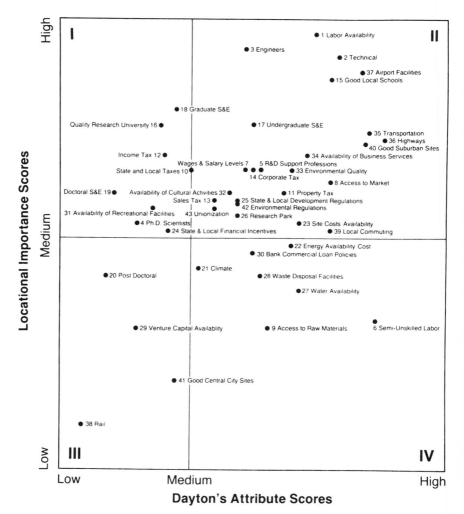

Figure 6–3.   Dayton's advanced technology sector locational matrix.

2.3 Hidden-Trend Breakers

Table 6–6 shows hidden trend-breakers. A hidden trend-breaker is defined as a three-digit industry that grew over 10 percent during 1979 to 1986

Table 6–6.   Hidden Trend-Breakers, 1979 to 1986

SIC	Name	Employment Change	Type
204	Grain Mill Products	211	A/G
344	Fabricated Structural Steel	−302	C/D
345	Screw Machine Products, Bolts	−114	C/D
351	Engines and Turbines	302	A/G
358	Refrigeration and Service Machiners	829	C/G
369	Misc. Electrical Equipment and Supplies	104	C/G
483	Radio and Television Broadcasting	190	A/G
489	Communications Services, NEC	408	CC/G
519	Misc. Nondurable Goods, Wholesale	−87	CC/D
573	Radio, Television, and Music Stores	133	C/G
596	Nonstore Retailers	−156	C/D
614	Personal Credit Institutions	−306	A/C
863	Membership Organizations	−102	C/D
864	Civic and Social Organizations	−140	C/D

Note: The type of employment change between 1979 and 1986 is the following: acyclical (A), cyclical (C), counter-cyclical (CC), growth (G), stable (S), and decline (D).
Source: Country Business Patterns.

while the two-digit group that it is part of declined by more than 10 percent during the same period, *or* a three-digit industry that declined by more than 10 percent while the two-digit industry grew by more than 10 percent. This restrictive definition avoids terming as "trend-breakers" three-digit, slight-growth industries in two-digit, slight-decline categories.

There were only six trend-breakers in the manufacturing sector: (1) grain mill products; (2) fabricated structural metal products; (3) screw machine products and bolts, nuts, screws, rivets, and washers; (4) engines and turbines; (5) service industry machines; and (6) miscellaneous electrical machinery equipment and supplies. The fact that there were relatively few trend-breakers indicates the extent that activities within the manufacturing sector are dependent upon each other.

The major trend-breakers in terms of overall growth were in SIC 35, Machinery, Except Electrical (SIC 351, 358). Shopsmith, successful producers of home woodworking machines, may account for some of the growth in this category. Also, machinery sold to the automotive sector is included in this category. Hence, these positive trend-breakers may reflect the strength of the automotive agglomeration.

2.4 Explaining Changes in Manufacturing

Five models are particularly useful in describing the changes in Dayton's manufacturing sector: (1) agglomeration, (2) post-industrial, (3) locational factors, (4) political, and (5) filtering. However, the models do not apply equally to all industry groups.

The automotive and the printing sectors (the term *information processing* may be more accurate) appear to have maintained the critical mass needed to achieve significant agglomeration economies with further growth potential. However, some local manufacturing sectors, such as rubber, suffered such large employment declines that they lost agglomeration economies. Individual firms may no longer benefit from opportunities that can result from a being near a group of related producers. One danger when an activity falls below a critical mass is that it will be more difficult to ". . . add new work to old" (Jacobs, 1970), so spinoffs are less likely.

Agglomeration economies are critical to urban development. Stigler (1951) said that geographic dispersion is a luxury that can be achieved only after industries have grown to the level where gains from specialization can be achieved at several production points. Once an industry starts to shrink, it must increase the degree of spatial concentration in order to maintain its agglomeration economies. Restructuring during decline rather than decline only is the best way to describe changes in manufacturing because some regions may experience employment gains in a declining industry. The growth within the automotive sector indicates that Dayton solidified its position as an agglomerative center of a restructured automobile industry.

Locational analysis indicated that the Dayton region is competitive with other sites in locational attributes that are important to automobile producers. The central location, skilled and semiskilled work force, and transportation accesses are strengths. Locational analysis also indicates strengths that could nurture advanced technology activities. The locational analysis not only helps explain what has happened but suggests changes that can make the region more competitive.

However, most of the manufacturing sectors have declined, although they recovered somewhat from recession lows. The future prospects of these cyclically stable or cyclically declining industries are likely to be tied closely to national trends. A few manufacturing industries, however, declined acyclically. Employment changes in these industries may be explained by new agglomerations centered in other regions and by the inability of Dayton to provide a critical mass necessary for sustainable growth. In the absence of an abrupt change, the future of the acyclically declining sectors is bleak. Theoretical insights on the general decline in the manufacturing sector may be provided by the postindustrial perspective of Daniel Bell (1973). He suggested that declines in manufacturing employment were part of a social and technological "long wave." This perspective may help explain the numerous small job losses, or slow growth, that have occurred in many of the cyclically declining manufacturing industries.

Political factors and local development efforts also explain a large part of the success of local advanced-tech activities and suggest potential threats. Efforts have been made to encourage Wright Patterson Air Force Base to extend contracts with local suppliers. Base policy has been changed to encourage such contracting in the belief that it is in the interest of the Air Force to build a local support system. Community business leaders have also been active in developing research facilities. The national budgetary priority placed on advanced weapons systems has also bolstered the local economy. Wright Patterson Air Force Base has several major contracts extended that are part of the confederation of research projects called SDI. The local economy has also benefited from research on the "space plane."

In addition to political factors, lack of production activity in advanced technology industries can be attributed to the traditional industrial filtering model. Employment in major corporations are near classic examples of a city spinning-off routine work. The region has several firms that are major forces in computers, business machines, and information technologies. Yet, they do little routine production in Dayton. Dayton has maintained the engineering, administrative, marketing research, and related functions.

3. Services

This section examines five service sector categories: transportation services, wholesale and retail services, producer services, social services, and personal services. Services have been performance stars for most urban areas during the 1979 to 1986 period, and the Dayton region is no exception. However, there are important differences among the service categories. Specifically, some services have contributed to the export base of the economy by generating dollars from outside the region, while other services appear merely to react to changes in local demand.

3.1 Transportation Services

The growth profile of the transportation sector is evident from table 6–4. All of the growth among transportation service providers is acyclical. Local and suburban transportation, air transportation, air transportation services, and freight forwarding all posted substantial employment gains. Most of this growth centers around Dayton International Airport, which has experienced considerable physical development. Emery Worldwide, the largest international air freight company in the United States, located its major hub in Dayton. Expansion of Emery's operations contributed significantly to the success of the transportation sector. However, most of the Emery jobs are part time, during the early morning hours, and are benefits-scarce. Consequently, they tend to attract young employees, especially college students. Fortunately, Emery normally loads and unloads at night and in the early morning, so those activities do not strain airport capacity.

Piedmont Airlines is another reason for the strength of the transportation sector. Dayton is a Piedmont hub. This designation has not only directly contributed to job growth, but has been a locational attraction for regional office and other activities that require quick access to distant cities.

The major firms in the air transportation sector are frequently under threat of corporate takeovers. Recently, Emery merged with Purolator, and Piedmont was taken over by U.S. Air. Fortunately for the region, the corporate restructuring has not yet adversely affected the economic vitality of the air transportation sector, but the threat continues.

Emery has been cash short after the merger, contributing to rumors of additional corporate change. The restructuring of the airline industry could result in the loss of Dayton's important hub function. In order to secure the advantages of a major airport, the community has invested heavily in promoting and physically upgrading the facility.

Trucking (SIC 921) and Warehouse (SIC 422) activities have been relatively stable. The stability resulted from two countervailing forces. On the one hand, the region is considered to offer excellent locational assets that appeal to trucking and distribution firms. Most importantly, Dayton is centrally located at the intersection of two major interstate highways, I-70 and I-75. On the other hand, nationally, distribution firms have undergone significant consolidation, and employment per dollar of service delivered has declined. The proximity to other major centers — Columbus and Indianapolis — has had mixed effect on trucking and warehousing activity by increasing markets that can be served from Dayton on the one hand, while providing sources of competition on the other.

The strength of distribution activities has provided a modest source of job growth in related areas. The distribution sector is an important element in the production of many products, so a strong distribution sector may give the region an advantage in attracting manufacturing and other distribution-sensitive industries. The distribution center for Honda is located in the area and helps anchor the important Japanese automobile complex. Dayton is also the site of the Defense Electronics Supply Center, a major distributor of electronic equipment for the Defense Department. The growth of the defense sector has contributed to increased distribution activity in this category.

3.2 Wholesale and Retail Trade

Table 6–4 shows the growth patterns among industry groups in the wholesale and retail services sector. There appear to be no clear growth patterns. The majority of industry groups showed employment patterns that matched the business cycle. On average, the job gains were only slightly higher than job losses. Based upon the large number of activities in the cyclical category that had a moderate level of employment growth, the wholesale and retail trade sector appears to conform to the growth of the regional economy. Thus, the traditional export base model appears to provide an important explanation for employment growth in wholesale and retail services. However, the export base model does not explain the large employment shifts among industry groups in the acyclical-growth and acyclical-decline classifications. Changes among industry groups in the acyclical-growth category probably reflect the growth of statewide distribution linked to changes in transportation services.

3.3 Producer Services

Job growth in the producer services sector has been strong. The producer services sector registered a net gain of 8,574 employees. The largest type of employment gain was among the acyclical-growth industry groups, whereas the largest declines occurred in the acyclical-decline category. The producer services appear to be less affected by the business cycle than most activities. There were only 13 industry groups in the cyclical category, compared to 19 industry groups in the acyclical category. Much of the growth in the advanced technology sector may be accounted for by components of producer services, such as Engineering Services (SIC 891).

3.4 Personal Services and Social Studies

Personal services were also a generally increasing category. Educational services were a major growth component of this sector. The region has made a substantial commitment to improving its educational infrastructure as part of a high-tech development strategy.

4. Trend-Breakers

The major trend-breakers for the service sectors are shown in table 6–6. Most of the trend-breakers were small, accounting for a net loss of only a few jobs. Many of the losses may be attributable to the region's proximity to Columbus and Cincinnati, which may have attracted some service activities that require large markets in order to be viable.

5. Explaining Changes in Services

Three models are useful in explaining changes in the service sector. First, a location-theory model that emphasizes minimizing transportation costs helps explain employment growth patterns in the distribution and producer services sector. Distribution firms tend to be very cost competitive, and they tend to locate near the "center of gravity" of their market. Seventy percent of the nation's population lives within 90 minutes of Dayton by air; 55 percent of the Canadian population also lives within 90 minutes air time. Thus, the region is well suited as a distribution center. The airport can accommodate air transport operations.

Dayton is also near major highways, so road distribution is good. The roads have been important in connection with air transportation because a commodity can be picked up later in the day on the East Coast, be unloaded at night in Dayton (most of Emery's deliveries are at night), and be delivered by truck the next day to cities within a five-hour trucking distance from Dayton. The popularity of just-in-time (JIT) inventory control has increased the importance of having a good highway system. Customers using JIT (including most of the Japanese automotive firms) hold fewer inventories, so they must be able to order and receive goods more quickly than in the past. While Dayton's central location is an advantage, it must compete with larger metropolitan areas that also have excellent locational attributes for the distribution sector.

Second, a postindustrial perspective, or "larger forces" model, explains that growth in the service sector in general. The postindustrial model contends that employment will shift away from manufacturing to tertiary (transportation, trade, finance, etc.) and higher-order (health, education, social services, arts, etc.) services. Kurt Vonnegut suggested an economy in which all goods (things) were produced by one machine. While we are still a long way from that point, the shift from production to nonproduction workers within particular establishments illustrates the trend.

Finally, the export-base theory suggests that activities that serve the local economy, especially retail and personal services, are linked to growth in the export sector (that is, sectors that sell goods and services outside the area). While the export sector has not been delineated in detail, large portions of the manufacturing sector, transportation and distribution and producer services are undoubtedly in the export sector. The export-base model is most appropriate in explaining subsectors of retail trade, business services, and personal services that closely followed the changes in the local business cycle.

6. Restructuring and Wages

The successful employment recovery has not translated into significantly higher incomes for Dayton families. In fact, the region has the second lowest average family income of any major region in the state.

The restructuring of Dayton's economy has had an adverse impact on the earnings of production and nonsupervisory personnel. The shift from the manufacturing sector toward the service sector has meant a shift from high-wage to low-wage jobs.

To estimate the impact of the shift in employment on wage income, we estimate what employment in each major sector would have been if each major sector maintained its 1979 percentage share of employment. The estimated employment, based on the 1979 proportions, was then subtracted from the actual 1986 employment, resulting in the change in employment in each major sector caused by restructuring. The results are shown in table 6–7.

Table 6–7. Changes in Earnings, 1979 to 1986

	Employment, 1986 (1,000s)			Weekly Average Earnings	$(4) \times (5)$
	Actual	Estimate	Difference		
Durable Goods	76.5	88.4	-11.9	$528.84	$ -6293.20
Nondurable Goods	19.3	37.3	-8.0	477.41	-3819.28
Construction	14.8	16.3	-1.5	466.75[a]	-700.13
Transportation and Utilities	14.9	16.7	-1.8	480.89[b]	-865.60
Wholesale	18.6	16.8	1.8	386.72	696.10
Retail	75.0	70.0	5.0	157.76	788.80
Finance, Insurance, and Real Estate	17.2	15.9	1.3	304.30[a]	395.59
Service	100.2	81.3	18.9	208.71[c]	5305.40
Total					-4492.31

Note: Superscript (a) denotes the national average; (b) equals 9,097 times communications, gas, and electric; and (c) equals .8305 times hospitals. See text for explanation.

Source: County Business Patterns.

A negative change in employment shows the sectors that have suffered relative declines. As expected, Dayton experienced declines in both durable and nondurable manufacturing, and in construction, transportation, and utilities. Positive changes indicate sectors that have increased their relative share. If wages across industries were equal, then these employment shifts would have no impact on earnings. However, as indicated in table 6–7, all of the sectors with negative employment changes had higher wages than all of the sectors with positive employment changes.

To calculate the decline in wage income caused by restructuring, the 1986 average weekly wage was multiplied by the change in employment in each sector. These figures were then multiplied by 52 and summed to arrive at an estimate of the wages lost in 1986. The results, shown in table 6–7, indicate that Dayton lost about $4.5 million dollars.

7. Shift-Share Analysis

The nature of the Dayton region's economic transition can be understood by comparing shift-share results for the 1978 to 1983 recession period with the 1983 to 1986 recovery. Table 6–8 shows the results. Between 1979 to 1983, the region lost about 34,000 jobs, although if the region had grown at the national average rate, it would have gained 18,072 jobs. The employment shift can be attributed to an industrial mix that included a high proportion of slow-growth industries and a poor competitive environment. For a variety of reasons, the Dayton area lacked the locational features necessary to attract and nurture business, as evidenced by the highly negative competitive component.

During the recovery period, the economy performed quite differently. Cyclically sensitive industries are likely to have high negative mix components during recessions but to have favorable mix components during

Table 6–8.   A Shift-Share Analysis: Summary Results for Employment of Major Group Levels

Time Period	Share	Mix	Competition	Actual Change
1979 to 1983	18,072	−23,775	−28,237	−33,940
1983 to 1986	17,409	20,337	2,614	40,360

Note: See text for explanation.
Source: County Business Patterns.

a recovery since they tend to rebound. Also, many of the acyclically declining industries declined to such a low level that they no longer exerted a major influence on the area's economy. Similarly, the industries that grew during the recession (the acyclically growing category) increased in relative importance. Consequently, they contributed to a positive industrial mix during the recovery period. (At the one-digit level, the manufacturing sector had a negative mix component, but when disaggregated the manufacturing sector had a positive mix component. This finding indicates that the region had a relative concentration in high-growth manufacturing activities).

The change in the competitive component is particularly important because it indicated that the region's environment is better able to attract and nurture activities than in the past. Part of the favorable competitive component may be attributable to policies intended to enhance the employment-generating capacity of the area. It may also reflect a general improvement in the Great Lakes economy.

8. Summary and Policy Outlook

During the 1979 to 1986 period, the Dayton-area economy grew slowly. The slow growth is the combined effect of employment declines between 1979 to 1983 and a strong recovery between 1983 to 1986. The expansion has continued through 1989. The slower-than-average growth was due to the fact that at the start of the period the region had an industrial mix that was disproportionally weighted toward slow-growth industries. Furthermore, most major industrial groups grew locally at rates below the national growth rate for that industry. Since 1983, the industrial mix has improved, as has the competitive component.

8.1 Lack of General Theory

Several models were used to explain employment shifts in various sectors. The following summarizes the models by industrial category:

Manufacturing

1. Agglomerative model (auto and related sectors).
2. Postindustrial perspective (general slow growth of the manufacturing sector)
3. Locational perspective (auto and related sectors).

4. Government supported (military-related sectors).
5. Industrial filtering (maintenance of corporate research development).

Services

1. Postindustrial perspective (general growth in personal, business, and social services).
2. Locational perspective (wholesale and related services).
3. Export-base model (cyclically sensitive retail, personal services).

The lack of a general theory of employment change is inelegant, but it may be more helpful to policymakers than a more comprehensive theory that is difficult to apply to specific situations. It is likely that explanations of regional growth may be better built from sectoral explanations that derived from a general theory. Thus, theories of changes for industrial sectors rather than comprehensive theories of regional changes properly represent the current state of the art.

8.2 Industries and Corporations

Employment changes in Dayton indicate that local analysts need to examine specific companies and establishments as much, or more, than industries for three reasons. First, individual establishments often do not fit well in the SIC classifications. Second, an individual establishment's growth or decline may be part of corporate strategy rather than the result of economic factors within the establishment or within the industry. Third, corporate as opposed to industrial trends are having even greater impact on local economies due to the merger movement. The possibility of takeovers is one of the major threats to the Dayton-area economy.

For local firms where corporate considerations are dominant, it will be nearly impossible to anticipate or explain major changes in local firms on the basis of three- to four-digit national industrial trends if corporate considerations dominate employment decisions. Many of the performance differences among the regions analyzed in this volume may be attributable to corporate factors rather than to market events in particular industries. The Dayton-area Chamber of Commerce, along with Wright State University, is currently developing a corporate information base to supplement the traditional standard that relies almost exclusively on trends in industrial categories.

A wit once said, if all you have is a hammer every problem looks like a nail. If local analysts need to emphasize behavior of corporations as much as the behavior of industries, the tools used may have to be expanded. Forecasting and related econometric techniques should be supplemented with tools of the corporate financial analyst and strategic planner.

The need to use corporate as well as industrial analysis is reinforced by some ambiguities in the Standard Industrial Code system. Several local establishments were contacted in an effort to determine which SIC category they fit. In every case, the local personnel department employees were uncertain which SIC category best described their firm and were doubtful about the use of SIC codes. This response lends support to the Phillips and Vidal (1970) concern regarding:

> . . . the ability of the standard industrial classification (SIC) system to adequately represent the character of metropolitan jobs. The system has received minor modification over the years, but its broad outlines have remained fixed. This greatly facilitates analysis of changes through time, but makes important and rapidly-evolving parts of urban economies difficult to monitor (p. 293).

9. Postscript and Prescripts

The tone of this commentary is intended to portray a region that has experienced major economic setbacks, including being hard-hit by the 1979 to 1983 recession. The recession and other events stimulated structural changes that left the region with above-average growth prospects. The strong recovery, particularly in key sectors, is partial (but not conclusive) evidence of successful restructuring.

Because the detailed data did not allow analysis beyond 1986, the full scope of the region's rebound was understated. Between January 1988 and January 1989, employment grew by 11,400 jobs or by over 2.5 percent. Durable goods manufacturing increased by about 2.7 percent. Just as impressive as the employment growth has been the continued physical growth of the community (including two major downtown office buildings) and the community efforts to enhance the local economy.

The historic reliance on a few business leaders setting the region's economic development agenda has changed in recent years, possibly reflecting the realization that the large corporate and federal institutions that dominate the export base of the economy have interests that transcend the area. This change does not imply that the business sector is inactive or unconcerned about the regional economy, but that the process has become more pluralistic. The 1979 to 1983 recession stimulated universities, broadly based business organizations, and other community groups to become active in economic development planning.

While the planning process is still in flux and exogenous events will undoubtedly cause changes in focus, several strategies are being actively discussed, including:

1. Improving the internal and external image of the region, particularly its image of labor-management conflicts.
2. Developing the Coldaynnatic (Columbus, Dayton, and Cincinnati) region. A larger region would draw more attention, offer greater resources to potential employers, and provide greater benefits to the components.
3. Strengthening international linkages by a variety of techniques, including internship or co-op programs between university foreign students and corporations seeking to operate abroad, and taking full advantage of the Japanese automobile agglomeration in the area.
4. Exploiting contracts and business spin-offs from Wright Patterson Air Force Base.
5. Addressing the relatively low income of the area. Recent literature (Warner, 1989) suggests that this might be accomplished by increasing the mix of human capital development in the current economic development package.
6. Recognizing the importance of politics to economic development by creating or nurturing political structures that can influence the region's economic development prospects directly and indirectly.

Notes

1. The Dayton region is defined as Clark, Greene, Miami, and Montgomery counties.
2. The Markusen classification was undertaken at the industry (four-digit) level, and data for the Dayton region were available primarily at the industry group (three-digit) level. Consequently, some judgment was employed in determining whether a local three-digit industry should be lumped into a high-tech category. No three-digit industries were classified as high-tech unless at least one of the four-digit subcomponents were included in the Markusen list.

7 DETROIT, MICHIGAN: AN ECONOMY STILL DRIVEN BY AUTOMOBILES

Kenneth P. Voytek and Harold Wolman

It has other uses and graces; but fundamentally modern Detroit exists to build and sell motor-cars, and once it quits doing that it will lose its chief reason for existence.

— *Arthur Pound (Detroit: Dynamic City, 1940)*

This chapter explores economic change in the Detroit Metropolitan Statistical Area (MSA) economy over the 1979 to 1986 period.[1] The performance of the Detroit MSA economy is largely a function of the performance of the automobile industry that dominates it. Any understanding of the modern automobile industry and its impact on urban economies must begin by recognizing two critical factors. First, even more than most durable goods industries, the automobile industry is highly cyclical in nature. Second, the domestic automobile industry is in the midst of a major restructuring that is bringing about profound long-term structural change in the area's economy (Abernathy, Clark, and Kantrow 1983, pp. 44–67). Understanding the Detroit MSA economy during this period requires sorting out conventional cyclical effects from the long-term structural effects that were simultaneously occurring.

The 1979 to 1986 period examined coincided with a major swing in the business cycle. From 1979 to 1982 the nation experienced a recession during which the U.S. unemployment rate increased from 5.8 percent in 1979 to 9.6 percent in 1982 or by 3.8 percentage points. Over the same period, the unemployment rate in the Detroit MSA increased from 7.9 percent to 15.9 percent or by 8 percentage points! Between 1979 and 1982 employment in the Detroit MSA fell by just under 229,000 jobs (approximately 16.3 percent), while employment nationally remained largely unchanged.

However, by 1986, the Detroit MSA unemployment rate had fallen to 8.2 percent (compared to 7.0 percent for the United States), and the MSA had gained back all of the lost jobs from 1979 to 1982 and added an additional 24,000 jobs. Nonetheless, this 1.7 percent increase in employment between 1979 to 1986 is scanty compared to the 11.8 percent increase in employment nationwide.

I. Background

This section compares population and selected other socioeconomic characteristics of the Detroit MSA to the characteristics of all U.S. MSAs in 1980. In addition, the performance of Detroit's major industrial divisions is compared to that of the United States over the 1979 to 1986 period.

1.1 Demographic and Socioeconomic

With a population of nearly 4.5 million in 1980, the Detroit MSA was the fifth largest metropolitan area in the United States. It was also one of the few to have experienced actual population decline. From 1970 to 1980, population in the Detroit MSA declined by 1.5 percent while population in all U.S. MSAs rose by 10.5 percent.

Per capita income in the Detroit MSA in 1980 was $11,584 (in constant 1983 dollars), higher than per capita income in all United States MSAs. Per capita income in the Detroit MSA grew slower over the 1969 to 1979 period (in constant 1983 dollars) than did real per capita income for all MSAs in the United States. The Detroit MSA was also characterized by lower education levels compared to other MSAs in the United States. The proportion of persons over 25 with 12 or more years of schooling in the Detroit MSA was slightly below that of all U.S. MSAs and those with 16 or more years of schooling in the Detroit MSA was significantly lower than that of all U.S. MSAs in 1980.

1.2 Employment [2]

As table 7–1 shows, the Detroit MSA deserves its classification as one of the quintessential manufacturing centers in the United States. Manufacturing employment accounted for 36.8 percent of 1979 total employment in the Detroit MSA. This disproportionate dependence on manufacturing as a source of employment in the Detroit MSA in 1979 resulted in its having lower shares of employment, compared to the United States, in all other nonmanufacturing industrial divisions.

Over the 1979 to 1986 period total employment in the Detroit MSA increased by 1.7 percent compared to 11.8 percent for the United States. Manufacturing experienced the largest percentage loss in employment (−23.4 percent). However, the highly cyclical nature of manufacturing in the Detroit MSA was readily apparent when comparing its performance during the 1979 to 1982 downturn (an employment decline of −33.2 percent) and during the 1982 to 1986 upturn (an employment gain of 14.7 percent). Producer services, the fastest growing sector, grew faster in the Detroit MSA than the United States over the 1979 to 1986 period. As a consequence of these different growth patterns between 1979 to 1986, manufacturing accounted for 27.7 percent of total employment, a significant decline from its 1979 level of 36.8 percent. Producer services, on the other hand, accounted for 21.0 percent of total employment in 1986, compared to only 15.5 percent in 1979. The remaining service divisions — transportation services, wholesale and retail trade, social services, and personal services — grew more slowly in the Detroit MSA than they did nationally from 1979 to 1986.

In summary, the Detroit MSA was characterized by sluggish growth over the 1979 to 1986 period as well as volatile performance over the course of the business cycle. It remains an economy dependent on manufacturing. Especially significant was the large loss in manufacturing employment and the subpar performance of nonmanufacturing (social services, personal services, transportation services) in the Detroit MSA relative to the United States over the 1979 to 1986 period.

Table 7–1. Employment Profile and Change by Industrial Division — Detroit MSA and the United States, 1979–1986

Industrial Division	Detroit MSA Employment				U.S. Employment				Percentage Change in Employment, 1979–1986	
	1979	% of Total	1986	% of Total	1979	% of Total	1986	% of Total	Detroit MSA	U.S.
Manufacturing	515,945	36.8	395,428	27.7	20,189,473	30.7	17,845,878	24.3	−23.4	−11.6
Transportation Services	47,373	3.4	39,664	2.8	2,474,434	3.8	2,583,935	3.5	−16.3	4.4
Wholesale and Retail Trade	280,799	20.0	292,588	20.5	15,007,057	22.8	16,622,648	22.6	4.2	10.8
Producer Services	217,344	15.5	299,144	21.0	11,283,608	17.2	15,067,739	20.5	37.6	33.5
Social Services	176,175	12.6	214,795	15.1	8,513,803	12.9	11,239,825	15.3	21.9	32.0
Personal Services	163,498	11.7	183,423	12.9	8,290,036	12.6	10,177,589	13.8	12.2	22.8
Total Employment	1,401,134		1,425,042		65,758,411		73,537,614		1.7	11.8

Source: 1979 and 1986 County Business Patterns.

2. Manufacturing

As noted above, even with its problems over the last several years, manufacturing remains important to the Detroit MSA economy. To examine the changes taking place within manufacturing in the Detroit MSA, we examine the performance of the 20 major manufacturing groups over the 1979 to 1986 period. Manufacturing employment was concentrated in four major groups — primary metals, fabricated metals, machinery, except electrical, and transportation equipment. These "metal-bending" groups accounted for three out of every four jobs in manufacturing within the Detroit MSA in 1979. Thus, the performance of Detroit manufacturing was largely dependent on how these four groups performed from 1979 to 1986. Two words sum up the performance of Detroit MSA manufacturing employment — *bleak* and *cyclical*. We classified these 20 major manufacturing groups into four categories based on their growth/decline pattern over the 1979 to 1986 period. The classification takes into account both their responses to the business cycle and long-term structural change over the course of the business cycle. The categories are:

Declining: Major manufacturing groups losing employment over the 1979 to 1986 period and employment decline in both subperiods (1979 to 1982 and 1982 to 1986).

Cyclical Declining: Major manufacturing groups losing employment over the 1979 to 1986 period as a result of employment loss suffered over the 1979 to 1982 period which was not offset by employment gains over the 1982 to 1986 period.

Cyclical Growing: Major manufacturing groups gaining employment over the 1979 to 1986 period. These groups lost employment over the 1979 to 1982 period and increased in employment over the 1982–1986 period sufficient to offset employment loss over the 1979 to 1982 period.

Growing: Major manufacturing groups gaining employment from 1979 to 1986 and in both subperiods (1979 to 1982 and 1982 to 1986).

Table 7–2 classifies the 20 major manufacturing groups based on their performance over the 1979 to 1986 period. Manufacturing as a whole was cyclical-declining. Employment in manufacturing fell by 33.2 percent over the 1979–1982 period and then increased by 14.7 percent from 1982 to 1986. Unfortunately, this was not enough to offset the earlier decline, and manufacturing employment fell by 23.4 percent over the 1979 to 1986 period.

Based on the four categories above, six major manufacturing groups were "declining", eight groups were "cyclical declining", four were "cy-

Table 7–2. Performance of Detroit MSA Major Manufacturing Groups, 1979–1986

Major Manufacturing Group	SIC Code	Detroit MSA Employment			Detroit MSA % Change in Employment			United States % Change in Employment		
		1979	1982	1986	1979–1986	1979–1982	1982–1986	1979–1986	1979–1982	1982–1986
Declining										
Food and Kindred Products	20	16,516	15,241	12,186	−26.2	−7.7	−20.0	−8.8	−5.1	−3.9
Textile Mill Products	22	1,133	1,066	858	−24.3	−5.9	−19.5	−23.1	−14.7	−9.8
Chemicals and Allied Products	28	13,351	9,030	8,798	−34.1	−32.4	−2.6	−9.8	−3.1	−6.9
Primary Metal Industries	33	48,252	26,316	25,795	−46.5	−45.5	−2.0	−39.4	−21.3	−23.0
Machinery, Except Electrical	35	87,336	71,814	67,057	−23.2	−17.8	−6.6	−19.4	−4.7	−15.4
Miscellaneous Manufacturing	39	4,082	3,775	3,572	−12.5	−7.5	−5.4	−17.6	−11.3	−7.1
Subtotal		170,670	127,242	118,266	−30.7	−25.4	−7.1	−19.6	−8.9	−11.8
Cyclical Declining										
Apparel and Other Textile Products	23	14,747	9,826	14,344	−2.7	−33.4	46.0	−18.8	−10.8	−8.9
Lumber and Wood Products	24	2,593	1,470	2,420	−6.7	−43.3	64.6	−13.7	−25.0	15.1
Furniture and Fixtures	25	2,309	1,597	2,359	2.2	−30.8	47.7	−2.7	−13.6	12.6
Paper and Allied Products	26	5,798	3,890	4,707	−18.8	−32.9	21.0	−5.3	−7.2	2.0

Printing and Publishing	27	20,689	16,720	20,180	−2.5	−19.2	20.7	16.0	3.7	11.8
Stone, Clay, and Glass Products	32	11,116	7,449	8,572	−22.9	−33.0	15.1	−16.6	−16.6	−0.0
Fabricated Metal Products	34	80,147	51,723	64,531	−19.5	−35.5	24.8	−14.2	−12.9	−1.4
Transportation Equipment	37	175,027	100,762	123,985	−29.2	−42.4	23.0	−9.6	−17.3	9.3
Subtotal		312,426	193,437	241,098	−22.8	−38.1	24.6	−8.4	−12.2	4.3
Cyclical Growing										
Tobacco Manufacturers	21	1	1	7	600.0	0.0	600.0	−18.9	0.2	−19.0
Petroleum and Coal Products	29	1,419	1,324	1,597	12.5	−6.7	20.6	−17.2	−3.9	−13.8
Rubber and Misc. Plastics Products	30	18,851	10,765	19,740	4.7	−42.9	83.4	−4.9	−15.2	12.2
Leather and Leather Products	31	283	187	296	4.6	−33.9	58.3	−41.6	−12.9	−32.9
Electric and Electronic Equipment	36	9,291	8,472	10,857	16.9	−8.8	28.2	2.9	0.6	2.3
Subtotal		29,845	20,749	32,497	8.9	−30.5	56.6	−3.7	−4.6	0.9
Growing										
Instruments and Related Products	38	3,004	3,392	3,567	18.7	12.9	5.2	−2.3	−0.1	−2.2
Total Manufacturing Employment		515,945	344,820	395,428	−23.4	−33.2	14.7	−11.6	−9.4	−2.5

Source: 1979, 1982, and 1986 County Business Patterns.

clical growing", and only one was "growing". The most striking feature
of many of the manufacturing groups was their pronounced cyclical behavior. This cyclical instability was evidenced by the fact that 13 of the
20 groups, representing 66.3 percent of 1979 Detroit MSA manufacturing
employment, lost employment over the l979 to 1982 period, while gaining
employment from 1982 to 1986. This cyclical instability was not too surprising based on the orientation of the Detroit MSA manufacturing base.
In 1979, 82 percent of Detroit MSA manufacturing was in durable goods
manufacturing compared to 62.1 percent in the United States. By 1986,
even while durable goods manufacturing employment had declined, it still
represented 79.1 percent of Detroit MSA manufacturing employment
compared to 60 percent for the United States.

Moreover, the four most important manufacturing groups to the Detroit MSA — primary metals, fabricated metals, machinery, except electrical, and transportation equipment — all lost employment and were
losing employment at a faster rate than they were in the United States.
Transportation Equipment (SIC 37), the dominant manufacturing group
in the Detroit MSA, representing 33.9 percent of manufacturing employment in 1979, lost more than 50,000 jobs (− 29.2 percent) between 1979
and 1986. The decline in the remaining three major groups was not too
surprising considering that they produce inputs for use in automobile
production.

The handful of manufacturing groups gaining employment represented
only 9.1 percent of all Detroit MSA manufacturing employment in 1986.
Of these, only rubber and miscellaneous plastic products (representing
nearly 20,000 employees in 1986) and electric and electronic equipment
(nearly 11,000 employees in 1986) had any substantial presence in the
Detroit MSA. Interestingly, both of these manufacturing groups (as well
as the other four) outperformed their counterparts nationally, suggesting
a possible competitive advantage for the Detroit MSA in these groups.

3. The Hidden Trend-Breakers

The previous section highlighted the decline in manufacturing, a decline
that has been substantial in many of the Detroit MSA's most important
major manufacturing groups. This section identifies those industry groups
that were "bucking the trends" — in most cases growing, even while the
major group was declining.[3] In all, 21 industry groups were identified that
were experiencing trends opposite to their major manufacturing group
and had 500 or more employees at any point over the l979–1986 period.
Table 7–3 presents these trend-breakers.

3.1 Growing Trend-Breakers

Against the rather bleak performance of many of the area's most important major manufacturing groups, there was a handful of industry groups
growing. In all, 15 industry groups grew over the 1979 to 1986 period,
while the major manufacturing group of which they were a part declined.
Clearly, even while these industry groups were growing, they did not offset declines in the remaining industry groups. Nonetheless, they may represent opportunities that can guide area development efforts. However,
some of these growing industry groups were the result of the "success"
of a particular firm, suggesting that they may not be as fruitful as initially
thought.

These growing trend-breakers represent a wide variety of different
types of activity. Of the 16 major manufacturing groups experiencing employment decline over the 1979 to 1986 period, 11 were represented in the
growing trend-breakers. The most interesting of those was Guided Missiles, Space Vehicles, and Parts (SIC 376) which grew by 109.1 percent
from 1979 to 1986 and added 1,319 jobs. The dramatic employment increase in this industry group was in large part due to one firm — Williams
International — which produces engines for cruise missiles. Employment
in Metal Services, NEC (Not Elsewhere Classified; SIC 347) increased
by 10.6 percent and added 510 jobs, while employment in Periodicals (SIC
272) grew by 78.9 percent (388 jobs) and in Miscellaneous Publishing (SIC
274) by 80 percent and added 749 jobs. The addition of 334 jobs in Flat
Glass (SIC 321) reflects the success of Guardian Industries which produces flat glass products for the automobile and construction equipment
markets (see table 7–3).

Several printing and publishing industry groups gained employment
over the 1979 to 1986 period. While technically classified as manufacturing, these industry groups are more like business services, and their
growth may reflect the greater usage of such services by area business.
Paper Mills, Except Building Paper (SIC 262), is another interesting case.
The growth in this industry group was concentrated primarily in one
county — St. Clair — and reflects the improved fortunes of two paper
mills in this county.

3.2 Declining Trend-Breakers

While a relatively small segment of the Detroit MSA's major manufacturing groups grew over the 1979 to 1986 period, a handful of industry groups
within them was declining. Employment in Fabricated Rubber Products,
NEC (SIC 306) has been nearly halved (a loss of 835 jobs), while employ-

Table 7-3. The Hidden Trend-Breakers — Manufacturing, Detroit MSA, 1979–1986

Industry Group	SIC Code	Detroit MSA Employment			Detroit MSA Percent Change in Employment			Major Manufacturing Group Performance Category
		1979	1982	1986	1979–1986	1979–1982	1982–1986	
Growing Trend-Breakers								
Meat Products	201	3,454	3,460	3,504	1.4	0.2	1.3	Declining
Preserved Fruits and Vegetables	203	608	733	700	15.1	20.6	-4.5	Declining
Millwork, Plywood, and Structural Members	243	936	477	1,178	25.9	-49.0	147.0	Cyclical declining
Paper Mills, Except Building Paper	262	751	947	914	21.7	26.1	-3.5	Cyclical declining
Periodicals	272	492	635	880	78.9	29.1	38.6	Cyclical declining
Miscellaneous Publishing	274	936	766	1,685	80.0	-18.2	120.0	Cyclical declining
Commercial Printing	275	6,650	5,326	7,418	11.5	-19.9	39.3	Cyclical declining
Printing Trade Services	279	931	1,052	1,170	25.7	13.0	11.2	Cyclical declining
Industrial Organic Chemicals	286	918	1,274	1,047	14.1	38.8	-17.8	Declining
Miscellaneous Chemical Products	289	2,203	1,854	2,594	17.7	-15.8	39.9	Declining
Flat Glass	321	1,502	516	1,836	22.2	-65.6	255.8	Cyclical declining

Metal Services, NEC	347	4,793	3,452	5,303	10.6	−28.0	53.6	Cyclical declining
General Industrial Machinery	356	6,964	6,743	7,195	3.3	−3.2	6.7	Declining
Misc. Machinery, Except Electrical	359	10,522	8,784	10,856	3.2	−16.5	23.6	Declining
Guided Missles, Space Vehicles, Parts	376	1,209	1,668	2,528	109.1	38.0	51.6	Cyclical declining

Declining Trend-Breakers

Fabricated Rubber Products, NEC	306	2,001	1,210	1,166	−41.7	−39.5	−3.6	Cyclical growing
Electric Distributing Equipment	361	974	870	603	−38.1	−10.7	−30.7	Cyclical growing
Electrical Industrial Apparatus	362	4,044	3,714	3,589	−11.3	−8.2	−3.4	Cyclical growing
Communication Equipment	366	842	1,059	555	−34.1	25.8	−47.6	Cyclical growing
Measuring and Controlling Devices	382	1,515	1,896	1,414	−6.7	25.1	−25.4	Growing
Medical Instruments and Supplies	384	721	684	667	−7.5	−5.1	−2.5	Growing

Source: 1979, 1982, and 1986 County Business Patterns.
Note: See earlier section for the definition of the performance categories.

ment in rubber and miscellaneous plastic products increased by nearly 5 percent. This may reflect the decline in demand for fabricated rubber products by the auto industry. Several "high-tech" industry groups have not done well in the Detroit MSA. Both Communication Equipment (SIC 366) and Electric Distributing Equipment (SIC 362) lost employment. Two other industry groups, Measuring and Controlling Devices (SIC 382) and Medical Instruments and Supplies (SIC 384), have also lost employment.

4. Earnings in Growing Versus Declining Major Manufacturing Groups

The Detroit MSA has traditionally been known as a high-wage economy, especially for many low-skilled blue-collar occupations. This reputation results from the importance of transportation equipment in the area economy and the high earnings prevailing in this industry and in many of its supplier industries. In addition, the significant presence of organized labor in the Detroit economy and its positive impact on earnings in other industries also inflates earnings in the Detroit MSA relative to other areas. In 1979, average manufacturing earnings in the Detroit MSA were $21,550 compared to $15,150 in the United States (1.42 times higher). How did the structural changes affecting the economy during the 1979 to 1986 period affect earnings; in particular, were earnings in growing industries as "good" as those in declining industries?

As table 7–4 shows, average manufacturing earnings in 1986 in the Detroit MSA were $30,445, an increase of 41.2 percent from 1979, while average manufacturing earnings in the United States increased by 55 percent to $23,490. Thus average manufacturing earnings in the Detroit MSA fell over this period relative to the United States — from 1.42 times the U.S. average in 1979 to 1.29 times the average in 1986.

Average earnings were lower in the growing major manufacturing groups than in the declining major manufacturing groups in the Detroit MSA. Average 1986 earnings in the growing manufacturing groups (which together comprised only 9.1 percent of total manufacturing employment in 1986) were $21,294 compared to $31,253 for the 14 declining manufacturing groups (which comprised 90.9 percent of total manufacturing employment). Average earnings in the growing manufacturing groups were also well below the Detroit MSA average manufacturing wage of $30,445. They were also below the national average manufacturing earnings of $23,490, or by approximately 10 percent.[4]

Of the growing manufacturing groups, only one (Petroleum and Coal

Table 7–4. Detroit MSA Average Earnings — Manufacturing, 1986

Major Manufacturing Group	SIC Code	Average Earnings 1986	Performance Category*	Above or Below Average	Earnings Rank-Ordered (Low to High)
Food and Kindred Products	20	$22,018	Declining	Below	6
Tobacco Manufacturers	21	—	Growing	—	—
Textile Mill Products	22	$16,388	Declining	Below	2
Apparel and Other Textile Products	23	$17,462	Declining	Below	3
Lumber and Wood Products	24	$18,830	Declining	Below	5
Furniture and Fixtures	25	$22,390	Declining	Below	7
Paper and Allied Products	26	$24,163	Declining	Below	10
Printing and Publishing	27	$26,192	Declining	Below	12
Chemicals and Allied Products	28	$29,497	Declining	Below	15
Petroleum and Coal Products	29	$36,316	Growing	Above	18
Rubber and Misc. Plastic Products	30	$18,484	Growing	Below	4
Leather and Leather Products	31	$6,988	Growing	Below	1
Stone, Clay, and Glass Products	32	$30,036	Declining	Below	14
Primary Metal Industries	33	$31,969	Declining	Above	17
Fabricated Metal Products	34	$27,882	Declining	Below	13
Machinery, Except Electrical	35	$31,031	Declining	Above	16
Electric and Electronic Components	36	$22,981	Growing	Below	8
Transportation Equipment	37	$37,527	Declining	Above	19
Instruments and Related Products	38	$26,168	Growing	Below	11
Miscellaneous Manufacturing	39	$23,251	Declining	Below	9

Notes: Average manufacturing earnings (employment weighted) = $30,445; growing average earnings = $21,294 (employment weighted); declining average earnings = $30,444 (employment weighted).

*Performance categories are a consolidation of the groups noted in section 5 and are growing (growing and cyclical growing) and declining (declining and cyclical declining).

**Note average earnings are total payroll divided by total employees.

Source: 1986 County Business Patterns.

Products, an industry that essentially has no presence in the area) had earnings above the Detroit MSA average for manufacturing, while one other (Instruments and Related Products) had earnings above the national average even though below the Detroit MSA average.

In summary, the significant restructuring of the Detroit MSA manufacturing base has also resulted in a changed earnings profile. First, earnings in manufacturing increased at a significantly slower rate in the Detroit MSA than in the nation between 1979 and 1986. Second, average earnings in the growing manufacturing groups were much lower than average earnings in the declining manufacturing groups. The difference was nearly $10,000 in 1986. Moreover, the average earnings in the growing manufacturing groups were also below that of the national average manufacturing earnings.

5. Services

As noted earlier, the performance of nonmanufacturing in the Detroit MSA was subpar compared to the United States over the 1979 to 1986 period. Service (defined as the nonmanufacturing sector excluding farm, agriculture and farm services, construction, government, and mining) employment increased by 16.4 percent in the Detroit MSA compared to 22.2 percent for the United States over the 1979 to 1986 period. Even though service employment grew, it was barely able to offset the loss of manufacturing employment over the 1979 to 1986 period.

In this section, we take a more detailed look at the performance of service employment in the Detroit MSA over the 1979 to 1986 period. Modifying the typology developed by Browning and Singelmann (1978), we examined the performance of five broad categories: (1) transportation services, (2) wholesale and retail trade, (3) producer services, (4) social services, and (5) personal services. The same classification scheme used to examine the pattern of growth/decline in manufacturing is used here — "declining", "cyclical declining", "growing", and "cyclical growing" — over the 1979 to 1986 period.

Over the 1979 to 1986 period, service employment increased by 16.4 percent in the Detroit MSA compared to 22.2 percent nationally. Service employment as a whole was cyclical growing, declining in the Detroit MSA by 6.5 percent from 1979 to 1982 and increasing by 24.4 percent from 1982 to 1986.

Employment in four of the five broad service categories (all but trans-

portation services) grew between 1979 and 1986. Producer services and
social services were "growing", while wholesale and retail trade and personal services were "cyclical growing", losing employment from 1979 to
1982, but more than making up for that loss from 1982 to 1986. Transportation services, however, was "cyclical declining" (see table 7–5).

Conventional wisdom suggests that service employment is less prone
to swings in employment over the business cycle. However, one of the
more striking features of many of the Detroit MSA major service groups
was their susceptibility to the economic downturn. Indeed, 27 of the 39
major service groups were cyclical, losing employment from 1979 to 1982,
then gaining employment from 1982 to 1986.

During the downturn, transportation services experienced the most
substantial percentage decline (37.4 percent), losing nearly 18,000 jobs.
Wholesale and retail trade employment fell by 13.1 percent, representing
just over 36,000 jobs, while employment in personal services dropped by
8.1 percent or 11,000 jobs. Employment in producer services rose slightly
(0.8 percent) and added almost 2,000 jobs, while employment in social
services rose by 4.6 percent and added just over 8,000 jobs.

The decline in employment in many of the Detroit MSA major service
groups reflects two phenomena. First, many of these major service
groups were closely linked to the area's manufacturing base. Second,
other major service groups, especially those in retail trade and personal
services, were dependent on consumer spending, which fell as the economy worsened from 1979 to 1982.

During the recovery from 1982 to 1986, job growth within services in
the Detroit MSA outpaced the national economy. Employment in services
grew by 24.4 percent in the Detroit MSA compared to 16.9 percent nationally from 1982 to 1986, adding over 202,000 jobs. Moreover, four of
the five broad service categories experienced more robust growth in the
Detroit MSA compared to their counterparts nationally from 1982 to 1986.
Only the rate of employment growth in social services was slower in the
Detroit MSA than it was nationally from 1982 to 1986. Producer services
employment rose by 80,000 while wholesale and retail trade increased by
48,000. The fairly broad trends mask the dynamics occurring within the
major service groups. Grouping the 39 major service groups for which
data are available into categories based on their growth/decline pattern
(see section 2) over the 1979 to 1986 period highlights this variability. Four
groups were "declining", seven were "cyclical declining", 20 were "cyclical growing", and eight were "growing" (see table 7–5).

Not unexpectedly, many of the major groups within transportation services exhibited a cyclical pattern over the course of the business cycle in

Table 7–5. Performance of Detroit MSA Major Service Groups, 1979–1986

Major Industry Group	SIC Code	Detroit MSA Employment			Detroit MSA % Change in Employment			Performance Category
		1979	1982	1986	1979–1986	1979–1982	1982–1986	
Transportation Services (Subtotal)		47,373	29,665	39,664	–16.3	–37.4	33.7	CD
Local and Interurban Passenger Transit	41	2,715	2,106	2,522	–7.1	–22.4	19.8	CD
Trucking and Warehousing	42	35,320	18,900	25,947	–26.5	–46.5	37.3	CD
Water Transportation	44	488	408	497	1.8	–16.4	21.8	CG
Transportation by Air	45	4,701	4,468	4,900	4.2	–5.0	9.7	CG
Pipe Lines, Except Natural Gas	46	0	0	0				—
Transportation Services	47	4,149	3,783	5,798	39.7	–8.8	53.3	CG
Wholesale and Retail Trade (Subtotal)		280,799	244,019	292,588	4.2	–13.1	19.9	CG
Wholesale Trade — Durable Goods	50	64,554	58,292	66,098	2.4	–9.7	13.4	CG
Wholesale Trade — Nondurable Goods	51	25,752	24,478	29,383	14.1	–4.9	20.0	CG
Building Materials and Garden Supplies	52	8,739	7,556	10,120	15.8	–13.5	33.9	CG
General Merchandise Stores	53	39,606	31,910	34,824	–12.1	–19.4	9.1	CD
Food Stores	54	36,584	35,874	40,374	10.4	–1.9	12.5	CG
Automotive Dealers and Service Stations	55	38,276	27,414	38,828	1.4	–28.4	41.6	CG

	Code							
Apparel and Accessory Stores	56	21,740	18,995	22,487	3.4	−12.6	18.4	CG
Furniture and Home Furnishing Stores	57	11,605	8,087	11,944	2.9	−30.3	47.7	CG
Miscellaneous Retail	59	33,943	31,413	38,530	13.5	−7.5	22.7	CG
Producer Services (Subtotal)		217,344	219,122	299,144	37.6	0.8	36.5	G
Communication	48	19,342	22,489	20,458	5.8	16.3	−9.0	CC
Electric, Gas, and Sanitary Services	49	22,894	20,053	19,618	−14.3	−12.4	−2.2	D
Banking	60	26,845	25,515	26,323	−1.9	−5.0	3.2	CD
Credit Agencies Other than Banks	61	13,315	12,805	14,587	9.6	−3.8	13.9	CG
Security, Commodity Brokers and Services	62	2,209	2,736	4,073	84.4	23.9	48.9	G
Insurance Carriers	63	18,561	23,127	24,989	34.6	24.6	8.1	G
Insurance Agents, Brokers, and Service	64	7,283	6,966	8,812	21.0	−4.4	26.5	CG
Real Estate	65	16,499	15,617	16,085	−2.5	−5.3	3.0	CD
Combined Real Estate, Insurance, etc.	66	188	138	119	−36.7	−26.6	−13.8	D
Holding and Other Investment Offices	67	1,541	1,530	2,756	78.8	−0.7	80.1	CG
Business Services	73	59,991	55,750	115,871	93.1	−7.1	107.8	CG
Legal Services	81	9,688	11,345	13,937	43.9	17.1	22.8	G
Miscellaneous Services	89	18,988	21,051	31,516	66.0	10.9	49.7	G
Social Services (Subtotal)		176,175	184,360	214,795	21.9	4.6	16.5	G
Health Services	80	122,469	132,157	146,662	19.8	7.9	11.0	G
Educational Services	82	11,631	11,240	15,735	35.3	−3.4	40.0	CG
Social Services	83	16,045	16,601	24,755	54.3	3.5	49.1	G
Membership Organizations	86	26,030	24,362	27,643	6.2	−6.4	13.5	CG

Table 7–5 continued

Major Industry Group	SIC Code	Detroit MSA Employment			Detroit MSA % Change in Employment			Performance Category
		1979	1982	1986	1979–1986	1979–1982	1982–1986	
Personal Services (Subtotal)		163,498	150,203	183,423	12.2	−8.1	22.1	CG
Eating and Drinking Places	58	91,809	87,264	111,514	21.5	−5.0	27.8	CG
Hotels and Other Lodging Places	70	11,422	9,358	10,378	−9.1	−18.1	10.9	CD
Personal Services	72	20,794	19,501	21,841	5.0	−6.2	12.0	CG
Auto Repair, Services, and Garages	75	13,970	11,440	15,619	11.8	−18.1	36.5	CG
Miscellaneous Repair Services	76	8,037	6,070	7,652	−4.8	−24.5	26.1	CD
Motion Pictures	78	1,959	2,313	2,935	49.8	18.1	26.9	G
Amusement and Recreation Services	79	14,019	13,325	13,218	−5.7	−5.0	−0.8	D
Museums, Botanical, Zoological Gardens	84	1,488	932	266	−82.1	−37.4	−71.5	D
Total	—	885,189	827,369	1,029,614	16.3	−6.5	24.4	CG

Source: 1979, 1982, and 1986 County Business Patterns.
Note: Performance categories are as follows: D = Declining, CD = Cyclical declining, CG = Cyclical growing, CC = Counter cyclical, G = growing.

the Detroit MSA. These services were tied closely to the distribution of highly cyclical manufacturing goods and, thus, would be expected to suffer when the economy turns down especially given the severity of the downturn in the Detroit MSA. The sharpest decline was in employment in Trucking and Warehousing (SIC 42), which fell by 26.5 percent (or nearly 10,000 jobs) over the 1979 to 1986 period. From 1979 to 1982, trucking and warehousing employment in the Detroit MSA fell by nearly 17,000 jobs, while adding just over 7,000 jobs from 1982 to 1986. Both Transportation by Air (SIC 45) and Transportation Services (SIC 47) were cyclical growing, losing employment from 1979 to 1982 while gaining back a sufficient number of jobs over the 1982 to 1986 period to offset the earlier loss. In addition, both of these groups grew more slowly in the Detroit MSA than they did nationally. The growth of transportation by air reflects the growing importance of Detroit Metropolitan Airport as a regional airport and the fact that Northwest Airlines established a hub there.

Similarly, the major groups within wholesale and retail trade were also cyclically sensitive (though less so than transportation services). All of the major groups in this category, except one, were cyclically growing, losing employment from 1979 to 1982, but adding enough jobs from 1982 to 1986 to offset the employment losses suffered earlier. The most cyclical of these groups was retail stores selling durable goods or "big ticket" items, purchases that were easily deferred by consumers.

Employment in producer services as a whole was growing faster in the Detroit MSA than it was in the United States. These rapid gains were led by Business Services (SIC 73) in which employment in the Detroit area nearly doubled, growing by 93.1 percent from 1979 to 1986, compared to a 58.9 percent growth rate nationally. Despite this startling overall gain, business services was cyclical, losing 7.1 percent of it's employment during the 1979 to 1982 downturn; it's rapid growth results entirely from a doubling of employment between 1982 to 1986. One contributor to this growth was the 1984 acquisition by General Motors of Electronic Data Systems (EDS), a firm based previously in Dallas, but whose operations were moved to the Detroit area after acquisition. However, the EDS move was estimated to have added approximately 8,000 jobs, only a small portion of the 60,000 business service jobs added in the Detroit area between 1982 and 1986. The rapid growth in temporary help establishments was also another major contributor to this rapid growth as firms find it more cost-effective to add to their labor force by hiring temporary workers.

Two producer service industry groups — Electric, Gas, and Sanitary Services (SIC 49) and Banking (SIC 60) — were anomalies in that their performance in the Detroit MSA was starkly different than their performance nationally. Employment in electric, gas, and sanitary services in the Detroit MSA fell by 14.3 percent while it grew by 15.3 percent in the nation from 1979 to 1986. The poor performance of this industry group in the Detroit MSA reflects two factors — (1) a decline in population as well as (2) industrial activity and financial problems in some of its major utilities resulting from ill-fated construction activity. Detroit MSA employment in banking dropped by 1.9 percent while nationally employment rose by 14.8 percent over the 1979 to 1986 period. The subpar performance of banking in the Detroit MSA may reflect peculiarities in bank regulation in Michigan.

The growth in social services as a whole from 1979 to 1986 (21.9 percent) lagged behind the national growth rate (32.0 percent). Detroit is a major regional health center, and employment in Health Services (SIC 80) grew by 19.8 percent, adding over 24,000 jobs to the Detroit MSA economy from 1979 to 1986. Nationally, however, health services grew at a substantially faster rate. The Detroit area's lagging growth rate in health services employment undoubtedly reflects its relatively stable population compared to that of the nation as a whole. However, Social Services (SIC 83) (one of the four major groups in the broad social services category) grew by 54.3 percent, resulting in the addition of over 8,000 jobs to the Detroit MSA economy over the 1979 to 1986 period. Nationally, social services grew by only 36.1 percent.

Personal services grew in the Detroit MSA but at a slower rate than the nation from 1979 to 1986. Personal services were also cyclical, reflecting the fact that spending on many of these services is discretionary.

6. The Hidden Trend-Breakers

The last section highlighted the diversity of services in the Detroit MSA and the variety of growth/decline patterns in many of these major service groups. Underlying the trends observed within the major groups, however, was the fact that specific industry groups may be bucking the trends — pointing to pockets of vitality within declining groups or instances of decline in growing groups.

In all, we identified 39 industry groups (with at least 500 employees) that exhibited a pattern of growth/decline different from the pattern observed for the major group of which they are a part. As table 7–6 highlights, a broad cross-section of industry groups was identified, representing 23 different major groups. Altogether eight industry groups gained employment from 1979 to 1986, even though the major group of which they are a part lost employment. There were 31 industry groups that lost employment during the 1979 to 1986 period, while the major group of which they were part was growing.

6.1 Growing Trend-Breakers

Within the handful of major service groups that lost employment over the 1979 to 1986 period, eight industry groups were growing. Both Public Warehousing (SIC 422) and Trucking Terminals (SIC 423) grew by 24.4 percent and 100.8 percent from 1979 to 1986, adding a total of 659 jobs between the two of them while the major group of which they were part — trucking and warehousing — lost employment (− 26.5 percent).

Two industry groups — Combination Electric and Gas and Other Utility Services (SIC 493) and Sanitary Services (SIC 495) — were growing by 30.5 percent and 23.7 percent even though the major group of which they were part lost employment from 1979 to 1986 (− 14.3 percent). These two groups added 856 jobs to the Detroit MSA economy. The growth of sanitary services was likely due to the greater propensity of local governments to contract out for municipal trash services as municipal financial resources were squeezed and the demand for disposal and removal of toxic wastes grew. Functions closely related to Banking (SIC 615) grew at a phenomenal rate, adding 851 jobs (483.5 percent), even though employment in the major group, banking, declined by 1.9 percent. This rapid increase in employment resulted from a curious blend of activities — growing demand for international financing activities and the "corner" check-cashing industry.

6.2 Declining Trend-Breakers

Given the more optimistic picture painted around services, there were some dark clouds on the horizon. Of the 39 trend-breakers identified, 31 were declining over the 1979 to 1986 period. While some churning was expected, the declines occurred in some rather surprising areas. Employment in Air Transportation, Certified Carriers (SIC 451) fell by 4.1 percent (or 179 jobs), even though employment in the major group, Transportation by Air, increased by 4.2 percent. It may be that the merger of Northwest and Republic Airlines, the area's two major air carriers, resulted in consolidations that reduced employment.

Table 7–6. The Hidden Trend-Breakers — Services, Detroit MSA, 1979–1986

Industry Group	SIC Code	Employment			% Change in Employment			Major Service Group Performance Category*
		1979	1982	1986	1979–1986	1979–1982	1982–1986	
Transportation Services								
Local and Suburban Passenger Transportation	411	828	888	1,362	64.5	7.2	53.4	CD
Public Warehousing	422	1,120	920	1,392	24.3	−17.9	51.3	CD
Trucking Terminal Facilities	423	384	301	771	100.8	−21.6	156.1	CD
Air Transportation, Certified Carriers	451	4,058	3,879	3,893	−4.1	−4.4	0.4	CG
Miscellaneous Transportation Services	478	1,029	596	825	−19.8	−42.1	38.4	CG
Wholesale and Retail Trade								
Wholesale Trade — Motor Vehicles and Auto Equipment	501	12,581	10,433	12,057	−4.2	−17.1	15.6	CG
Wholesale Trade — Furniture and Home Furnishings	502	2,542	1,880	1,805	−29.0	−26.0	−4.0	CG
Wholesale Trade — Lumber and Other Construction Material	503	3,590	2,402	3,187	−11.2	−33.1	32.7	CG
Wholesale Trade — Sporting, Recreational, Hobby Goods	504	1,322	1,240	1,206	−8.8	−6.2	−2.7	CG
Wholesale Trade — Metals and Minerals, Except Petroleum	505	6,923	5,761	6,377	−7.9	−16.8	10.7	CG
Wholesale Trade — Hardware, Plumbing, Heating Equipment	507	4,248	3,473	3,821	−10.1	−18.2	10.0	CG
Wholesale Trade — Misc. Durable Goods	509	3,988	3,097	3,652	−8.4	−22.3	17.9	CG

Wholesale Trade — Petroleum and Petroleum Products	517	2,034	1,760	1,424	−30.0	−13.5	−19.1	CG
Hardware Stores	525	3,144	2,654	2,839	−9.7	−15.6	7.0	CG
Meat and Fish Markets	542	1,370	1,513	1,200	−12.4	10.4	−20.7	CG
Candy, Nut and Confectionary Stores	544	1,001	843	789	−21.2	−15.8	−6.4	CG
Motor Vehicle Dealers	551	17,749	12,308	17,490	−1.5	−30.7	42.1	CG
Men and Boys' Clothing and Furnishings	561	4,061	2,600	2,543	−37.4	−36.0	−2.2	CG
Shoe Stores	566	4,425	3,884	4,011	−9.4	−12.2	3.3	CG
Furniture, Home Furnishings, and Equipment Stores	571	7,342	4,963	6,752	−8.0	−32.4	36.0	CG
Producer Services								
Telephone Communication	481	17,071	17,179	16,075	−5.8	0.6	−6.4	CG
Combination Electric and Gas and Other Utility Services	493	1,907	1,367	2,489	30.5	−28.3	82.1	DC
Sanitary Services	495	1,156	929	1,430	23.7	−19.6	53.9	DC
Functions Closely Related to Banking	605	176	815	1,027	483.5	363.1	26.0	CD
Personal Credit Institutions	614	5,534	5,523	5,032	−9.1	−0.2	−8.9	CG
Business Credit Institutions	615	1,895	1,479	1,693	−10.7	−22.0	14.5	CG
Life Insurance	631	7,335	7,223	6,743	−8.1	−1.5	−6.6	GR
Pension, Health, and Welfare Funds	637	631	262	438	−30.6	−58.5	67.2	GR
Credit Reporting and Collection	732	995	801	886	−11.0	−19.5	10.6	CG
Noncommercial Research Organizations	892	670	603	376	−43.9	−10.0	−37.6	GR
Social Services								
Schools and Educational Services, NEC	829	1,206	987	651	−46.0	−18.2	−34.0	CG
Business Associations	861	1,197	1,231	983	−17.9	2.8	−20.1	CG
Labor Organizations	863	7,116	4,711	4,933	−30.7	−33.8	4.7	CG
Civic and Social Organizations	864	4,514	4,472	4,266	−5.5	−0.9	−4.6	CG

Table 7–6 continued

Industry Group	SIC Code	Employment			% Change in Employment			Major Service Group Performance Category
		1979	1982	1986	1979–1986	1979–1982	1982–1986	
Personal Services								
Photographic Studios, Portrait	722	8,177	7,113	7,428	-9.2	-13.0	4.4	CG
Funeral Services and Crematories	726	2,207	1,786	2,075	-6.0	-19.1	16.2	CG
Miscellaneous Personal Services	729	835	601	710	-15.0	-28.0	18.1	CG
Automotive Repair Shops	753	751	1,141	1,091	45.3	51.9	-4.4	DC
Misc. Amusement and Recreational Services	799	6,143	6,303	6,767	10.2	2.6	7.4	DC

Source: 1979, 1982, and 1986 County Business Patterns.
*See table 7-5 for definition of the performance categories.

Several wholesale and retail trade industry groups were losing employment as well while their major groups were adding jobs. The employment decline in wholesale trade — Motor Vehicles and Auto Equipment (− 4.2 percent) — is none too surprising given the decline in automobile production in the area. Motor Vehicle Dealers (SIC 551) also lost employment over the 1979 to 1986 period, losing 259 jobs (− 1.5 percent). Both the wholesale and retail ends of Furniture and Home Furnishings (SICs 502 and 571) lost employment from 1979 to 1986 in the Detroit MSA (− 29.0 percent and − 8.0 percent), accounting for a loss of 1,327 jobs. Wholesale trade — Metals and Minerals (SIC 505) — lost 546 jobs (− 7.9 percent), reflecting the decline in manufacturing in the Detroit MSA that produces and purchases its products.

Telephone Communication (SIC 481) lost 996 jobs (− 5.8 percent) over the 1979 to 1986 period, even though the major group of which it is a part, communications, gained 5.8 percent. This employment decline was attributable to the deregulation of the phone system and the employment cutbacks that resulted. Both Personal (SIC 614) and Business Credit Institutions (SIC 615) lost employment (− 10.7 percent and − 9.1 percent), combining for a loss of 794 jobs. Credit Reporting and Collecting (SIC 732) lost employment as well, declining by 109 jobs (− 11.0 percent) from 1979 to 1986. In addition, both Business Associations (SIC 861) and Labor Organizations (SIC 863) lost employment (− 17.9 percent and − 30.7 percent). These losses reflect the tough times faced by these organizations — many unions saw their ranks decimated, and businesses cancelled their membership or did not join areawide business associations.

Thus, there was a substantial degree of churning within the Detroit MSA service economy. Many of the industry groups can be grouped into somewhat larger constellations of activity that reflect general trends in a set of activities.

7. Average Earnings in Declining Versus Growing Major Service Groups

This section compares the average earnings in declining versus growing major service groups and examines whether employment growth in services has occurred, as frequently alleged, primarily in low-wage jobs.

In 1979, average earnings for all major service groups were $12,577 in the Detroit MSA, compared to $11,006 nationally, a ratio of 1.14. By 1986 average earnings for all major service groups were $18,148 in the Detroit

MSA compared to $17,055 nationally, a ratio of 1.06. Thus, while service earnings were higher in the Detroit MSA compared to the national average, service earnings nationally increased at a faster rate than in the Detroit MSA (55 percent increase nationally versus 44.3 percent increase in the Detroit MSA) from 1979 to 1986.

As table 7–7 suggests, there was a wide variation in average earnings in the major service groups — ranging from a low of $8,187 in Eating and Drinking Places (SIC 58) to a high of $45,957 in Security, Commodity Brokers, and Services (SIC 62) in 1986. In addition, the "weighted" average earnings in each of the broad service categories (transportation, wholesale and retail, producer, social, and personal services) were also characterized by large variation. Rank ordering the five categories from high to low, transportation was ranked number one ($23,510), producer services was second ($22,682), wholesale and retail trade was number three ($18,099), social services was fourth ($17,515), and personal services was last ($10,414).

Average earnings were lower in the growing major service groups than in the declining ones. The weighted average earnings in the 28 growing major groups in the Detroit MSA were $17,959 in 1986 compared to $19,204 for the 11 declining major groups. The growing major service groups represented 84.8 percent of total service employment in 1986 compared to 15.2 percent for the declining groups.

Within producer services (the fastest growing by far of the five service categories), the nine growing major groups had a weighted average earnings of $22,322 compared to $24,056 for the four declining major groups. In personal services, however, the four growing major groups had average earnings of $9,503, considerably below the weighted average of $14,812 for the four declining major groups. This results from rapid employment growth in eating and drinking places (21.5 percent, nearly 20,000 jobs), which had the lowest average earnings ($8,187) of any of the major service groups. However, it is important to keep in mind that average earnings are calculated by simply dividing total payroll by total employees, including part-time employees. Since eating and drinking places have a disproportionate number of part-time employees, average earnings in this group may appear lower, relative to other groups, than was actually the case.

Has most of the employment growth in services occurred in jobs characterized by low earnings? The answer appears to be "yes." From 1979 to 1986, the 28 major service groups experiencing employment growth added a total of 166,496 jobs. In 15 of the 28 growing major service groups, representing 36.8 percent of all the job growth in major service groups, average earnings were above the Detroit MSA average ($18,148)

Table 7–7. Average Earnings in Major Service Groups, Detroit MSA, 1986

Major Group	SIC Code	Average Earnings 1986*	Performance Category**	Above or Below Overall Weighted Wage	Rank Order (Low to High)
Transportation Services					
Local and Interurban Passenger Transit	41	$11,820	CD	Below	10
Trucking and Warehousing	42	$25,478	CD	Above	30
Water Transportation	44	$28,031	CG	Above	33
Transportation by Air	45	$25,042	CG	Above	29
Pipelines, Except Natural Gas	46				
Transportation Services	47	$18,107	CG	Below	19
Weighted Average		$23,510			
Wholesale and Retail Trade					
Wholesale Trade — Durable Goods	50	$29,848	CG	Above	34
Wholesale Trade — Nondurable Goods	51	$26,165	CG	Above	31
Building Materials and Garden Supplies	52	$12,872	CG	Below	11
General Merchandise Stores	53	$10,380	CD	Below	6
Food Stores	54	$11,370	CG	Below	9
Automotive Dealers and Service Stations	55	$20,464	CG	Above	23
Apparel and Accessory Stores	56	$9,085	CG	Below	2
Furniture and Home Furnishing Stores	57	$15,247	CG	Below	15
Miscellaneous Retail	59	$10,956	CG	Below	8
Weighted Average		$18,099			
Producer Services					
Communication	48	$31,554	CG	Above	36
Electric, Gas, and Sanitary Services	49	$36,552	D	Above	37
Banking	60	$19,130	CD	Above	22
Credit Agencies Other than Banks	61	$21,488	CG	Above	26

Table 7-7 continued

Major Group	SIC Code	Average Earnings 1986	Performance Category	Above or Below Overall Weighted Wage	Rank Order (Low to High)
Security, Commodity Brokers and Services	62	$45,957	GR	Above	39
Insurance Carriers	63	$23,924	GR	Above	27
Insurance Agents, Brokers and Services	64	$24,451	CG	Above	28
Real Estate	65	$16,918	CD	Below	18
Combined Real Estate, Insurance, etc.	66	$18,601	DC	Above	21
Holding and Other Investment Offices	67	$29,595	CG	Above	35
Business Services	73	$16,326	CG	Below	17
Legal Services	81	$34,111	GR	Above	38
Miscellaneous Services	89	$27,994	GR	Above	32
Weighted Average		$22,682			
Social Services					
Health Services	80	$20,518	GR	Above	24
Educational Services	82	$13,113	CG	Below	12
Social Services	83	$10,104	GR	Below	3
Membership Organizations	86	$10,735	CG	Below	7
Weighted Average		$17,515			
Personal Services					
Eating and Drinking Places	58	$8,187	CG	Below	1
Hotels	70	$10,351	CG	Below	5
Personal Services	72	$10,259	CD	Below	4

Auto Repair, Services, and Garages	75	$16,141	CG	Below	16
Miscellaneous Repair Services	76	$20,823	CD	Above	25
Motion Pictures	78	$18,537	GR	Above	20
Amusement and Recreation Services	79	$14,862	DC	Below	14
Museums, Botanical, and Zoological Gardens	84	$13,491	DC	Below	13
Weighted Average		$10,414			
Overall Weighted Average		$18,148			

Source: 1986 County Business Patterns.
*Average earnings are total payroll divided by total employees.
**See table 7-5 for definition of performance categories.

Table 7–8. Manufacturing Versus Service Employment Growth, Detroit MSA, 1979 to 1986

	Employment			Absolute Change		
Sector	1979	1982	1986	1979–1986	1979–1982	1982–1986
Manufacturing	515,945	344,820	395,428	−120,157	−171,125	50,608
Services*	885,189	827,369	1,029,614	144,425	−57,820	202,245
Total	1,401,134	1,172,189	1,425,042	23,908	−228,945	252,853

*See earlier definition of Services.
Source: 1979, 1982, and 1986 County Business Patterns.

for all service jobs in 1986. They were above the average earnings for the United States in 1986 as well. These service sector jobs were clearly not poorly paying ones.

By comparison, employment growth in major service groups having below-average earnings represented 63.2 percent of all service employment growth between 1979 and 1986, and employment growth in major groups with average earnings of less than the $15,000 represented 27.4 percent of all service job growth.[5]

8. Manufacturing and Service Groups —
From Metal Bending to Mind Bending

Over the last several years, several researchers have put forth the thesis that the U.S. economy was entering a "post-industrial era" (Bell, 1973), that the United States was deindustrializing (Bluestone and Harrison, 1982), and that the U.S. economy was undergoing substantial structural change (Reich, 1983). Others have argued that this case was overstated (Lawrence, 1983; Cohen and Zysman, 1987).

Given the employment decline in manufacturing and the rapid service employment growth, has service employment growth offset the decline in manufacturing employment? As the table 7–8 indicates, from 1979 to 1986 the growth in service employment, as defined here, offset the decline in manufacturing employment. Growth in these service groups accounted for 144,425 jobs between 1979 to 1986, making up for the 120,517 jobs lost in manufacturing. As a consequence, the Detroit metropolitan area registered a small net gain of 23,908 jobs between 1979 and 1986.

Service employment experienced a roller-coaster ride over the business cycle — service employment fell from 1979 to 1982 — but not nearly as dramatically as the decline in manufacturing (service employment fell by 57,820 jobs while manufacturing employment fell by 171,125 jobs). Service employment was able to bounce back over the 1982–1986 period and actually add jobs over the entire 1979 to 1986 period. Manufacturing employment increased over the 1982 to 1986 period but was unable to generate additional jobs to offset the loss over the 1979 to 1982 period.

What has been the effect on earnings of the employment decline in manufacturing and the service employment growth? In 1979, weighted average earnings for all manufacturing and service groups in the Detroit MSA were $15,881 compared to $12,405 for the United States, a ratio of 1.28. By 1986, weighted average earnings for manufacturing and services groups in the Detroit MSA were $21,560, while in the United States it had risen to $18,616, a ratio of 1.16. Thus, from 1979 to 1986 average earnings in the Detroit MSA fell from 1.28 times that of the United States to 1.16 times that of the United States.

Average earnings in manufacturing in the Detroit MSA in 1986 remained substantially higher than average earnings in services ($30,445 compared to $18,148). Moreover, weighted average earnings in the growing major service groups ($17,959) were substantially below those of the declining major manufacturing groups ($30,444) in 1986.

In short, while the Detroit area has successfully replaced lost jobs in manufacturing with service jobs, it has also become relatively poorer in the process. Average earnings in the Detroit MSA were still substantially higher than they are nationally. However, they were considerably less above the national average in 1986 than they were in 1979.

9. Shift-Share Analysis

The previous sections have highlighted the significant change taking place in the Detroit MSA economy over the 1979 to 1986 period. The Detroit MSA economy was characterized by a highly cyclical economy, and the period under examination — 1979 to 1986 — included both a severe recession (1979 to 1982) and a vigorous expansion (1982 to 1986). Detroit's economy, as has traditionally been the case, exceeded the national economic swing both in the depths to which it fell during the recession and the vigor of its recovery.

However, an examination of Detroit's performance over the course of the business cycle indicates that important structural change has also been taking place. Manufacturing — and particularly transportation equipment — has been steadily losing employment, while employment in services, particularly in producer services, has been increasing. Over the entire period, gains in service employment exceeded losses in manufacturing employment, and the Detroit MSA had a small net employment gain over the 1979 to 1986 period. However, since the jobs lost in manufacturing had, on average, higher earnings than jobs in the growing service sector, average real earnings fell by 6.5 percent in constant 1982 dollars.

Most of the analysis presented earlier has been cast in terms of simple job growth or decline in the Detroit MSA. However, these job changes tell only part of the story. It is also important to know in which major groups the Detroit MSA economy possesses a competitive advantage. In order to examine this question, we performed a shift-share analysis of the area's major manufacturing and service groups.

Over the 1979 to 1986 period, the Detroit MSA economy suffered from both an adverse industrial mix and an adverse differential shift. Had employment in each of the area's major groups grown at the same rate as total employment in the national economy, the Detroit MSA economy would have gained 165,753 jobs (national effect). Had employment in each of the major groups grown at the same rate in the Detroit MSA as employment in that group did nationally, the area would have gained only 129,564 jobs. Thus, the Detroit MSA's set of industries was growing more slowly than the national economy as a whole. As a result, the Detroit MSA had a negative industrial mix of 36,189 jobs (165,723 minus 129,564).

In fact, the Detroit MSA economy gained only 23,908 jobs instead of the expected gain of 129,564 which would have resulted had each of its major groups grown at the same rate in the Detroit MSA as it had nationally — a negative differential shift of 105,657 jobs. Thus, the Detroit MSA economy produced 100,000 fewer jobs than would have been expected based on industrial structure. This suggests that Detroit MSA manufacturing and service groups were, in aggregate, suffering a serious competitive disadvantage relative to other areas in the United States.

Moreover, each of the major industrial divisions experienced a substantial negative differential shift (see table 7–9). Manufacturing had a negative differential of 49,557 jobs (− 9.6 percent), while services had a negative differential of 56,100 jobs (− 6.3 percent).

Manufacturing also had a negative industrial mix effect of 131,996 jobs. Thus, even if the major manufacturing groups in the Detroit MSA changed at the same rate as each did nationally, manufacturing in the area would have fallen by 70,960 jobs, or 131,996 jobs less than would have been expected had it grown at the same rate as the national economy (in which case it would have gained 61,036). In short, manufacturing in the Detroit MSA economy appeared to be experiencing the worst of all possible worlds: manufacturing employment was declining nationally and, at the same time, Detroit was becoming less competitive (that is, they were declining even more rapidly in Detroit than in the United States).

Despite this generally abysmal performance, some major groups registered positive differential shifts, indicating growing competitiveness, over the 1979 to 1986 period. Of the ten major manufacturing groups registering positive differential shifts, however, only electrical and electronic equipment (14 percent) was also growing nationally. Instruments and Re-

Table 7–9. Shift-Share Analysis of Detroit MSA Economy (Percentages Are Relative to 1979 Base Employment)

	Overall Change		National Effect		Industrial Mix Effect		Differential Shift	
1979–1986								
Manufacturing	−120,517	(−23.4%)	61,036	(11.8%)	−131,996	(−25.6%)	−49,557	(−9.6%)
Services	144,425	(16.3%)	104,717	(11.8%)	95,807	(10.8%)	−56,100	(−6.3%)
Total	23,908	(1.7%)	165,753	(11.8%)	−36,189	(−2.6%)	−105,657	(−7.5%)
1982–1986								
Manufacturing	50,608	(14.7%)	39,639	(11.5%)	−46,970	(−13.6%)	57,933	(16.8%)
Services	202,245	(24.4%)	95,110	(11.5%)	45,055	(5.4%)	62,087	(7.5%)
Total	252,853	(21.6%)	134,739	(11.5%)	−1,915	(−0.2%)	120,020	(10.2%)

Source: 1979, 1982, and 1986 County Business Patterns.

lated Products (SIC 38) had a positive differential of 21.1 percent and declined slightly nationally (− 2.3 percent) from 1979 to 1986. The remaining eight major manufacturing groups with positive differential shifts — tobacco manufacturers, apparel and other textile products, lumber and wood products, furniture and fixtures, petroleum and coal products, rubber and miscellaneous plastic products, leather and leather products, and miscellaneous manufacturing — were all losing employment nationally from 1979 to 1986. Moreover, in three of these major groups — apparel and other textile products, lumber and wood products, and miscellaneous manufacturing — employment fell in the Detroit MSA but at a slower rate than elsewhere. The remaining major groups showed only modest job growth in the Detroit MSA.

Among major service groups there were some hopeful signs. In producer services, both insurance carriers (26.5 percent) and business services (34.3 percent) had positive differential shifts as did social services (18.2 percent), educational services (7.2 percent), and wholesale trade — nondurable goods.

However, a shift-share analysis of the more recent 1982 to 1986 period of economic expansion shows many more hopeful signs. During that period, the area had a very positive differential shift and an essentially neutral industrial mix (see table 7–9). During the 1982 to 1986 period, the Detroit MSA gained 252,854 jobs (21.6 percent) as it rebounded from the recession (see table 7–9). Had employment in each of the area's major groups grown at the same rate as total employment in the national economy, the Detroit MSA would have gained 134,739 jobs. Had employment in each of the major groups grown at the same rate in the Detroit MSA as it did nationally, the area would have gained 132,824 jobs. The MSA's mix of industries thus did about as well in the national economy as did the national economy. In short, the Detroit MSA did not suffer because of its industrial structure.

More importantly, the MSA actually added 252,854 jobs, 120,020 more than expected. This positive differential shift of 10.2 percent suggests increased competitiveness in the Detroit MSA over the 1982 to 1986 period; major service and manufacturing groups were, in aggregate, performing better than the same groups elsewhere in the United States.

The 1982 to 1986 shift-share results were particularly telling for manufacturing. Probably for the first time in this century, Detroit had a negative industry mix effect in manufacturing during the upturn of a business cycle. Manufacturing in the Detroit MSA grew at a slower rate than it did nationally. As a consequence, had each of the major manufacturing groups in the Detroit MSA grown at the same rate as that group nationally, Detroit would have lost more than 46,000 jobs from 1982 to 1986. Manufacturing employment in the Detroit MSA was disproportionately engaged in activities losing employment nationally.

However, manufacturing employment in the Detroit MSA in fact increased by just over 50,000 jobs. The Detroit MSA had a positive differential shift in manufacturing of nearly 58,000 jobs (16.8 percent), pointing to increased competitiveness in manufacturing relative to the rest of the nation. The Detroit MSA also had a positive differential shift (7.5 percent) in services.

Among the major manufacturing groups with positive differential shifts from 1982 to 1986 were transportation equipment (13.8 percent), fabricated metals (26.2 percent), rubber and miscellaneous plastic products (71.2 percent), electric and electronic equipment (25.9 percent), and furniture and fixtures (35.1 percent). Among major service groups with positive differential shifts were business services (65.5 percent), trucking and warehousing (27.6 percent), wholesale trade — durable goods (2.8 percent), educational services (22.9 percent), and social services (19.0 percent).

Some obvious caveats must be attached to efforts to interpret such analyses, and particularly the 1982 to 1986 shift-share results. Clearly the automobile industry was engaging in some "outsourcing" shifting functions (and employment) that were once accomplished inside the firm and thus inside the auto industry to firms in other industries (for example, plastics, textiles, business services, and miscellaneous services). As a consequence, both the negative industry-mix effect in transportation equipment and the positive differential shift in the major groups to which outsourcing occurred might be overestimated. (This assumes the automobile industry was outsourcing more rapidly than other industries.)

It was also possible that several of the major groups that showed positive differential shifts from 1982 to 1986 did so because they were much more closely tied to the automobile industry in the Detroit MSA than they were nationally. This might be true either of major groups that provide inputs to the auto industry (fabricated metals, plastics, glass) or of major groups that feed off the health of the auto industry in terms of secondary spending (retail stores, eating and drinking places). Thus, if these groups were less tied to the highly cyclical auto industry nationally than in Detroit, it was probable that they did not suffer as substantial employment declines during the 1979 to 1982 downturn. This means that, nationally, their recovery from the recession could be expected to be lower (in percentage terms) than in the Detroit MSA. As a consequence, the industry-mix effect for these groups would register as artificially low in the Detroit area from 1982 to 1986, and the differential shift effect would register as artificially high.

Shift-share analysis at the state level for the 1982 to 1986 period shows the same pattern as in the Detroit MSA in terms of substantial differential shift gains in manufacturing. Analysis of previous recovery periods in the state (1975 to 1979, 1970 to 1973) emphatically do not show this pattern; instead, in both periods, Michigan had positive industry-mix effects and negative competitive shifts. Since Detroit MSA employment accounts for over 50 percent of total Michigan employment in 1986, it was likely that the same pattern prevailed in Detroit. This strongly suggests that the positive differential shift observed from 1982 to 1986 in the Detroit MSA cannot be attributed to the tight links of other industries to the auto industry, unless they have become more tightly coupled in the 1980s than before.

10. Summary

Detroit's economy is clearly in a period of transition as the automobile industry undergoes a restructuring process that is not yet completed. The data can be interpreted to yield either near catastrophic or modestly hopeful scenarios for the future. In the former, the U.S. automobile industry succumbs to international competition and surplus world capacity and continues, indeed accelerates, its decline with equally dire impacts on automobile supplier industries. The Detroit MSA economy enters a downward spiral from which it will be difficult to emerge.

In the latter, the automobile industry is able to continue to achieve productivity gains, to hold, or even to increase, its market share, and begin to stabilize its employment. Suppliers continue to thrive in the area; business and professional services locate near the headquarters of the major automobile firms; and high-tech firms related to the automobile industry (instruments, robotics, machine vision, etc.) are drawn to an increasing agglomeration of such industries in the Detroit-Ann Arbor "automation alley" corridor. Detroit-area firms are able to capture a substantial amount of outsourcing from the automobile industry and are able to use their automobile-related business as the base from which they are able to diversify into a range of nonmotor-vehicle-related markets.

In short, in this scenario Detroit is transformed from an area dependent on the automobile industry characterized by low-skilled (albeit highly paid) workers engaged in routine production processes. It becomes, instead, an area that, drawing on the automobile industry as a base, contains a more diverse set of manufacturing and service employment

opportunities characterized by workers engaged in more complex production processes requiring greater skills. However, as the analysis in this
chapter suggests, the price of this transformation, if it occurs, will be paid
in terms of lower average earnings; it is clear that the high-wage, low-
skilled routine production work in the Detroit economy will become an
increasing anomaly.

Notes

1. The Detroit MSA is composed of the following seven counties: Lapeer, Livings-
ton, Macomb, Monroe, Oakland, St. Clair, and Wayne as defined by the U.S. Office of
Management and Budget in 1984.

2. We chose to use County Business Patterns (CBP) data rather than E.S. 202 data
for a variety of reasons. First, this data base was readily available and accessible by the
authors and permitted the comparison of the experiences of the Detroit MSA to the
United States over the same time period. Second, the CBP data are geographically specific when allocating establishment employment to particular counties. Third, the CBP
data separately break out Administrative and Auxiliary employment from industry employment totals. Fourth, the CBP data used (purchased from Northern Illinois University) avoid disclosure problems down to the three-digit SIC code. CBP data focus,
however, exclusively on private sector employment and thus their coverage is less than
that of the E.S. 202 file.

3. Because County Business Patterns is not a longitudinal file based on the linking of
data over time for particular establishments, it is possible that some changes in employment at this detailed level may reflect the reclassification of employment in an establishment from one three-digit SIC code to another. Thus, especially in cases where
employment declines or increases by a large amount (i.e., 100 percent), the numbers
should be approached cautiously.

4. It is important to emphasize that the differences between Detroit and national manufacturing earnings reflect both differences in industrial structure and differences in
wages paid within similar industries. It is highly probable that most of the difference in
average earnings reflect differences in industrial structure.

5. However, these conclusions are extremely sensitive to year-to-year variations.
When the same analysis was done for the 1979 to 1985 period, the opposite conclusion
was reached: 63.4 percent of the service sector job growth occurred in service industry
groups with average wages above the Detroit MSA average for all service sector jobs.
This primarily results from the switch of Business Services (SIC 73) from having above-
average earnings in 1985 to below-average earnings in 1986. Part of this may reflect the
rapid growth in temporary employment services.

8 MILWAUKEE, WISCONSIN: ALL IS NOT LOST

James R. Paetsch and Sammis B. White

Milwaukee appears at first blush to be the epitome of the "rust belt" city. The metropolitan population has been virtually stagnant at 1.4 million, while the central city has lost some 18 percent of its 1960 population. The mix of the population has changed, especially in the central city. The minority, largely black, population has grown from 5 percent in 1960, to 24 percent in 1980, to an estimated 27 percent in 1986. The minority population in the city schools has grown even faster, passing the 60 percent mark in 1986. The suburban black population is, by contrast, virtually nonexistent at less than 1 percent.

Iron and steel products were the heart of Milwaukee's industry. The largest, single, two-digit industry was SIC 35, Non-Electrical Machinery. In 1979, it employed some 65,300 workers in the metropolitan area. By 1986, that figure had dropped by some 22,000 jobs. Factories were idle and rusting. But the rust was not confined only to SIC 35. Manufacturing was the business of Milwaukee. As is shown by the location quotients in table 8–1, Milwaukee had a higher concentration of manufacturing employment (1.20) than the rest of the United States in 1979, and a particularly high concentration (1.53) of durable goods manufacturing. And Milwaukee's largest manufacturing industry, non-electric machinery, had

209

Table 8–1.   Locations Quotients: United States versus Milwaukee Metro Area, 1979–1986

Industry	1979	1986	Change
Mining	0.04	0.04	0.00
Construction	0.64	0.56	−0.08
Manufacturing	1.20	1.17	−0.03
Durable Goods	1.53	1.40	−0.13
Nondurable Goods	0.70	0.83	0.13
Services	0.99	1.02	0.03
Transportation	0.83	0.94	0.11
Wholesale and Retail Trade	0.81	0.81	0.00
Producer Services	0.86	0.94	0.08
Social Services	1.68	1.65	−0.03
Personal Services	0.84	0.86	0.02

Sources: Urban Research Center, UWM, Employment Database, 1979–1987; and U.S. Dept. of Commerce, Bureau of the Census, County Business Patterns.

Note: We want to thank the Urban Research Center at the University of Wisconsin — Milwaukee for their support of this work.

a location quotient of 3.04 in 1979. Unfortunately, Milwaukee lost market share in all three of these sectors between 1979 and 1986. But the metropolitan area remains more heavily involved in manufacturing than the rest of the nation. It is also considerably more involved in social services, another sign of the decline in the rust belt.

But all is not gloom and doom, nor is it all rust in this metropolitan area. The metropolitan area went through some very difficult times in the 1979 to 1986 period (see figure 8–1). Its low point was 1983, when metropolitan employment dropped 10 percent below that of 1979 and the unemployment rate was 10.4 percent. But buoyed by rapid service-sector growth, most notably in producer and social services, total metropolitan employment grew after March 1983. By 1986 employment was only 2 percent below 1979, and by 1987 total employment exceeded that of 1979. Unfortunately, the growth rate of the metro area had not matched that of either the rest of the United States or the rest of Wisconsin, basically because the city of Milwaukee had not yet recovered from the loss of jobs in the 1979 to 1983 period. But by 1989 even the city was very close to its 1979 employment level.

That cannot be said for the metro area's major industrial sector, manufacturing. Manufacturing employment is still more than 50,000 jobs be-

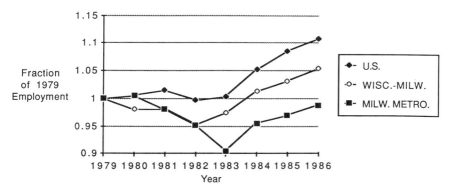

Figure 8–1.   Total employment index, 1979–1986: Metropolitan Milwaukee, Wisconsin, and the United States.
Sources: Urban Research Center, UWM, Employment Database, 1979–1987; U.S. Department of Labor, Bureau of Labor Statistics, *Employment & Earnings.*

low that of 1979. The vast majority of these jobs were lost from large, older firms in the central city and first-ring suburbs. Such losses dropped manufacturing from 34 percent of the jobs in the economy to 26.5 percent, and helped the suburban job base pass the city base in total employment.

Unlike many other metropolitan areas in the rust belt, Milwaukee has numerically recovered its employment base. The mix of industries has changed, as have the rates of pay and total payroll. But rust is not as prevalent because of dramatic growth in services and the stabilization of employment in manufacturing at a lower, yet very important level.

1. Manufacturing — Major Group Analysis

In the last decade, manufacturing employment in Milwaukee peaked in 1979, when 218,483 persons, or 34 percent of the work force, were employed in the manufacturing sector. The post-1979 low point for manufacturing was hit in 1983 when 56,800 fewer workers were employed in this sector. Since 1983, there has been some recovery in manufacturing employment, but Milwaukee's recovery still lags behind those of the United States and the rest of the state of Wisconsin.

Milwaukee has been able to recover only 77 percent of its 1979 manufacturing employment while the rest of Wisconsin and the United States have reached 93 percent and 90 percent, respectively (see figure 8–2). The fact remains that since 1979, Milwaukee has experienced a net loss of almost 50,000 manufacturing jobs, and manufacturing employment has dropped to one-quarter of total area employment.

The decline in manufacturing, however, did not affect all industries. A closer examination of manufacturing at the two-digit SIC level (from here on referred to as "major group") can help to pinpoint where severe declines and unexpected growth have occurred. Table 8–2 shows employment for each major group using a traditional durable and nondurable goods classification scheme.

Durable goods industries are responsible for the largest portion of manufacturing job losses in the metro area. These industries comprised 77 percent of the manufacturing employment base in 1979, yet were responsible for 96 percent of total manufacturing job losses from 1979 to 1986 (−47,817 jobs). Although durable goods have lost a significantly larger number of jobs than nondurable goods, the pattern of decline for each has been the same: decline from 1979 to 1983, and stabilization, and even modest growth, from 1984 to 1986.

Loss of manufacturing jobs can primarily be attributed to declines in four durable goods groups: (1) Primary Metal Products (SIC 33); (2) Fabricated Metal Products (SIC 34); (3) Machinery, Except Electric (SIC 35), and (4) Electric and Electronic Equipment (SIC 36). These groups accounted for 70 percent of all job loss, or 43,839 jobs. In 1979, these four

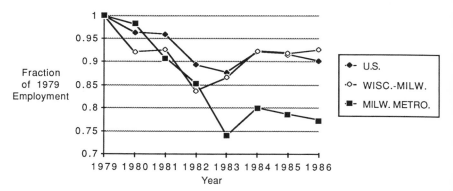

Figure 8–2.   Manufacturing employment index, 1979–1986: Metropolitan Milwaukee, Wisconsin, and the United States.
Sources: Urban Research Center, UWM, Employment Database, 1979–1987; U.S. Department of Labor, Bureau of Labor Statistics, *Employment & Earnings.*

sectors also accounted for 66 percent of all manufacturing employment. Machinery (SIC 35) alone lost 22,631 jobs, accounting for 41 percent of total manufacturing decline. Nearly all of these losses occurred from 1979 to 1983. In fact, since 1983 these four groups have actually added 3,944 jobs.

Large job losses in declining major groups have not been offset by gains in "growing" groups. Even where increases have occurred, they have been small in comparison to the staggering losses in these four declining groups. Three of the five groups boasting net employment gains experienced increases of less than 600 jobs each. The two groups that grew the most, Printing and Publishing (SIC 27) and Rubber and Plastics (SIC 30), together added fewer than 4,000 jobs. Printing and Publishing alone accounted for 54 percent of all manufacturing growth. The hard fact is that for each manufacturing job gained since 1979, 11 were lost.

2. Manufacturing — Industry Trend-Breakers

Although Milwaukee's manufacturing sector has passed through a troublesome period, there have been some bright spots. Several four-digit SICs (from here on referred to as "industries") have experienced steady growth, while others have increased employment exponentially. What follows is a description of these growing industries, as well as a discussion of industries that have experienced unusually severe declines.

When manufacturing employment is disaggregated to the industry level, 331 different industries are located in the Milwaukee area. Nearly 40 percent of all these industries experienced some growth between 1979 and 1986. But only 31 (9 percent) of these industries had 500 or more persons employed sometime in that period and also experienced growth in employment between 1979 and 1986. Despite the gross loss of almost 60,000 manufacturing jobs between 1979 and 1986, the 31 growing industries added 10,839 jobs to the local economy.

Table 8–3 lists the 10 industries that added the most employees between 1979 and 1986. The standout among all of the growing industries has been Commercial Printing, Lithograph (SIC 2752), which by itself has added 2,971 jobs, increasing its employment by 67 percent. One firm, Quad/Graphics, accounted for almost one-half of the growth in this industry. Miscellaneous Plastic Products (SIC 3079) has also created a sizeable number of jobs, adding 1,101 and increasing its employment by 31 percent.

Instruments (SIC 3811) led all industries in terms of relative growth

Table 8-2. Milwaukee Metropolitan Area Durable and Nondurable Manufacturing Employment by Major Group, 1979–1986

Major Group Description	Employment			Change			Percent		
	1979	1983	1986	1979 to 1986	1979 to 1983	1983 to 1986	1979 to 1986	1979 to 1983	1983 to 1986
Durable Goods									
24 Lumber	975	861	1,156	181	-114	295	19	-12	34
25 Furniture	1,970	1,105	1,384	-586	-865	279	-30	-44	25
32 Stone, Clay, Glass	1,857	1,321	1,603	-254	-536	282	-14	-29	21
33 Metals	14,208	7,242	7,514	-6,694	-6,966	272	-47	-49	4
34 Metal Products	28,462	19,465	20,187	-8,275	-8,997	722	-29	-32	4
35 Machinery	65,301	39,078	42,670	-22,631	-26,223	3,592	-35	-40	9
36 Electrical Equip.	35,141	29,544	28,902	-6,239	-5,597	-642	-18	-16	-2
37 Transport Equip.	13,043	10,390	9,372	-3,671	-2,653	-1,018	-28	-20	-10
38 Instruments	3,986	3,770	4,578	592	-216	808	15	-5	21
39 Misc. Mfg.	3,448	3,129	3,208	-240	-319	79	-7	-9	3
Total	168,391	115,905	120,574	-47,817	-52,486	4,669	-28	-31	4

Nondurable Goods

20 Food	16,488	14,750	12,625	-3,863	-1,738	-2,125	-23	-11	-14
21 Tobacco	2	2	0	-2	0	-2	-100	0	-100
22 Textiles	979	757	767	-212	-222	10	-22	-23	1
23 Apparel	1,858	1,702	1,552	-306	-156	-150	-16	-8	-9
26 Paper	4,644	4,031	4,055	-589	-613	24	-13	-13	1
27 Printing	13,649	13,462	16,338	2,689	-187	2,876	20	-1	21
28 Chemicals	3,607	3,364	4,078	471	-243	714	13	-7	21
29 Petroleum	238	131	97	-141	-107	-34	-59	-45	-26
30 Rubber/Plastic	4,494	4,046	5,539	1,045	-448	1,493	23	-10	37
31 Leather	4,133	3,533	3,286	-847	-600	-247	-20	-15	-7
Total	50,092	45,778	48,337	-1,755	-4,314	2,559	-4	-9	6
Total Mfg. Employment	218,483	161,683	168,911	-49,572	-56,800	7,228	-23	-26	4

Source: Urban Research Center, UWM, Employment Database, 1979–1987.

Table 8–3. Milwaukee Metropolitan Area Fastest Growing Manufacturing Industries Ranked by Job Growth

Rank	SIC	Description	Employment			Change			Percent		
			1979	1983	1986	1979 to 1986	1979 to 1983	1983 to 1986	1979 to 1986	1979 to 1983	1983 to 1986
1	2752	Commercial Printing, Lithographic	4,419	4,869	7,390	2,971	450	2,521	67	10	52
2	3079	Miscellaneous Plastic Products	3,507	3,529	4,608	1,101	−248	1,349	31	−7	41
3	3693	X-Ray Apparatus and Tubes	4,217	5,730	5,193	976	1,513	−537	23	36	−9
4	381	Engineer and Scientific Instruments***	121	92	1,073	952	−29	981	787	−24	1,066
5	3662	Radio and TV Communication Equipment	1,844	2,266	2,509	665	422	243	36	23	11
6	3499	Fabricated Metal Products, NEC	684	858	1,142	458	174	284	67	25	33
7	2051	Bread, Cake, and Related Products**	1,419	1,605	1,821	402	186	216	28	13	13
8	369	Miscellaneous Elec. Equip. and Supplies*	897	1,399	1,264	367	502	−135	41	56	−10
9	2011	Meat Packing Plants	1,604	2,027	1,945	341	423	−82	21	26	−4
10	3612	Transformers	1,884	1,809	2,136	252	−75	327	13	−4	18

*Because of the small number of firms in the four-digit industry, we've reported only the name and number at the three-digit level. The employment figures, however, are at the four-digit level.

**Each industry has grown basically because of an SIC code change. Virtually all employment in 381 switched in 1985; all of the gain in 2051 is attributable to one firm's switch from retail to wholesale bakery.

Source: Urban Research Center, UWM, Employment Database, 1979–1987.

rate, increasing employment by an astounding 787 percent, translating into 952 new jobs. Unfortunately, other industries with high relative growth rates were unable to generate enough jobs to qualify their industries for analysis in this section where industries must have had 500 workers sometime between 1979 and 1986. Small 1979 base employment figures can create deceiving growth rates that are not indicative of the small number of jobs actually generated. For example, even instruments, which had added 952 jobs by 1986, still constituted only 0.6 of 1 percent of manufacturing employment in that year. Nevertheless, the simple fact that growth industries do exist in the manufacturing sector is encouraging, considering the demise of the environment around them.

It is even more encouraging to note that 24 of the 31 larger growth industries (77 percent) are found among major groups that are declining. This is not surprising, considering the diverse product mix in each major group. Interestingly, nearly two-thirds of the growth industries found among declining major groups were concentrated in three of the same four groups that accounted for 79 percent of manufacturing employment loss: Fabricated Metal Products (SIC 34), Machinery (SIC 35), and Electrical Equipment (SIC 36). Thus, even in the most difficult of times, a handful of manufacturing industries has been able to prosper in Milwaukee.

Declining manufacturing industries, on the other hand, have been abundant. Job losses were experienced by 63 of the larger industries, double the number that recorded growth. Rates of decline ranged from 5 to 100 percent with the median decline being 32 percent. The industries that experienced the largest absolute losses of jobs appear in table 8–4.

All but one of these industries are found among the four major groups that have dominated manufacturing decline: Primary Metal Products (33), Fabricated Metal Products (SIC 34), Machinery (SIC 35), and Electrical Equipment (SIC 36). Declines in many of these industries can be explained by severe job losses among a small group of firms that used to form the backbone of Milwaukee's manufacturing economy, but that have since fallen on hard times. For example, Allis-Chalmers accounted for 76 percent of the decline in farm machinery and equipment (− 2,200 jobs), 25 percent of the decline in mining machinery (− 900 jobs), 16 percent of the decline in motors and generators (− 300 jobs), and the loss of another 1200 jobs in pumps and pumping equipment. In all, Allis-Chalmers lost 4,600 jobs.

Other large manufacturing firms have faired almost as poorly as Allis-Chalmers. Allen-Bradley, which lost 2,500 jobs, was responsible for 69 percent of the decline in industrial controls. Harnischfeger, which made cranes and drag lines in Milwaukee, accounted for 35 percent of the decline in construction machinery (− 1,500 jobs). Nearly all of the losses in

Table 8–4. Milwaukee Metropolitan Area Fastest Declining Manufacturing Industries Ranked by Job Decline

Rank	SIC	Description	Employment			Change			Percent		
			1979	1983	1986	1979 to 1986	1979 to 1983	1983 to 1986	1979 to 1986	1979 to 1983	1983 to 1986
1	3519	Internal Combustion Engines, NEC	18,007	10,360	11,330	−6,667	−7,647	970	−37	−42	9
2	3531	Construction Machinery	8,214	3,373	3,904	−4,310	−4,841	531	−52	−59	16
3	3622	Industrial Controls	12,512	8,467	8,276	−4,236	−4,045	−191	−34	−32	−2
4	2082	Malt Beverages	7,354	5,696	3,313	−4,041	−1,658	−2,383	−55	−23	−42
5	3532	Mining Machinery and Equipment	5,324	2,862	1,741	−3,583	−2,462	−1,121	−67	−46	−39
6	3462	Iron and Steel Forgings	5,697	2,900	2,673	−3,024	−2,797	−227	−53	−49	−8
7	3523	Farm Machinery and Equipment	4,084	2,126	1,186	−2,898	−1,958	−940	−71	−48	−44
8	3325	Steel Foundries, NEC	3,881	1,740	1,797	−2,084	−2,141	57	−54	−55	3
9	3621	Motors and Generators	3,940	2,340	2,013	−1,927	−1,600	−327	−49	−41	−14
10	3566	Speed Changers, Drivers, and Gears	5,014	2,937	3,183	−1,831	−2,077	246	−37	−41	8

Source: Urban Research Center, UWM Employment Database, 1979–1987.

malt beverages can be explained by the closing of one major brewery, Schlitz, which caused a loss of over 2,000 jobs, and severe employment declines in two others, Pabst and Miller, which combined lost another 2,000 jobs. Virtually all of these jobs are lost from the Milwaukee economy for good.

3. Manufacturing Earnings

The average annual earnings of workers in durable groups, where employment declines have been most severe, are greater than those earned by workers in nondurable groups. This is due, at least in part, to the du-

Table 8–5. Milwaukee Metropolitan Area Durable and Nondurable Manufacturing Major Groups Ranked by Earnings, 1986

Rank	Major Group Description	Earnings 1986 $	Employment Change 1979 to 1986
1	37 Trans. Equip.	33,771	−3,671
2	35 Machinery	28,608	−22,631
3	29 Petroleum	28,538	−141
4	36 Elec. Equip.	28,131	−6,239
5	20 Food	27,251	−3,863
6	38 Instruments	25,280	592
7	26 Paper	25,248	−589
8	28 Chemicals	25,218	471
9	34 Metal Prods	25,115	−8,275
10	32 Stone, Clay, Glass	24,515	−254
11	33 Metals	23,160	−6,694
12	27 Printing	22,304	2,670
13	25 Furniture	21,314	−586
14	30 Rubber/Plastic	20,570	1,045
15	31 Leather	19,116	−847
16	39 Misc. Mfg.	18,529	−240
17	23 Apparel	17,238	−306
18	24 Lumber	16,256	181
19	22 Textiles	13,474	−212
20	21 Tobacco	0	−2
	Nondurable	23,383	−1,774
	Durable	27,319	−47,817

Source: Urban Research Center, UWM, Employment Database, 1979–1987.

rable groups' propensity to lay off less-senior workers, to the nondurable firms' propensity to hire nonsenior workers, and to the fact that decline is greatest in the older, more entrenched industries that are considered high-wage.

Earnings for durable groups are only slightly greater than the average earnings for all manufacturing workers. This can be explained by the fact that Milwaukee's manufacturing landscape is still dominated by industries that are declining.

A breakdown of earnings at the major group level further demonstrates that groups that have experienced severe declines in employment tend to offer higher earnings. Table 8–5 ranks major groups by average annual earnings and compares earnings with employment trends in each respective major group. Note that the three durable groups that offer the highest average earnings also lost 32,541 jobs. Only two major groups that experienced employment gains since 1979 appear among the top ten groups ranked by average earnings, and these two groups generated only 1,062 jobs. Printing and Publishing (SIC 27), which added 2,670 jobs to Milwaukee's economy, paid average earnings that were $3,889 less than the mean manufacturing earnings of $26,193. Conversely, Machinery (SIC 35), which lost 22,631 jobs, paid an annual salary $2,415 greater than the manufacturing average.

4. Services-Major Group Analysis

Contrary to trends in manufacturing, the service sector has experienced considerable growth. Milwaukee, though, still lags in the United States and the rest of Wisconsin in the rate of this growth (see figure 8–3). Since 1979, the service sector, as defined by Browning and Singlemann (1978), has gained 44,552 jobs, an 11 percent increase.

A further breakdown of services into five categories shows where the growth has been concentrated. These categories — transportation, wholesale and retail, producer, social, and personal services — and their respective employment levels are shown in table 8–6.

Similar to manufacturing, the largest portion of service growth occurred from 1983 to 1986. During this period, 41,495 jobs were added. In the 1979 to 1983 period, service employment increased by only 3,057 jobs.

Producer services, which include finance, insurance, real estate, and various business services, have generated the largest number of jobs (+24,082) and have exhibited the highest growth rate (32 percent) in the service sector. Only wholesale and retail services, which lost only 337 jobs, failed to regain its 1979 employment level.

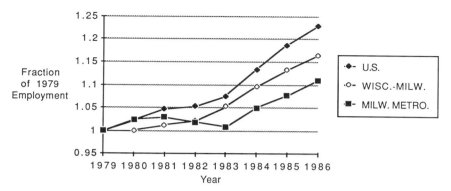

Figure 8–3.   Service employment index, 1979–1986: Metropolitan Milwaukee, Wisconsin, and the United States.
Sources: Urban Research Center, UWM, Employment Database, 1979–1987; U.S. Department of Labor, Bureau of Labor Statistics, *Employment & Earnings.*

   The overall composition of the service sector has remained the same. Social and personal services share of employment has remained constant while there has been a slight shift from wholesale and retail to producer services (approximately 3 percent), a result of producer services' higher growth rate.
   Over one-half of the growth in producer services comes from Miscellaneous Business Services (SICs 67,73,899), which added 13,540 jobs. Included in these SICs are Holding and Other Investment Offices (SIC 67), Business Services (SIC 73), and Other Nonclassifiable Services (SIC 899). Banking (SICs 60–62), which added 3,892 jobs, and Insurance (SICs 63–64), which added another 2,878, accounted for 16 percent and 12 percent of the growth in producer services, respectively. Medical Services (SICs 801–805,807–809) accounted for 73 percent of the growth in social services (9,489 jobs). The Eating and Drinking category (SIC 58) was responsible for 75 percent of the growth in personal services (6,812 jobs).

5. Services — Industry Trend-Breakers

As would be expected, the service sector has a large number of growing industries (95) with 500 or more employees, outnumbering declining industries (SIC 51) by nearly two to one. These 95 growing industries added 65,573 jobs to the Milwaukee labor market. Individual industry gains are

Table 8–6. Milwaukee Metropolitan Area Service Sector Employment, 1979 to 1986

Description	SIC	Employment			Change			Percent		
		1979	1983	1986	1979 to 1986	1979 to 1983	1983 to 1986	1979 to 1986	1979 to 1983	1983 to 1986
Transportation Services		17,313	15,703	19,025	1,712	−1,610	3,322	10	−9	21
Transportation	40–42, 44–47	17,313	15,703	19,025	1,712	−1,610	3,322	10	−9	21
Wholesale and Retail Services		104,253	95,410	103,916	−337	−8,843	8,506	0	−8	9
Wholesale Trade	50–51	36,024	34,278	36,669	675	−1,746	2,421	2	−5	7
Retail Trade	52–57,59	68,229	61,132	67,217	−1,012	−7,097	6,085	−1	−10	10
Producer Services		81,860	88,737	105,942	24,082	6,877	17,205	29	8	19
Communications	48–49	13,450	14,283	13,989	539	833	−294	4	6	−2
Banking	60–62	15,833	17,489	19,725	3,892	1,656	2,236	25	10	13
Insurance	63–64	15,477	17,241	18,355	2,878	1,764	1,114	19	11	6
Real Estate	65–66	5,148	5,810	5,521	373	662	−289	7	13	−5
Engineering and Architect.	891	2,373	2,112	2,855	482	−261	743	20	−11	35
Accounting	893	2,344	2,815	3,236	892	471	421	38	20	15
Misc. Business Services	67, 73, 892, 899	23,504	24,560	37,044	13,540	1,056	12,484	58	4	51
Legal Services	81	3,731	4,427	5,217	1,486	696	790	40	19	18
Social Services		146,208	151,165	157,252	11,044	4,957	6,087	8	3	4
Medical Services	801–805, 807–809	21,390	25,169	30,879	9,489	3,779	5,710	44	18	23

Hospitals	806	27,551	31,286	26,753	−798	3,735	−4,533	−3	14	−14
Education	82	46,052	45,380	47,235	1,183	−672	1,855	3	−1	4
Welfare	832	636	813	879	243	177	66	38	28	8
Non-Profit	86	5,491	5,506	5,450	−41	15	−56	−1	0	−1
Postal Services	43	4,638	4,417	4,913	275	−221	496	6	−5	11
Government	91–99	32,698	31,001	31,567	−1,131	−1,697	566	−3	−5	2
Miscellaneous	833–839	7,752	7,593	9,576	1,824	−159	1,983	24	−2	26
Personal Services		58,765	60,441	66,816	8,051	1,676	6,375	14	3	11
Domestic	88	310	418	490	180	108	72	58	35	17
Hotels	70	4,791	4,701	4,476	−315	−90	−225	−7	−2	−5
Eating and Drinking	58	33,080	35,544	39,892	6,812	2,464	4,348	21	7	12
Repair	753, 76	3,390	3,401	3,775	385	11	374	11	0	11
Laundry	721	2,920	2,501	2,579	−341	−419	78	−12	−14	3
Barber and Beauty Shop	723–724	3,218	3,453	4,282	1,064	235	829	33	7	24
Entertainment	78–79, 84	7,395	7,121	7,000	−395	−274	−121	−5	−4	−2
Miscellaneous	722, 725–729, 751–752, 754	3,661	3,302	4,322	661	−359	1,020	18	−10	31
Total Service Employment		408,399	411,456	452,951	44,552	3,057	41,495	11	1	10

Source: Urban Research Center, UWM. Employment Database, 1979–1987.

encouraging as well: 19 industries added more than 1,000 jobs, eight added more than 2,000, and three added more than 3,000. Growth rates exhibited by several of these industries were also impressive: 30 industries increased employment by at least 50 percent, 15 industries at least doubled employment, and seven industries tripled their 1979 employment.

Wholesale and retail services accounted for 34 percent of all growth industries (32 industries), Producer services for 33 percent (31 industries), social services for 19 percent (18 industries), personal services for 11 percent (10 industries), and transportation services for 4 percent (4 industries). As shown in table 8–7, the ten service industries that have added the most jobs to the Milwaukee economy represent several areas of the service economy. Most of the growth in these industries has come from employment gains in a large number of relatively small firms and also from a handful of larger firms.

The largest absolute growth occurred in the largest service industry, Eating and Drinking Places (SIC 5810). One firm alone added 1,038 jobs. This was followed by growth in Temporary Help Services (SIC 7362). Four firms were responsible for the largest portion of growth in this industry: Kelly Services, DJ Nugent, Flexi-Force, and Bisco Services.

The growth in these first two industries cannot match that found in the combined medical-service area, which includes medical insurance, physicians' offices, nursing homes, and new health services. Together they added 9,538 jobs. Among the better-known firms that have prospered in these industries are: Blue Cross-Blue Shield, We Care Nursing Services, American Medical Services, Villa Clement Nursing Services, and Milwaukee Medical Clinic.

There is some overlap between industries that experienced both high absolute and high relative growth. Medical Service and Health Service (SIC 632) and Data Processing Services (SIC 7374), which grew 617 and 267 percent, respectively, appear on both lists. But the top industry in terms of relative growth was Communication Services, NEC (SIC 4899), which increased employment eightfold.

The service sector does have a considerable number of declining industries and, in some cases, decline has been worse than in manufacturing. Overall, 51 service industries with more than 500 workers lost 23,028 jobs during the 1979 to 1986 period. Most of these losses were modest: 47 industries lost fewer than 1,000 employees, 40 less than 500, and 20 less than 300. The losses were spread over all five subsectors. Half of the declining industries were in wholesale and retail services (26 industries). Social services accounted for 20 percent of all declining industries, and

Table 8–7. Milwaukee Metropolitan Area Fastest Growing Service Industries Ranked by Job Growth

Rank	SIC	Description	Employment			Change			Percent		
			1979	1983	1986	1979 to 1986	1979 to 1983	1983 to 1986	1979 to 1986	1979 to 1983	1983 to 1986
1	5810	Eating and Drinking Places	33,080	35,544	39,892	6,812	2,464	4,348	21	7	12
2	7362	Temporary Help Supply Services	6,002	4,332	10,417	4,415	−1,670	6,085	74	−28	140
3	822	Colleges and Universities*	845	4,452	4,500	3,655	3,607	48	433	427	1
4	632	Medical Service and Health Insurance*	430	2,972	3,081	2,651	2,542	109	617	591	4
5	8091	Health and Allied Services, NEC	673	960	3,232	2,559	287	2,272	380	43	237
6	8011	Offices of Physicians	5,366	6,530	7,618	2,252	1,164	1,088	42	22	17
7	5411	Grocery Stores	7,677	8,474	9,910	2,233	797	1,436	29	10	17
8	8051	Skilled Nursing Care Facilities	9,067	10,327	11,143	2,076	1,260	816	23	14	8
9	7374	Data Processing Services	664	1,339	2,439	1,775	675	1,100	267	102	82
10	6123	State Associations, Insured	1,903	2,393	3,666	1,763	490	1,273	93	26	53

*Because of the small number of firms in the four-digit industry, we've reported only the name and number at the three-digit level. The employment figures, however, are at the four-digit level.
Source: Urban Research Center, UWM, Employment Database, 1979–1987.

Table 8–8. Milwaukee Metropolitan Area Fastest Declining Service Industries Ranked by Job Decline

Rank	SIC	Description	Employment			Change			Percent		
			1979	1983	1986	1979 to 1986	1979 to 1983	1983 to 1986	1979 to 1986	1979 to 1983	1983 to 1986
1	5311	Department Stores	17,009	13,260	12,476	-4,533	-3,749	-784	-27	-22	-6
2	8249	Vocational Schools, NEC**	3,341	79	68	-3,273	-3,262	-11	-98	-98	-14
3	9131	Executive and Legislative Combined	28,410	26,843	27,271	-1,139	-1,567	428	-4	-6	2
4	8062	General Medical and Surgical Hospitals	25,213	28,601	24,196	-1,017	3,388	-4,405	-4	13	-15
5	6321	Accident and Health Insurance	2,184	879	1,255	-929	-1,305	376	-43	-60	43
6	8059	Nursing and Personal Care, NEC	1,520	940	650	-870	-580	-290	-57	-38	-31
7	612	Savings and Loan Associations*	919	846	54	-865	-73	-792	-94	-8	-94
8	8211	Elementary and Secondary Schools	30,863	29,113	30,100	-763	-1,750	987	-2	-6	3
9	4811	Telephone Communication	6,420	6,050	5,730	-690	-370	-320	-11	-6	-5
10	6361	Title Insurance	991	237	303	-688	-754	66	-69	-76	28

*Because of the small number of firms in the four-digit industry, we've reported only the name and number at the three-digit level. The employment figures, however, are at the four-digit level.

**This was merely a reclassification out of this SIC.

Source: Urban Research Center, UWM, Employment Database, 1979–1987.

producer and personal services each accounted for 15 percent of the industries.

Table 8–8 lists the industries that lost the greatest absolute number of jobs. Department stores lead the list by a long shot: J.C. Penney and Sears Roebuck were most affected. The second biggest loser was a combination of health care industries (hospitals, health insurance, and one form of nursing care), which lost jobs as health care is being restructured. The rest of the losers are spread across industry subsectors and reveal only modest declines.

6. Service Earnings

A breakdown of annual average earnings by sector reveals few, if any, notable trends (see table 8–9). Transportation services were tops in earnings among service sectors, while personal services earned the lowest. When broken down into major groups, however, service earnings vary quite widely. For example, Security Brokers (SIC 62) earned an average of $51,797 per year and Water Transportation (SIC 44) workers earned $50,171. At the low end of the spectrum, workers in Eating and Drinking Establishments (SIC 58) earned an average of only $5,866 annually. Thus, even though service earnings are generally lower than manufacturing earnings, there is an enormous range, with some industry average earnings more than double those found in manufacturing.

Table 8–9.   Milwaukee Metropolitan Area Service Sectors Ranked by Earnings, 1986

Rank	Sector	Earnings 1986 $	Employment Change 1979 to 1986
1	Transportation Service	26,178	1712
2	Wholesale Trade	24,535	675
3	Producer Services	22,093	24,082
4	Social Services	19,174	11,044
5	Retail Trade	11,616	− 1,012
6	Personal Services	7,855	8,051
	Total	17,554	44,552

Source: Urban Research Center, UWM, Employment Database, 1979–1987.

7. Services Versus Manufacturing

This section will address two critical questions. First, is the growth in service sector jobs keeping pace with the loss of manufacturing jobs? In Milwaukee, the answer to this question is both "yes" and "no." From 1979 to 1986, service gains were not able to offset manufacturing losses (see table 8–10).

Note that the gap between services and manufacturing was greatest in 1979 to 1983, when manufacturing lost 56,800 jobs and even the service sector gained only 3,057 jobs. But in 1984 to 1986, both services and manufacturing gained jobs, combining to add 48,723 jobs. By 1987, the net number of jobs exceeded the 1979 total.

The second of these questions is the following: are earnings in growing services (especially in producer services) as high as the earnings in declining manufacturing groups? Earnings in declining manufacturing industries still remain far greater than earnings in all services combined or producer services. Workers in declining manufacturing groups earned $27,027 per year in 1986, while workers in all services and producer services earned $17,554 and $22,093, respectively.

8. Shift-Share Analysis

We have seen changes in employment in all industries over our study period. One technique that gives us additional insight into the causes of these changes is a shift-share analysis, which helps to identify the competitiveness of the region in relation to the United States in each industrial sector. To increase the insight, we have broken the study period in two: 1979 to 1983, the recession, and 1983 to 1986, the initial recovery. The

Table 8–10. Changes in Manufacturing and Service Employment, 1979–1983, 1983–1986

| | Employment Change | | |
Sector	1979 to 1986	1979 to 1983	1983 to 1986
Manufacturing	− 49,572	− 56,800	7,228
Service	44,552	3,057	41,495
Total Gain/Loss	− 5,020	− 53,743	48,723

Source: Urban Research Center, UWM, Employment Database, 1979–1987.

employment change by industrial sector and relative cause is shown in table 8–11 for both periods.

The first period reveals employment losses across many sectors. But whether a sector gained or lost employment, the negative signs in the last column show that Milwaukee was not as competitive as the rest of the United States in any sector. In manufacturing, for example, the area lost some 56,800 jobs. Some 30,500 jobs were lost because of a national decline, and some 25,600 jobs were lost because of the uncompetitiveness of Milwaukee relative to the rest of the country. In every other industry, Milwaukee either lost additional jobs or gained fewer jobs than it might have because of its lack of competitiveness during this period. Even in producer and social services in which jobs were added, the competitive effect is negative, indicating that conditions for growth were more favorable elsewhere.

In the 1983 to 1986 period, the Milwaukee economy added employment in all industrial sectors, and some of these gains were attributable to the competitiveness of the area. The only sizable gains (greater than 800 jobs), however, that can be attributed to local competitiveness were in nondurable manufacturing, construction, transportation, and producer services. The area was just marginally more competitive in these sectors; and despite adding employment in all other sectors, the area was less competitive in these sectors than the rest of the country.

9. Why Has Change Occurred?

The biggest change in the Milwaukee economy between 1979 and 1986 was the net loss of some 50,000 manufacturing jobs. Over 41,500 jobs were lost in major groups that were either involved in the making of metal parts or metal machinery (SICs 33–35, 37). Eight of the 10 industries experiencing the largest job losses, totaling 26,174 positions, were members of these four major groups. The reasons for the dramatic loss of one-quarter of the manufacturing base appear to be multifold. No one theory can cover the changes, although product life cycle, export base, structure change, and cumulative causation may all contribute.

Most of the decline in these industries began in late 1979 and continued through 1983. Transportation equipment employment declined throughout the period. A domestic recession accounted for most of the initial decline, but other factors contributed. One factor that grew increasingly important as a reason for Milwaukee employment declines was increasing foreign competition. Milwaukee was home to several industries with

Table 8–11. Milwaukee Metropolitan Area Shift-Share Analysis: 1979 to 1983 and 1983 to 1986

Industry	1979 to 1983				
	Employment Change	Growth Effect	Mix Effect	Share Effect	Competitive Effect
Mining	-119	-1	14	13	-132
Construction	-7,993	-65	-2,840	-2,906	-5,087
Manufacturing	-56,800	-649	-30,512	-31,162	-25,638
Durable Goods	-52,486	-500	-30,276	-30,777	-21,709
Nondurable Goods	-4,314	-149	-4,046	-4,194	-120
Services	3,057	-1,214	31,509	30,295	-27,238
Transportation	-1,610	-51	-836	-888	-722
Wholesale and Retail Trade	-8,843	-310	-385	-695	-8,148
Producer Services	6,877	-243	11,858	11,614	-4,737
Social Services	4,957	-434	24,181	23,747	-18,790
Personal Services	1,676	-175	5,319	5,144	-3,468

1983 to 1986

Industry	Employment Change	Growth Effect	Mix Effect	Share Effect	Competitive Effect
Mining	52	26	−49	−22	74
Construction	4,617	1,790	1,992	3,783	834
Manufacturing	7,228	20,741	−11,424	9,317	−2,089
Durable Goods	4,669	14,869	−4,696	10,172	−5,503
Nondurable Goods	2,559	5,873	−5,000	873	1,686
Services	41,495	52,783	7,658	60,440	−18,945
Transportation	3,322	2,014	497	2,511	811
Wholesale and Retail Trade	8,506	12,239	93	12,332	−3,826
Producer Services	17,205	11,383	4,885	16,268	937
Social Services	6,087	19,382	−3,927	15,464	−9,377
Personal Services	6,375	7,754	2,258	10,011	−3,636

Source: Authors.

which manufacturers in other parts of the world felt they could compete. Internal combustion engines, construction machinery, farm machinery, and automobiles and parts were all experiencing increased foreign competition by 1980. This competition usually was in the form of lower prices and often equivalent, if not superior, quality. What began as mild intrusions in the markets rapidly became massive competition as the value of the dollar rose, making U.S. products uncompetitive both domestically and internationally. Even firms like Caterpillar Tractor could not compete. The major reason for the increased valuation of the dollar was U.S. policy — the creation of enormous debt and the reliance on foreign borrowing to fund the debt.

The higher dollar exacerbated the uncompetitiveness of most U.S. manufacturers, Milwaukee's included. Virtually all of the local firms in the metals industries were inefficient, having made little investment in existing plants and equipment and having created a work force that was highly paid and inflexible. In some cases, the products manufactured were not competitive. U.S. autos are perhaps the best example. In other cases, the management of the firms in these industries could not see the need to change or to invest until it was too late. Management was not proactive; it was not even reactive. Firms sat on large cash surpluses, not knowing what to do. Once the area's largest employer at 17,500 workers, Allis-Chalmers, for example, was unable to respond to save its markets. Today it has fewer than 500 workers in Milwaukee and is attempting to work out its bankruptcy.

Firms like Allis-Chalmers were also affected by another set of forces in one particular market, agriculture. During these same years, American agriculture became increasingly unprofitable. Other countries that had received U.S. aid to increase agricultural productivity finally became more productive, reducing their demand for U.S. agricultural products. Second, with the increased value of the dollar, U.S. farm products became too expensive, so other countries with lower production costs stepped in to fill the international need for foodstuffs. Third, the high domestic interest rates made it difficult for farmers already suffering a financial downturn to purchase new farm equipment made in the United States.

The results of these many factors were a loss in employment for Milwaukee's metal products industries. Companies cut back on production, moved production to other parts of the country or world, cut back on employment and increased efficiency locally, or simply went out of business. Metal products industries remain the dominant employer among manufacturers in the area, but they are much smaller than they were. And despite modest, more recent job growth, the industry will never regain its size. Many of the major employers in internal combustion engines, construction equipment, farm machinery, motor vehicle parts, and their local jobbers and suppliers no longer operate these industries in Milwaukee.

Only one of the two other major industries that have experienced substantial job loss, industrial controls, suffered decline because of the same set of factors afflicting the metals industries. Employment is smaller because of a slow change to competitive products, a move to make Milwaukee operations more efficient by reducing the labor input here, and a move to make the companies more efficient by moving manufacturing to newer plants in lower labor cost areas of the United States and world. Malt beverages, the industry that also lost in excess of 4,000 employees, has suffered from competition and lack of investment in local plant operations, but the industry has also suffered because of marketing errors. Schlitz folded in Milwaukee, in part because of an inefficient brewery but more importantly because it changed its flavor and could not sell it. Pabst has lost market share and has had to reduce its work force substantially.

The overwhelming force that has undermined manufacturing in Milwaukee is increased competition. That competition has hurt Milwaukee because of the high value of the dollar (which killed markets), the high real interest rates, which precluded reinvestment that may have made more firms competitive, and poor business decisions made by managers who were unprepared for the keenness of the competition. The reaction of employers to that competition covers the continuum from outright closing to making local operations and products competitive. But clearly the overall impact is lower levels of employment in the area's traditional major industries. Starting in 1987, the effects of the cheaper dollar have been felt in the surviving industries. Employment has increased modestly. How long that continues is a function of the value of the dollar, the steps taken by local industry to become even more competitive, and changes in the national business cycle.

Manufacturing employment grew in 40 percent of the industries in Milwaukee. But in only two, printing and plastics, was the growth substantial in an absolute sense. Why these two industries grew as much as they did is unclear at this time. Printing grew from 2 percent to over 4 percent of manufacturing jobs. This may be due to a comparative advantage attributable to Wisconsin's being the leading papermaking state. It could also be due to smart business decisions by a few firms that have invested heavily in the new technology of presses and satellite transmission. Perhaps it is only the business cycle or some combination of the above. A comparison with other communities should be revealing. Plastics may have grown for a similar set of reasons, or its growth could be related to an abundance of inexpensive water or to the general substitution of plastics for metals in auto and similar industries. Again comparisons with other communities will give additional insight.

Collectively, four of the top ten growth industries in manufacturing are electronics-related. These are growth areas nationally. The growth locally can be attributed in part to new product developments from local companies. In 1980, for example, Milwaukee was characterized by the Rand Corporation as the national center of medical technology development. The presence of General Electric, with its CAT scanners and magnetic resonance machines, its spin-offs, and suppliers, have contributed to this growth. Significantly, very little of this electronics growth is defense-related. Milwaukee does not have, nor has it ever had, much defense-based industry. It missed entirely the growth in the area.

The three food products industries that have grown the most have gained in part because of consolidation of ownership of local grocery chains and their suppliers, but more importantly, they have grown because of new product development that has allowed a move to national distribution. New breads and meat products that have been developed to appeal to a more health-conscious market have grown to serve a much broader cross-section of America.

In the service sector, the growth that has occurred in Milwaukee appears to mirror largely the growth found in the United States as a whole. Temporary help, eating and drinking establishments, and health-care-related industries all experienced dramatic growth in the United States over this period. The growth in two of these, temporary help and health care, is due in large measure to restructuring. Temporary help workers are employed in a variety of other industries, industries that probably reported declines in employment. Thus, some industries' employment figures are undercounted, but there is no way to correct for this. In health care we can note that several of the industries reporting the largest declines were those whose business was taken by the health industries reporting the greatest growth. If we examine only the largest gainers and losers, however, it appears that some 7,000 net jobs were added in the health-care field in Milwaukee.

The growth in education, elementary and secondary schools, reflects more children and decreasing pupil-teacher ratios at the elementary and secondary levels. The other major growth industries — grocery stores, data processing services, and legal services — reflect a mix of forces. Grocery store employment has grown substantially in Milwaukee because of the success of some local chains in capturing more of the market, which generates central office and food packing jobs locally. Also the increased competition from these chains has forced out of business the mom-and-pop stores that were not previously counted in the ES202 data because they were family-run operations.

The growth in the data processing industry is not unique to Milwaukee, given the proliferation of computers. Where its growth stands relative to other communities remains to be seen. But it is possible that the general growth in service industries in Milwaukee and information needs in these industries may be driving the growth in data processing. The legal services growth is most closely linked to the general increase in litigation in American society. It is focused in Milwaukee because Milwaukee houses one of the two law schools in the state and is by far the largest city in the state.

In examining the reasons for decline in the service sector, a similar theme emerges — increased competition. Department stores, hospitals, insurance companies, telecommunications, hotels, car dealers, and gas stations all faced changing and increasing competition. The result was a marked decline in employment in all of these industries. For Milwaukee, by far the biggest declines came in department stores. Several local headquarters were closed in acquisitions, and the changing nature of retail to specialty and discounting demolished the labor-intensive department store. Hotels and gas stations have become less service-oriented. Car dealerships have been consolidated. Hospitals have had to compete, and many have been unable. It is somewhat ironic that the loss of many of the jobs in the service sector is attributable to the uncompetitiveness of providing real service.

The service sector has changed because of the infusion of more capital in some industries and a basic consumer change in demand in other industries. Price consciousness has prevailed to a greater degree than previously, and markets have segmented. If individuals want service, they must pay for it. If others do not, they have many options where they can pump their own gas, pick out their own clothes, chose a minimal service hotel, and even decide what hospital to use. The result has been a restructuring. For example, department store employment is down, but discount, specialty, and mail order employment is up. Other substitutions are not as obvious, in part because the effects of pumping our own gas are not as focused. But the results of the changes, declines in employment in certain service sectors, are related to growth in other sectors and help to explain some of that growth.

Several factors, many of them related, have helped to push the dramatic restructuring of the Milwaukee economy. Where it will end up is difficult to predict. Manufacturing is still a major sector of the economy, and it seems to be surviving, albeit at lower levels of employment. Production and productivity continue to increase. The attitude of manufacturers is more positive—they think that they can compete, and many are taking the steps they see as necessary to succeed. The biggest unknown for them is the future value of the dollar. Much of their recovery is dollar-value related. If the dollar remains lower in value long enough, manufacturers should be able to earn profits that will allow further reinvestment to occur and further productivity gains to emerge. Time will tell.

The future changes in service will certainly be influenced by changes in manufacturing. But change will also be influenced by such factors as demographic change. Milwaukee has, for example, an older, white population that could well demand further increases in the health-care sector. And a baby boomlet is just beginning to affect education. The changes in services will have to be examined at this detailed level because of the complex interaction of forces determining their futures. As of 1989, though, total metro area employment, because of service growth, has surpassed that of 1979 and is continuing to grow.

9 PITTSBURGH, PENNSYLVANIA: FROM STEEL TOWN TO ADVANCED TECHNOLOGY CENTER

Joan Fitzgerald

Pittsburgh has come a long way from the dirty steel town of the first half of the century to recognition by Rand McNally's *Places Rated Almanac* as the nation's most livable city in 1985. Two public-private partnership programs, Renaissance I and II, are responsible for the physical transformation of the central city.

Pittsburgh is also publicized as a city that has made a phenomenal transformation from a manufacturing to a high-tech economy. Employment data suggest, however, that the economic transition has not been as successful as the physical transformation of downtown Pittsburgh. The forces behind economic trends in the Pittsburgh Primary Metropolitan Statistical Area (PMSA) are those leading to the rise and decline of the steel industry. This chapter examines these trends and, using ES202 employment data compiled by the Pennsylvania Department of Labor and Industry, analyzes economic change from 1979 to 1986.

1. Economic Restructuring

Pittsburgh has been going through a demographic and economic transformation directly related to the ongoing restructuring of the U.S. Steel industry that began about 30 years ago and that has been marked by wrenching changes in the mid to late 1970s and the 1980s.

During the last 100 years, Pittsburgh became almost totally concentrated in steelmaking and related industries. The concentration did not serve the city well when market changes resulted in plant closings and the loss of tens of thousands of jobs in the industry. For example, U.S. Steel announced in 1979 that it would permanently close 12 steel plants, half of which were in the Pittsburgh area. Total employment in these facilities went from 22,554 in 1980 to 8,000 in 1983.

From a demographic standpoint, Pittsburgh has been losing its young adult population, largely as a result of outmigration in response to the decline of the manufacturing sector. The fastest growing age group is people aged 55 and over.

As a result of the decline in manufacturing, the sectorial composition of the Pittsburgh PMSA has changed dramatically during the study period, 1979 to 1986. The dominant change has been the shift from a manufacturing to a service-based economy. In 1976, the manufacturing sector comprised 30.4 percent of total employment, but it has steadily declined each year since then to its 1986 level of 16.3 percent. Surprisingly, manufacturing now comprises a smaller percentage of total employment in the Pittsburgh PMSA than in the nation as a whole (19.1 percent). Despite the drastic decline in the steel industry, manufacturing employment still is concentrated in primary metals, which comprised 20.8 percent of manufacturing employment in 1986.

The service sector is the fastest growing employer in the Pittsburgh PMSA. However, the increase in service sector employment has not compensated for decline in manufacturing in either income or employment. While 97,457 jobs were lost in manufacturing, service sector employment increased by only 35,473 during the 1979 to 1986 period.

Employment in mining and transportation has fallen with manufacturing, with total job loss of 6,236 and 12,576, respectively, since 1979. Construction has stayed relatively stable, hovering close to 5 percent for the entire period. Wholesale and retail trade have grown, 5.4 and 0.9, respectively, but at considerably slower rates than in the nation as a whole. Nationally, employment in wholesale and retail trade has increased by 10.2 and 19.1 percent, respectively. Employment in finance, insurance, and real estate (FIRE) has increased by 15.3 percent during the 1979 to 1986 period, far less than the 26.5 national increase during the same period.

Unemployment in the Pittsburgh PMSA has remained persistently above both state and national levels for the entire study period. High unemployment rates from 1982 to 1984 were due to drastic cutbacks in the steel industry. Unemployment rates in the steel-producing Monongahela Valley (Allegheny County) during this period were easily twice that of the PMSA as a whole (Fitzgerald, 1988). One effect of the decline in manufacturing has been a reversal in the unemployment-rate patterns between men and women, with females having lower unemployment rates than males since 1985. While increased female labor force participation in the 1970s is consistent with increases nationally, increases in the 1980s are probably also associated with displacement of males in the higher-paying manufacturing sector.

2. The Manufacturing Sector

To examine trends in manufacturing employment, three categories of change are used: continuous decline, relatively little change, and growth. During the 1979 to 1986 period, the Pittsburgh PMSA lost 97,457 manufacturing jobs, a decline of 43.1 percent (see table 9–1). Of the 19 major groups in manufacturing represented in the Pittsburgh PMSA, only one experienced growth during the period (see table 9–2). Nine of ten durable goods industries, and seven of 10 nondurable goods industries, were classified as being in continuous decline. Durable goods employment went from 181,672 to 93,532 over the period, a drop of 48.5 percent, while employment in nondurable goods went from 44,421 to 35,104, a drop of 21 percent.

Table 9–1. Location Quotients: Pittsburgh PMSA, 1979, 1986

Industry	Empl. 1979	Empl. 1986	% Change 1979 to 1986	L.Q. 1979	L.Q. 1986
Mining	12,845	6,598	− 48.6	1.15	.78
Construction	45,667	39,823	− 12.8	.98	.92
Manuf.	226,093	128,636	− 43.1	.89	.68
Trans/Comm.	53,543	40,967	− 23.5	.98	.85
Wh. Trade	48,949	49,412	0.9	.78	.87
Re. Trade	153,670	162,041	5.5	.86	.94
Fire	44,196	50,973	15.3	.76	.85
Services	280,582	316,055	12.6	1.50	1.52

Source: Computed by the author using Commonwealth of Pennsylvania, Department of Labor and Industry ES202 files.

Table 9-2. Manufacturing Employment and Earnings in the Pittsburgh PMSA, 1979 to 1986

SIC	Industry	Durable–Nondurable	1979	1983	1986	Total % Change 1979–1986	1986 % of Manf. Employ.	Average Earnings in 1986
Continuous Decline								
(20)	Food and Kindred	N	10,995	9,451	8,060	−26.7	6.3	$24,290
(22)	Textile Mills	N	363	193	221	−39.1	0.2	16,156
(23)	Apparel	N	3,899	2,762	2,067	−47.0	1.6	10,675
(24)	Lumber and Wood	D	1,450	940	1,190	−17.9	0.9	13,158
(25)	Furntr. and Fixt.	D	1,933	1,212	1,482	−23.3	1.1	18,687
(26)	Paper and Allied	N	2,901	2,014	2,093	−27.9	1.6	22,481
(28)	Chemicals	N	10,123	8,881	8,711	−13.9	6.8	31,581
(29)	Petro. Refining	N	3,563	2,765	680	−81.0	0.5	44,163
(31)	Leather	N	51	27	19	−62.7	—	17,313
(32)	Stone, Clay, and Glass	D	16,641	11,810	10,097	−39.3	7.8	29,666
(33)	Primary Metals	D	72,172	39,703	26,817	−62.8	20.8	33,608
(34)	Fabricated Metals	D	21,051	13,393	11,849	−43.7	9.2	27,364
(35)	Ind. and Comm. Mach.	D	22,552	15,506	16,380	−27.4	12.7	28,728
(36)	Elctrc. and Oth. Elec.	D	23,393	19,851	12,471	−46.7	9.7	33,671
(37)	Trans. Equip.	D	14,063	9,600	6,309	−55.1	4.9	30,905
(38)	Meas. Cntrl. Instr.	N	7,274	6,294	5,922	−18.6	4.6	28,140
(39)	Miscellaneous	D	1,143	981	1,015	−11.2	0.8	23,128
Relatively Little Change								
(27)	Prnt. Pub. and Allied	N	9,120	8,933	8,992	−1.4	3.3	23,486
Growth								
(30)	Rubber and Misc.	N	3,406	3,452	4,261	25.1	7.0	19,483
Total			226,093	157,768	128,636			

Source: Commonwealth of Pennsylvania, Department of Labor and Industry ES202 files

Seventeen major groups have shown continuous decline over the 1976 to 1986 period. Primary and Fabricated Metals (SICs 32, 33) have been the hardest hit industries in the Pittsburgh area. These two categories comprised 41.2 percent of manufacturing employment at the beginning of the period, and fell to 30 percent by 1986. Within primary and fabricated metals, only one industry, Coating, Engraving and Allied Services (SIC 3479), has not lost employment. Two major groups tied to the primary metals industry, Transportation Equipment (SIC 37) and Industrial and Commercial Machinery (SIC 35), declined by 7,754 (55.1 percent) and 6,273 (27.4 percent), respectively, over the period. Paper and Allied (SIC 26), which is concentrated in production of Corrugated and Solid Fiber Boxes (SIC 2653), has also experienced employment loss.

Although Printing and Publishing (SIC 27) has shown relatively little change, one industry within this major group, Nonlithographic Commercial Printing (SIC 2751), has declined by almost 30 percent. In contrast, Lithographic Commercial Printing (SIC 2752) has increased by 9.3 percent. Slight growth has also occurred in Business Forms (SIC 2761) and Loose Leaf Binder (SIC 2782) production.

One major group, Rubber and Miscellaneous Plastics Products (SIC 30), has shown continuous employment growth in Pittsburgh and in the nation as a whole over the 1979 to 1986 period. Employment in this major group is concentrated in Miscellaneous Plastic Products (SIC 3079), in which employment has increased by 29.3 percent over the seven-year period to its 1986 level of 4,022. Although any manufacturing growth is welcomed, SIC 30 accounted for only 3.3 percent of manufacturing employment in 1986.¢

With 72.7 percent of 1986 manufacturing employment in major groups in continuous decline, it would be encouraging if several hidden trend-breaker industries within them could be identified. Indeed, a few industries seem to be defying trends at the broader majorgroup level. Although Industrial and Commercial Machinery (SIC 35) declined 27.4 percent, four industries within it are growing. Specialty Dies, Jigs Fixtures, and Molds (SIC 3544) declined from 1979 to 1983, but exceeded 1979 employment by 11.5 percent by 1986, employing 1,732 workers. Miscellaneous Machinery (SIC 3599) increased by 26 percent.

While employment in Chemicals (SIC 28) declined by 13.9 percent over the period, two industries within this major group experienced growth. Employment in Plastic Materials (SIC 2821), which employed 2,317 in 1986, increased by 10 percent from 1979 to 1986, and Paints and Allied Products (SIC 2851) increased 11.6 percent. Both of these industries are growing nationally and are likely to remain strong in the Pittsburgh area.

However, at 1986 employment levels of 2,317 and 1,661, respectively, they will not be a major source of new jobs.

2.1 Manufacturing Earnings

Unfortunately, the highest-paying jobs in the Pittsburgh PMSA are in the declining manufacturing industries. Average earnings in durable goods for 1986 were $26,546, and in nondurable goods, $23,777. Earnings in primary metals ($33,608) are still among the highest in manufacturing, exceeded only by electrical machinery ($33,671) in durable goods. The lowest-paying jobs in the declining manufacturing industries are in nondurable goods. Specifically, textile mills ($16,156), apparel ($10,675), and leather ($17,313) provide annual earnings considerably less than the manufacturing average in the Pittsburgh PMSA ($25,088). However, two major groups in nondurable goods, chemicals ($31,581) and petroleum refining ($44,163), have higher earnings than the manufacturing average.

3. The Service Sector

A modification of Browning and Singelmann's (1978) typology is used to analyze change in the Pittsburgh PMSA service sector. The categories include: transportation, wholesale and retail trade, producer services, social services, and personal services. Total service sector employment has increased by 33,304 from 1979 to 1986, an increase of 5.6 percent. Changes in employment during the 1979 to 1986 period and average earnings in 1986 are presented in table 9–3.

Transportation includes Railroad (SIC major group 40), Motor Freight and Warehousing (SIC 42), Water (SIC 44), Air (SIC 45), and Pipeline (SIC 46) Transportation, as well as Transportation Services (SIC 47) and Local and Suburban Transit (SIC 41). Total employment loss from 1979 to 1986 was 9,632. The only group within this major group that grew was transportation services, which employed 2,183 in 1986, a 29.7 percent increase from 1979. Air transportation, which is not included in the 1986 transportation total, employed 5,009 in 1985, the most recent year reported. Most of the employment loss in transportation can be attributed to its strong association with the manufacturing sector.

Wholesale trade declined by 4.8 percent between 1979 and 1983, following the decline in the related manufacturing sector. Although it grew by 6.0 percent between 1983 and 1986, whole trade is performing much worse than in the nation as a whole, where it increased by 10.2 percent over the 1979 to 1986 period. The same pattern of decline and growth is evident in retail trade. Its growth of 6.8 percent over the 1979 to 1986 period is considerably less than the national average of 19.1 percent, and can also be traced to the decline of the manufacturing sector.

Some of the highest growth rates are in producer services, the only category to increase throughout the 1979 to 1986 period. Accounting, miscellaneous business services, and legal services have experienced phenomenal growth. The relatively small gain in real estate can be attributed to outmigration in search of employment.

Social services declined by 6.9 percent between 1979 and 1983, but increased by 18.5 percent between 1983 and 1986. Social services employ more people than any of the other service categories. Four of the components of social services experienced continuous growth throughout the period. They include medical services, hospitals, welfare, and miscellaneous services. The decline in education is attributable to declining student populations due to outmigration.

Personal services comprise the smallest of the service categories. Employment declined by 3.1 percent between 1979 and 1983, but increased by 14.4 percent between 1983 and 1986. Employment in Eating and Drinking Establishments (SIC 58), the top industry in Pennsylvania in terms of jobs, has increased by 10,744. While Domestic Services (SIC 88) and Barber and Beauty Shops (SICs 723–724) have increased significantly percentage-wise, the actual numbers employed are low.

3.1 Service Sector Earnings

The highest average service sector earnings in 1986, $27,526, were in producer services. There is great variation within the category, with a range of $12,100. Earnings in accounting, miscellaneous business services, and legal services are among the highest in the service sector, and bring the entire producer services category earnings to a level significantly higher than the others.

Wholesale and retail services and social services have similar average earnings, at $17,724 and $17,472, respectively. The range of earnings within the categories is high. The difference between wholesale and retail trade is $10,765, which is due in part to more part-time employment in retail. The range in social services is $13,358. Within the category, Medical Services (SICs 801–805, and SICs 807–809) varies from $47,473 in Physicians and Surgeons (SIC 801) to $11,720 in Nursing and Personal Care Services (SIC 805).

All of the jobs in personal services are relatively low-paying. Average

Table 9–3. Service Sector Employment, 1979–1986, Pittsburgh PMSA

Name of Sector	SIC	1979	1983	1986	% Change 1979–1986	1986 Avg. Earnings
Transportation	40-42, 44-47	29,367	24,394	19,735	-32.8	$21,047
Wholesale and Retail Services						
Wholesale Trade	50-51	48,949	46,597	49,412	.9	23,106
Retail Trade	52-57, 59	110,850	103,884	108,477	6.8	12,341
Subtotal		159,799	150,481	157,889	-1.2	$17,724
Producer Services						
Comm. Elec/Gas/San.	48-49	24,176	23,695	21,232	-12.2	30,366
Banking	60-62	22,471	25,020	27,401	21.9	29,874
Insurance	63-64	12,522	12,557	13,520	8.0	22,807
Real Estate	65-65	8,403	12,557	7,773	7.5	
Eng. and Arch.	891	9,009	9,646	10,172	12.9	34,210
Accounting	893	2,398	3,093	3,941	64.3	22,110
Misc. Bus. Services	67, 73, 892, 899	32,450	33,966	47,905	17.6	24,771
Legal Services	81	4,224	5,508	6,301	49.2	27,519
Subtotal		115,653	121,065	130,472	12.8	$27,526

Social Services						
Medical	801–805, 807–809	22,581	26,871	33,616	48.9	23,133
Hospitals	806	47,356	54,472	56,201	18.7	19,996
Education	82	69,170	64,113	65,586	−5.2	20,027
Welfare	832	3,418	4,064	5,431	58.9	14,497
Non-Profit	86	11,026	9,400	9,336	−15.3	10,228
Government	91–97	45,271	24,927	47,522	5.0	23,586
Misc.	833–839	5,586	6,514	7,849	40.5	10,837
Subtotal		204,408	190,361	225,551	10.3	17,472
Personal Services						
Domestic	88	763	975	992	30.0	7,714
Hotels	70	8,188	7,657	7,973	2.6	8,928
Eating and Drinking	58	42,820	48,607	53,564	25.1	6,380
Repair	725, 753, 76	8,706	5,795	6,498	−25.4	14,176
Laundry	721	3,350	3,039	3,205	−4.3	10,013
Barber and Beauty	723–724	3,656	3,969	4,087	11.8	8,517
Entertainment	78–79, 84	10,869	10,593	9,434	−13.2	11,279
Misc.	722, 726–729	4,144	4,995	5,627	35.8	14,138
Subtotal		82,496	79,912	91,380	10.8	$10,143

Source: Compiled by the author from Commonwealth of Pennsylvania Department of Labor and Industry ES202 Files.

1986 earnings were $10,143. Employment in personal services is more likely to be part time than in any other category. This is especially evident in eating and drinking establishments, with average 1986 earnings of $6,380.

The number of jobs created in the service sector has not been sufficient to replace jobs lost in manufacturing. Between 1979 and 1986, the Pittsburgh PMSA lost 97,457 jobs in manufacturing and gained 33,304 jobs in the service sector. Even if the service sector could absorb all those displaced from manufacturing, incomes would be below those in manufacturing. Not only do jobs pay less in the polarized service sector but they also offer fewer fringe benefits and are more likely to be part time than jobs in the manufacturing sector (Harrison and Bluestone, 1988). In Pittsburgh, 1986 average earnings in services were $18,782, far below the manufacturing average of $25,088.

4. Shift-Share Analysis

Shift-share analysis is used to partition a region's growth rate in a defined time period into three components:

1. National share, the rate at which the region would have grown if its growth rate were identical to that of the nation.
2. Industry mix, the difference between the national growth rate and the national growth rate for the region's particular industry mix.
3. Competitive, the difference between the rate at which the region's industry mix grows nationally and the rate at which it grows in the region.

The results of the shift-share analysis for the Pittsburgh PMSA are presented in table 9–4. The analysis reveals that Pittsburgh is less competitive than the nation. The relative health of the region is revealed in the competitive component column. The mix of industries in the Pittsburgh PMSA is weighted toward slow-growth industries. Competitive advantage in some industries has shifted. Total shift (national share) reveals what the region's employment increase would have been if growth for each industry had occurred at the same rate as the total national employment rate. The industry mix component reveals whether the regional employment shift was due to national or regional economic forces. A positive number in the regional component column (proportional shift) reveals a rapid-growth industry in the region in an industry. A positive number in

Table 9–4.   Shift-Share Components of Employment Growth, Pittsburgh PMSA, 1979–1984 and 1984–1986

Industry	Empl. Change 1979 to 1984	National Share	Industry Mix	Regional Component
Mining	− 5,774	748.9	− 296.4	− 6,226.5
Construction	− 7,889	2,662.4	− 3,915.8	− 6,635.6
Manuf.	− 77,072	13,181.2	− 33,218.4	57,304.8
Trans./Comm.	− 5,022	3,121.6	− 786.8	− 7,356.7
Wh. Trade	− 1,520	2,853.7	57.3	− 4,431.1
Re. Trade	3,896	8,959.0	3,884.6	− 8,947.6
Fire	3,838	2,576.6	4,303.4	− 3,041.9
Services	8,989	16,357.9	47,431.6	− 54,800.5

Industry	Empl. Change 1984 to 1986	National Share	Industry Mix	Regional Component
Mining	− 4,200	445.5	− 1,195.6	277.1
Construction	− 31,180	2,380.0	2,676.7	− 3,011.7
Manuf.	− 109,198	9,388.3	− 10,139.9	− 19,633.4
Trans./Comm.	− 80,115	3,056.8	− 1,183.9	− 9,427.1
Wh. Trade	− 6,462	2,988.0	− 654.2	− 350.0
Re. Trade	108,154	9,926.7	3,894.9	− 9,346.6
Fire	114,007	3,026.1	1,369.6	− 1,456.8
Services	8,989	18,242.9	23,649.0	− 4,407.9

Source: Computed by the author from ES202 data.

the industry mix (differential shift) column means that the industry is doing better in the region than in the nation as a whole. In every industry group, the regional shift component is negative, indicating that no industry in the Pittsburgh PMSA is performing as well as in the nation as a whole.

5. A High-Tech Future?

In anticipation of the decline of the steel industry, two major economic development strategies were implemented in the 1980s. Both strategies concentrate on advanced technology employment. In 1984, the Allegheny Conference of Community Development (ACCD) produced "Strategy for Growth: An Economic Development Program for the Pittsburgh Region."

In 1985, the combined efforts of Pittsburgh's Mayor Richard Caliguiri, the Allegheny Board of Commissioners, the University of Pittsburgh, and Carnegie Mellon University culminated in "Strategy 21: Pittsburgh/Allegheny Economic Development Strategy to begin the 21st Century."

"Strategy for Growth" proposes that the Pittsburgh area could become a regional center in the following areas: (1) international corporate headquarters and finance; (2) health care, education, and business support services; and, (3) high-tech research and development. In order to attract new businesses and to expand existing businesses, the strategy proposes to retrain displaced workers and to support efforts to improve the labor climate. The last component of the strategy calls for improvements in the crumbling infrastructure of the region, including highways, the Greater Pittsburgh International Airport, and public transportation. Although the need to maintain manufacturing is mentioned, the emphasis of the program is on high-tech, advanced technology development.

"Strategy 21" lists four economic development goals for the Pittsburgh area: (1) reinforce the region's traditional economic base as a center for the metals industry; (2) convert underutilized land, facilities, and laborforce components to new uses, especially those involving advanced technology; (3) enhance the region's quality of life, thereby attracting new residents and increasing tourism; (4) expand opportunities for women, minorities, and the structurally unemployed.

To realize these goals five separate projects are proposed. They include modernization, expansion, and improvement of highway linkages to the Greater Pittsburgh International Airport, development of the riverfront area of downtown Pittsburgh for tourism; and improvement of infrastructure in the Mon Valley communities.

In addition, Pennsylvania's Ben Franklin Partnership for Advanced Technologies, initiated in 1982, has been an active partner in promoting high-tech development in the area. This public-private partnership is supported by state monies, with matching funds from Advanced Technology Centers and the private sector. The partnership supports entrepreneurial development, particularly high-tech, and has allotted funds for retraining displaced workers in areas of anticipated growth in the state economy.

Through the Ben Franklin Partnership, four Advanced Technology Centers have been created in the Commonwealth. Through these centers, research universities work in collaboration with the private sector to provide research and development and assistance and education for entrepreneurs in growing high-tech sectors. Funds for the centers have increased from $1 million in the program's first year to $28 million in 1987 (Berry et al., 1987).

Carnegie-Mellon and the University of Pittsburgh, along with several smaller universities, colleges, and private enterprises, form the Western Pennsylvania Advanced Technology Center (WPATC). Research at the center has focused on robotics and computer-aided manufacturing and biotechnology (Berry et al., 1987). Since 1983 the center has assisted the formation of 96 firms, providing 1,200 new jobs in addition to assisting expansion and retention of existing businesses (Albrandt and Weaver, 1987, p. 453). The WPATC provided funds to 15 organizations that assist the development of the high-tech sector in various ways. Among the programs offered by these organizations are management assistance, including training on bidding on government contracts, marketing, and promotion (Albrandt and Weaver, 1987).

Despite these programs, the decline in the traditional manufacturing industries has not been offset by growth in high-tech industries. A total of 19 high-tech industries had employment over 500 in the Pittsburgh PMSA in 1986.[1] Of these, seven are among those identified by Markusen, Hall, and Glasmeier (1986) as fast-growing (see table 9–5). Although total employment increased from 16,693 in 1976 to 27,005 in 1979 (61.2 percent), by 1986 it had fallen to 18,445, a drop of 31.7 percent since 1979. Six of the fastest-growing high-tech industries nationally are declining in the Pittsburgh PMSA.

High-tech employment in major SIC group 28 (Chemicals and Allied Products) has declined by 20.5 percent over the 1979 to 1986 period. Of the 11 industries represented in this major group, six have lost employment and five have gained. Industrial Inorganic Chemicals (SIC 2819) has gained significantly, while Soap and Other Detergents (SIC 2841) has almost disappeared. Several industries are remaining stable or increasing slightly (SICs 2821, 2851, 2891) or growing (SICs 2821 and 2851). Although Chemicals, Chemical Preparations NEC (SIC 2899) appears to have declined significantly, the majority of the decline is from reclassification of two previously unclassified firms.

Although 18 industries in major SIC group 35 (Industrial and Commercial Machinery and Computer Equipment) are represented, only six have employment over 500. Of the six, five have declined in employment, some quite severely (SICs 3532, 3545, 3547, 3567). Of the 11 fast-growing industries within this major group, eight are represented in the Pittsburgh PMSA, with five having employment of less than 500. Of the three with more than 500 employees, one is increasing (SIC 3544) and two are declining (SICs 3545, 3573) in employment.

Total employment in major SIC group 36 (Electronic and Other Electrical Equipment and Components, Except Computer Equipment) has declined by 34.3 percent during the 1979 to 1986 period. Of the five industries represented, three have employment over 500, with two show-

Table 9–5. Employment in High-Tech Industries, Pittsburgh PMSA

SIC	Industry Name	1979 Empl.	1986 Empl.	% Change 1979 to 1986
^2813	Industrial Gases	385	347	− 9.9
2816	Inorganic Pigments	334	0	− 100.0
^2819*	Ind. Inorg. Chemicals	25	1,016	3,964
2821	Plastic Materials, Synthetic Resins	2,108	2,317	9.9
2841	Soap, Other Detergents	1,212	18	− 98.5
2842	Special Cleaning, Polishing Preparations	32	59	84.4
2844	Perfumes, Cosmetics, Toilet Preparations	132	0	− 100.0
2851	Paints, Varnishes, Lacquers	1,489	1,661	11.6
2869	Ind. Org. Chems., NEC	12	0	− 100.0
2891	Adhesives, Sealants	77	80	3.9
2899	Chemicals, Chemical Preparations, NEC	1,691	465	− 72.5
2911	Petroleum Refining	3,035	227	− 92.5
3511	Steam, Gas, Hydraul. Turbines	37	0	− 100.0
3531*	Construction Machine Equip.	0	205	
3532	Mining Machinery Equip.	1,719	993	− 42.2
3533*	Oilfield Machinery Equip.	0	77	
3537	Indus. Trucks, Tractors	99	0	− 100.0
^3541*	Machine Tools, Metal Cutting Types	316	89	− 71.8
^3542	Machine Tools, Metal Forming Types	175	93	− 46.9
^3544*	Specialty Dies, Die Sets, Jigs Fixtures, Industry Molds	1,554	1,732	11.5
^3545*	Machine Tool Accessories, Measuring Devices		1,366	− 40.2
^3547	Rolling Mill Machinery Equip.		1,270	− 64.8
3549*	Metalworking Machinery, NEC	223	250	12.1
^3562*	Ball, Roller Bearings	313	97	− 69.0
3564	Blowers, Exhaust, Vent. Fans	105	36	− 65.7
3565	Industrial Patterns	223	57	− 74.4
3566	Speed Changers, Ind. High Drives, Gears	208	96	− 53.8
3567	Industrial Process Furnaces, Ovens	1,860	728	− 60.9
3569*	Gen. Ind. Machinery Equip., NEC	321	457	42.4
^3573*	Electronic Computing Equip.	1,476	1,360	− 7.9
3613	Switch Gear, Switchboard Apparatus	2,033	269	− 86.8

Table 9–5 continued

SIC	Industry Name	1979 Empl.	1986 Empl.	% Change 1979 to 1986
3622*	Industrial Controls	374	535	43.0
^3662*	Radio, TV Transmitting, Signal Detection Equip.	3,477	1,777	− 48.9
^3674*	Semiconductors, Related Devices	0	1,234	
^3679*	Electronic Components, NEC	653	476	− 27.1
^3728*	Aircraft Parts, Aux. Equip., NEC	0	61	
^3811	Engineering, Lab., Scientific Research Instruments	0	678	
3823*	Ind. Inst. for Measurement and Display	129	306	137.2
^3825*	Instruments, Measuring, Testing Electrical, Elec. Signals	0	50	
3829	Meas. Controlling Devices, NEC	454	0	− 100.0
^3832*	Optical Instruments, Lenses	225	446	98.2
3841*	Surgical, Med. Instr. Appar.	0	33	
3843	Dental Equip. Supplies	0	11	
3861*	Photographic Equip., Supplies	219	109	− 50.2
	Total	7,005	18,445	− 31.7

Source: Commonwealth of Pennsylvania, Department of Labor and Industry ES202 Files.
*Identified by Markusen, Hall, and Glasmeier (1986) as one of the 30 fastest growing high-tech industries.
^Defense-related, as defined by Markusen and Bloch (1985).

ing employment gains (SICs 3622, 3674) and one showing decline (SIC 3662). The decline in Radio and Television Transmitting, Signaling and Detection Equipment (SIC 3662) is significant, with total loss of 1,700 employees over the period. The area employed 1,234 workers in Semiconductors and Related Devices (SIC 3674) in 1986, but the growth rate cannot be calculated, since employment was disclosed prior to 1986. Of the seven fast-growing industries in this major group, four are represented in Pittsburgh, with two declining and two growing.

Major SIC group 38 (Industrial and Commercial Machinery) is the only high-tech sector that has shown total employment gain over the 1979 to 1986 period (59.0 percent). However, of the eight industries represented, only one had employment over 500 in 1986. That only one of the five nationally fast-growing industries in this sector is declining in the Pittsburgh PMSA is perhaps an encouraging sign for future growth.

One weakness of the occupational definition of high-tech employment is that it ignores service sector employment. In order to establish whether this bias minimizes the extent of high-tech employment in the Pittsburgh PMSA, employment figures using a product-sophistication definition (Vinson and Harrington, 1979) are presented in table 9–6. This definition includes, at the industry group (three-digit) level, many of the same industries as in the occupational definition. In addition, it contains the nonmanufacturing industries Computer Programming (SIC 737), Commercial R&D Laboratories (SICs 7391,7397), Business Management and Consulting Services (SIC 7392), Engineering and Architectural Services (SIC 891), and Nonprofit Educational, Scientific, and Research Organizations (SIC 892).

Total employment in the Pittsburgh PMSA in 1986 was 28,559, compared to 18,445 using the occupational definition. While the occupational definition shows a 31.7 percent decline in high-tech employment over the 1979 to 1986 period, the product-sophistication definition reveals a 7.8 percent increase. However, part of the difference is the result of using three-digit rather than four-digit classifications. If totaled at the three-digit level, high-tech employment using the occupational definition is 22,699 in 1986, rather than the 18,445 obtained at the four-digit level. Inclusion of some three-digit categories (for example, SIC 891, Miscellaneous Services) may inflate actual high-tech employment. Still, employment in the nonmanufacturing sectors alone (product-sophistication definition) was 19,645 in 1986.

To date, the programs have not resulted in significant gains in high-tech employment in the Pittsburgh PMSA. Albrandt and Weaver (1987, p. 457) argue that employment gains resulting from the efforts of the various public-private partnerships will not be realized for several years because of the lag time from program inception to actual job creation. Yet Carnegie Mellon is a relatively late starter in high-tech research partnership. Past university-industry research was associated with the traditional manufacturing sector in Pittsburgh.[2] The conditions created in the nation's most prominent high-tech centers, Silicon Valley and Boston's Route 128, are not likely to be replicated, and future growth is likely to favor those already existing concentrations (Malecki, 1986).

Furthermore, the planning focus on high-tech is not supported by all groups in the Pittsburgh community. Tri-State Conference on Steel, an organization working to prevent the decline of the local manufacturing sector, questions proposals for worker training or retraining for jobs in the high-tech and service sector. Tri-State's position is that a transition to a service economy cannot be sustained without a strong manufacturing sector (see Cohen and Zysman, 1987).

Table 9–6.   High-Technology Employment, Pittsburgh PMSA, 1976–1986
(Product-Sophistication Definition)

SIC	Industry	Emp. 1976	Emp. 1986	% Change 1976 to 1986
281	Industrial Inorganic Chemicals	765	1,655	116.3
282	Plastics and Synthetics Resins	1,663	2,317	39.3
283	Drugs	0	0	—
351	Engines and Turbines	63	0	− 100
357	Office Computing Machines	1,086	1,360	25.2
361	Electrical Transmission Equipment	4,847	0	− 100
362	Electrical Industrial Apparatus	0	0	—
366	Communications Equipment	2,562	1,777	− 30.6
367	Electronic Components and Assembly	1,040	1,721	65.4
372	Aircraft and Parts	0	61	
376	Space Vehicles and Guided Missiles	0	0	—
381	Engineering, Laboratory Instruments	551	678	23.0
382	Measuring and Controlling Instruments	2,176	3,054	40.3
383	Optical Instruments and Lenses	269	446	65.8
385	Photographic Equipment	282	308	9.2
737	Computer Programming Sesrvices	1,058	4,758	349.7
7391, 7397	Commercial R&D Laboratories	0	706	
7392	Business Management and Consulting	2,986	3,757	25.8
891	Engineering and Architectural Services	9,632	10,172	5.6
892	Non-Profit Educational, Scientific	487	252	− 48.3
Total		26,481	28,559	7.8

Indeed, workers in primary metals are less likely to find reemployment in other sectors than workers in other industries (Flaim and Sehgal, 1985). The reemployment success of displaced workers is more sensitive to local growth in the industry of displacement than to total local employment, suggesting that manufacturing workers are not readily absorbed by other industries (Harris, 1984; Howland, 1988, p. 130). The figures presented here and in other studies (Jacobson, 1987) suggest that, for those who are reemployed, overall job quality has been reduced (also see Hoerr, 1987). Survey research in the Pittsburgh area (Fitzgerald, 1988) and nationally (Flaim and Sehgal, 1985) reveals that close to half of reemployed displaced workers earn less than in their previous job. This suggests that a strategy of replacing manufacturing with jobs in high-tech and services is not enough for cities like Pittsburgh. Economic development strategies must address the fact that these sectors cannot replace manufacturing, either in income or numbers. There is a great need for this issue to be addressed in the economic development strategies proposed for Pittsburgh.

Notes

1. High-tech industries are defined by occupational structure, specifically, industries in which the proportion employed as engineers, engineering technicians, computer scientists, life scientists and mathematicians, exceeds the manufacturing average (Markusen, Hall, and Glasmeier, 1985, p. 16).

2. The past concentration of Carnegie Mellon in research associated with Pittsburgh's traditional manufacturing sector supports Chinitz's argument that innovation in new sectors is not likely to occur in cities dominated by one industry.

10 SYRACUSE, NEW YORK: A REFLECTION OF THE NATIONAL ECONOMY

Michael Wasylenko

The major theme of this research is to determine whether the jobs created in the Syracuse metropolitan area have the same earnings as the jobs that have been lost, principally in manufacturing. There is a controversy about whether the economic restructuring that has taken place in recent years has harmed living standards. Bluestone and Harrison have recently argued that economic restructuring has harmed living standards in the United States, and that our society has become increasingly polarized as income shifts from middle income to those in the highest income quintile.[1]

While data on individuals are not available, this analysis can examine whether average earnings in the three-county Syracuse area have declined as a result of economic restructuring or whether the jobs created in Syracuse are at least as good as the jobs that are lost.

The development of the Syracuse area dates back to immediately after the Revolutionary War, when settlers were awarded land around what was to become Syracuse as partial payment for fighting on the side of the Colonies. Much of Syracuse's development after that time was linked to its placement along major transportation routes. The completion of the Erie Canal in 1819 brought a large boom in commerce and trade. As the railroads followed the pathways of the Canal, Syracuse maintained its

255

transportation advantage, which attracted manufacturing and other industries. Transportation remains central to Syracuse's development. Two major highway systems, the New York Thruway and Interstate 81, crisscross through Syracuse, giving it access to major markets both east and west and north and south.

The metropolitan area, including Onandaga, Madison, and Oswego counties, had a total population of 642,971 in 1980. Syracuse's population profile differs in many respects from the statewide average. Population increased only 1 percent between 1970 and 1980, and grew another 1 percent between 1980 and 1986. Population declined about 2.5 percent for New York State during the 1970 and 1986 period. Syracuse's population is 4.8 percent black compared to 13.7 percent for New York State, and 0.9 percent of Syracuse's population is Hispanic origin compared to 9.5 percent for New York State. In addition, the median age of the Syracuse population is 29.1 and almost three years younger than that for the state as a whole. The number of households has increased by 16.4 percent between 1970 and 1980, compared to an increase of only 7.2 percent for the state as a whole.

The per capita income of Syracuse was $6,906 in 1979, which was almost $600 less than that for the state as a whole. Nonetheless, only 7.3 percent of Syracuse families had income below the poverty level in 1979, compared to 10.8 percent of families with income below the poverty level in the state.

The Syracuse economy is undergoing a period of economic restructuring. Several of its large manufacturing firms have recently downsized and others have closed completely. For example, Bristol Laboratories, even though it remains a major employer in the area, moved the Syracuse portion of its research and development to Connecticut. On the other hand, Allied Chemical recently closed a large soda ash plant. Despite these recent employment losses, the metropolitan area still has 20 employers with more than 1,000 employees, including a major private university (Syracuse), several hospitals (Community-General, Crouse Irving Memorial, St. Joseph's, and State University of New York (SUNY) Health Science Center), a public utility (Niagara-Mohawk), several auto parts producers (FisherGuide and New Process Gear), and several metals producers (Crouse-Hinds and Crucible Metals), as well as Agway headquarters, Bristol Labs, Carrier Corporation, Carrols, Fay's Drug, General Electric, Miller Brewing, MONY Financial Services, New York Telephone, and "P and C" — a major regional food retailer and wholesaler.[2] Many of these corporations are not manufacturing-based, which gives the area some diversity from manufacturing. In addition, Syracuse is a regional hub for several major airlines.

1. Economic Structure — Location Quotients

The changing structure of Syracuse's economy can be seen by examining location quotients between 1979 and 1986. The location quotients for industrial divisions in table 10–1 show that, overall, the Syracuse economy has more employment in the Service and Transportation, Communication and Public Utility industrial divisions than the nation as a whole, and that Syracuse has about an average presence of manufacturing in its employment structure. When major industry groups are examined, the employment structure appears much more concentrated. For example, while most manufacturing employment is underrepresented compared to the United States as a whole, Syracuse has much heavier relative employment concentrations in Primary Metals, Machinery, Except Electrical, and Electric and Electronic Equipment. The relatively large decline in the location quotient for chemicals between 1979 and 1986 is due to the closing of the Allied Chemical plant.

In nonmanufacturing industries, Syracuse has a large employment concentration in Electric, Gas, and Sanitary Services (SIC 49) due to the presence of Niagara-Mohawk — a large utility company. Syracuse shows no significant employment concentration in the transportation component of this industrial division.

Syracuse has a relatively high concentration of employment for insurance carriers mainly due to the large and growing presence of MONY financial services in downtown Syracuse. But the employment in services is due mainly to a very heavy concentration of employment in educational services, which employs 7.45 times as many people in Syracuse compared to what would be expected based on the nation's employment structure.

The presence of Syracuse University with about 4,000 employees, a campus of the State University of New York, several liberal arts colleges, and an extensive primary and secondary education system gives Syracuse its heavy concentration in educational services. Syracuse has mainly below-average employment concentrations in other service categories. Moreover, this large concentration of educational services in Syracuse is a relatively stable component of the employment base, as educational services employment is not as cyclical as the manufacturing sector of the economy.

Table 10–1. Location Quotients for Syracuse, by Major Group, 1979 and 1986

		Location Quotients			
SIC	Major Group	1979	1986	Difference 1986–1979	1986 Employment
Total Nonagricultural Employment		1.00	1.00	0.00	280,490
Mining		D	D	D	D
Construction					
15	General Building Contractors	0.80	0.96	0.17	14,704
16	Heavy Construction Contractors	0.45	0.74	0.29	3,086
17	Special Trade Contractors	1.36	1.67	0.30	3,914
	Manufacturing	0.78	0.88	0.10	7,704
		0.83	0.82	−0.01	54,293
Durable Goods		0.94	0.95	0.01	37,488
24	Lumber and Wood Products	0.31	0.35	0.05	836
25	Furniture and Fixtures	D	D	D	D
32	Stone, Clay, and Glass Products	0.94	0.88	−0.05	1,756
33	Primary Metal Industries	1.14	1.66	0.52	4,277
34	Fabricated Metal Products	0.41	0.46	0.05	2,321
35	Machinery, Except Electrical	1.29	1.11	−0.18	8,175
36	Electric and Electronic Equipment	1.54	1.61	0.07	12,005
37	Transportation Equip. Excluding Motor Vehicles	0.79	0.68	−0.11	4,845
38	Instruments and Related Products	0.65	0.82	0.18	2,062
39	Miscellaneous Manufacturing Industries	0.67	0.74	0.07	927
Nondurable Goods		0.66	0.63	−0.04	16,805
20	Food and Kindred Products	1.21	1.17	−0.03	6,382
21	Tobacco Manufactures	D	D	D	D

22	Textile Mill Products	D	D	D	D
23	Apparel and Other Textile Products	D	D	D	D
26	Paper and Allied Products	0.89	0.83	−0.05	1,961
27	Printing and Publishing	0.67	0.67	0.00	3,394
28	Chemicals and Allied Products	1.07	0.74	−0.33	2,676
29	Petroleum and Coal Products	D	D	D	D
30	Rubber and Miscellaneous Plastics Products	0.65	0.60	−0.05	1,645
31	Leather and Leather Products	D	D	D	D
	Transportation	1.04	1.13	0.09	19,188
40	Railroad Transportation	D	D	D	D
41	Local and Interurban Passenger Transit	1.00	1.17	0.18	1,202
42	Trucking and Warehousing	0.85	0.92	0.07	4,352
44	Water Transportation	D	D	D	D
45	Transportation by Air	0.56	0.52	−0.04	987
46	Pipelines, Except Natural Gas	D	D	D	D
47	Transportation Services	1.15	0.85	−0.31	821
48	Communications	0.92	0.76	−0.16	3,464
49	Electric, Gas, and Sanitary Services	1.46	2.04	0.58	6,459
	Wholesale Trade	1.00	0.92	−0.07	18,383
50	Wholesale Trade (Durable Goods)	1.19	1.06	−0.13	12,514
51	Wholesale Trade (Nondurable Goods)	0.72	0.72	0.01	5,869
	Retail Trade	0.77	0.81	0.05	49,345
52	Building Materials and Garden Equipment	0.59	0.75	0.16	1,751
53	General Merchandise Stores	0.71	0.73	0.02	5,914
54	Food Stores	1.00	1.04	0.04	10,209
55	Automotive Dealers and Service Stations	0.69	0.76	0.07	5,054

Table 10–1 continued

SIC	Major Group	Location Quotients			1986 Employment
		1979	1986	Difference 1986–1979	
56	Apparel and Accessory Stores	0.75	0.78	0.03	2,835
57	Furniture and Homefurnishings Stores	0.78	0.77	−0.01	2,052
58	Eating and Drinking Places	0.78	0.80	0.03	15,755
59	Miscellaneous Retail Stores	0.67	0.75	0.08	5,775
	Finance, Insurance, and Real Estate	0.93	0.92	−0.01	19,180
60	Depository Institutions	0.77	0.81	0.05	4,906
61	Nondepository Institutions	0.27	0.24	−0.02	682
62	Security and Commodity Brokers	D	D	D	D
63	Insurance Carriers	1.67	1.90	0.23	8,289
64	Insurance Agents, Brokers, and Services	1.04	0.87	−0.16	1,720
65	Real Estate	0.77	0.76	−0.02	2,996
67	Holding and Other Investment Companies	D	D	D	D

	Services				
70	Hotels and Other Lodging Places	1.32	1.24	−0.09	89,903
72	Personal Services	0.70	0.59	−0.11	2,692
73	Business Services	0.68	0.83	0.14	3,200
75	Auto Repair, Services, and Garages	0.82	0.79	−0.03	12,784
76	Miscellaneous Repair Services	0.82	0.73	−0.09	1,906
78	Motion Pictures	0.58	0.68	0.09	753
79	Amusement and Recreation Services	D	D	D	D
80	Health Services	0.83	0.84	0.01	2,230
81	Legal Services	0.91	0.97	0.06	21,808
82	Educational Services	0.82	0.79	−0.03	1,996
83	Social Services	7.24	7.45	0.21	30,875
84	Museums, Botanical, and Zoological	1.23	0.97	−0.25	4,298
	Gardens	D	D	D	D
86	Membership Organizations	1.22	1.04	−0.18	2,667
88	Private Households	D	D	D	D
89	Miscellaneous Services	0.97	0.95	−0.02	4,168

Note: "D" indicates that disclosure rules prevent reporting information for the major group. The major group has fewer than 500 employees.

Source: Author's tabulations based on unpublished ES202 data provided by the New York State Department of Labor and the U.S. Department of Labor, Bureau of Labor Statistics.

2. Manufacturing Employment[3]

Table 10–2 lists the annual employment growth rates of Syracuse's manufacturing industries by major group. The employment growth rates for each major group are calculated from 1979 to 1986, from 1979 to 1984, and from 1984 to 1986. Each two-digit industry is put into one of five groups according to its employment growth pattern during the 1979 to 1986 period: (1) decline over the time period of 1979 to 1986; (2) decline during the 1979 to 1984 period followed by growth for 1984 to 1986; (3) relatively little change during the 1979 to 1986 period; (4) continuous growth during the 1979 to 1986 period; and (5) growth from 1979 to 1984 followed by decline from 1984 to 1986. Also listed in table 10–2 are the 1986 employment levels and the average 1986 annual earnings.

Five major manufacturing groups had continuously declining employment over the 1979 to 1986 period. These major groups included Primary Metals; Machinery, Except Electrical; Transportation Equipment; Chemicals and Allied Products; and Rubber and Miscellaneous Plastics Products. These five major groups accounted for about 40 percent of the 1986 level of total manufacturing employment in the Syracuse metropolitan area. Employees in two of these five major groups — Transportation Equipment, and Chemicals and Allied Products — had average annual earnings of $37,882 and $39,862, respectively, which were the two highest average annual earnings among the manufacturing major groups in the Syracuse metropolitan area. Employees in Primary Metals and Machinery, except Electrical, had about average annual manufacturing earnings or earn $28,983 and $28,657, respectively. Employees in the fifth major group, Rubber and Miscellaneous Plastics Products, earned about $18,397 annually or about $10,000 less than the average manufacturing employee in the Syracuse metropolitan area.[4]

Five manufacturing major groups followed a pattern of declining employment from 1979 to 1984 and employment growth between 1984 and 1986. These industries included Lumber and Wood Products; Stone, Clay, and Glass Products; Fabricated Metal Products; Miscellaneous Manufacturing Products; and Paper and Allied Products. Each of the two most rapidly growing industries in this group — Lumber and Wood Products, and Miscellaneous Manufacturing Products — had total employment of less than 1,000; and, as a whole, the major groups in this growth category accounted for only 13 percent of total manufacturing in the Syracuse metropolitan area. The 1986 average annual earnings ranged between $15,889 and $25,707 for major groups in this employment growth category, and employees in the two more rapidly growing major groups in this growth category were the lowest paid, earning less than $20,000 per year.

Table 10–2. Manufacturing Employment and Earnings: Growth Rates, Levels, and Earnings as a Percent of Average Manufacturing Earnings

		Annual Employment Growth Rate					Earnings	
SIC	Major Group	1979–1984	1984–1986	1979–1986	1986 Employment	1986 Employment Share	1986 Annual Earnings	Percent of Average Annual Earnings
Continuous Decline		−2.19	−7.45	−3.72	21,618	39.82	31,395	109.98
33	Primary Metal Industries (Durable)	−1.91	−3.57	−2.39	4,277	7.88	28,938	101.53
35	Machinery, Except Electrical (Durable)	−2.34	−9.60	−4.47	8,175	15.06	28,657	100.39
37	Transportation Equipment (Durable)	−3.40	−1.11	−2.75	4,845	8.92	37,882	132.70
28	Chemicals and Allied Products (Nondurable)	−0.89	−18.30	−6.21	2,676	4.93	39,862	139.64
30	Rubber and Miscellaneous Plastics Products (Nondurable)	−1.28	−0.75	−1.13	1,645	3.03	18,397	64.44

Table 10–2 continued

		Annual Employment Growth Rate				1986 Employment Share	Earnings		
SIC	Major Group	1979–1984	1984–1986	1979–1986	1986 Employment		1986 Annual Earnings	Percent of Average Annual Earnings
Decline Followed by Recovery								
24	Lumber and Wood Products (Durable)	−3.35	2.82	−1.62	7,801	14.37	22,957	80.42
		−3.00	9.91	0.52	836	1.54	15,889	55.66
32	Stone, Clay, and Glass Products (Durable)	−5.28	0.43	−3.69	1,756	3.23	24,786	86.83
34	Fabricated Metal Products (Durable)	−1.95	2.02	−0.83	2,321	4.27	23,541	82.46
39	Miscellaneous Manufacturing Products (Durable)	−4.05	4.68	−1.63	927	1.71	18,589	65.12
22	Textile Mill Products (Nondurable)	D	D	D	D	D	D	D
26	Paper and Allied Products (Nondurable)	−2.70	1.41	−1.55	1,961	3.61	25,707	90.05
Neither Growth nor Decline								
	None							

Continuous Growth	2.16	3.05	5.30	5,456	10.05	20,657	72.36
38 Instruments and Related Products (Durable)	3.48	5.89	4.16	2,062	3.80	23,796	83.36
27 Printing and Publishing (Nondurable)	1.30	4.69	2.25	3,394	6.25	18,750	65.68
29 Petroleum and Coal Products (Nondurable)	D	D	D	D	D	D	D
Growth Followed by Decline	1.32	−3.53	−0.09	18,387	33.87	30,613	107.24
25 Furniture and Fixtures (Durable)	D	D	D	D	D	D	D
36 Electrical and Electronic Equipment (Durable)	1.49	−1.09	0.75	12,005	22.11	30,352	106.32
20 Food and Kindred Products (Nondurable)	0.66	−7.07	−1.61	6,382	11.75	31,104	108.96
23 Apparel and Other Textile Products (Nondurable)	D	D	D	D	D	D	D
Unable To Classify							
31 Leather and Leather Products (Nondurable)	−22.25	D	D	D	D	D	D
Total Manufacturing	−0.96	−3.66	−1.73	54,293	100.00	28,547	100.00

Note: "D" indicates that disclosure rules prevent reporting information for the major group. The major group has fewer than 500 employees.

Source: Author's tabulations based on unpublished ES202 data provided by the New York State Department of Labor.

None of the manufacturing industries fits into the neither-growth-nor-decline category. But two major groups, Instruments and Related Products and Printing and Publishing, are in the continuous-growth category of table 10–2. These two major groups account for about 10 percent of total manufacturing employment in Syracuse. Average annual earnings were $23,796 in Instruments and Related Products and only $18,750 in Printing and Publishing; both of these figures were below the 1986 average annual earnings in manufacturing in the Syracuse metropolitan area of about $28,547.

In two manufacturing major groups, Electrical and Electronic Equipment and Food and Kindred Products, employment grew between 1979 and 1984 and then declined between 1984 and 1986. These two groups account for about 34 percent of manufacturing employment in the Syracuse metropolitan area. Employees in both of these major groups had annual earnings in the low $30,000 range, which is above the 1986 average for all manufacturing in the Syracuse metropolitan area.

From this examination of the major groups in manufacturing, it appears that major groups with the highest earnings wages were either in the continuous-decline employment category or in the growth-and-then-decline category. Moreover, industries in these two categories accounted for about 74 percent of the manufacturing employment in the Syracuse metropolitan area. By contrast, the manufacturing major groups that were either in the continuous-growth or in the decline-followed-by-growth categories accounted for about 26 percent of manufacturing employment; employees in these industries had annual earnings that were between 56 percent and 90 percent of the average annual earnings for the manufacturing sector as a whole. Thus, in the Syracuse metropolitan area manufacturing employment growth occurred in the low-wage jobs, while manufacturing employment declined in the higher paying manufacturing sectors.

While employment has declined in the seven major industry groups with the highest earnings, two major groups — Primary Metals, and Electrical and Electronic Equipment — have declined at a slower pace than national employment in these same major groups. This fact is evidenced in the location quotients reported for these major groups in table 10–2. Thus, the overall fortunes for manufacturing employment do not appear that different from those of the nation as a whole. However, although the message for the Syracuse metropolitan area is similar to that for the nation as a whole, the message is that Syracuse lost relatively high-earnings jobs and replaced some of them with manufacturing jobs that pay less.

3. Underlying Trends in Manufacturing Employment

Hidden trend-breakers include manufacturing industries for which employment changes varied from the patterns of their major group and that had 500 or more employees during the 1979 to 1986 period. For example, in table 10–2 Primary Metals; Machinery, Except Electrical; Transportation Equipment; Chemicals and Allied Products; and Rubber and Miscellaneous Plastics were listed as major groups with employment continually declining between 1979 and 1986. However, although confidentiality prohibits disclosure of the exact growth rates, four industries within three of these major groups did not have continual employment decline during the 1979 to 1986 period. Employment in Aluminum Sheet, Plate and Metal, and in Nonferrous Wire Drawing and Insulating grew between 1979 and 1986. To be specific, employment in these two industries grew between 1979 and 1984, but then employment declined between 1984 and 1986. In addition, employment in Paper Industries Machinery declined during the 1979 to 1984 period, but then increased by 1.9 percent per annum between 1984 and 1986.

In the decline-followed-by-recovery category, two industries, Vitreous China and Manufacturing Industries, not elsewhere classified, had continuously declining employment. In the continuous growth category, two industries, Newspapers and Blankbooks and Looseleaf Binders, had employment decreases between 1979 and 1986, but employment rebounded in these industries during the 1984 to 1986 period. In the growth-followed-by-decline category, three industries — Noncurrent-Carrying Wiring Devices, Chocolate and Cocoa Products, and Malt Beverages — had continually declining employment. One industry, Semiconductors and Related Devices, had declining employment between 1979 and 1984, and employment growth between 1984 and 1986. Another industry, Radio and TV Communication Equipment, had continual employment growth during the 1979 to 1986 period.

Thus, there appear to be three additional areas for optimism about manufacturing employment growth in Syracuse. Radio and TV Communication Equipment, and Semiconductors and Related Devices, had relatively high employment growth rates during the 1984 to 1986 period, and those employed in the corresponding major group had annual average earnings of $30,352, which is 6 percent above the average annual earnings in manufacturing (see table 10–2). In addition, Paper Industries Machinery also had substantial employment gains between 1984 and 1986. Employees in this major group had about average annual manufacturing earnings of $28,657.

The three industries described in the last paragraph employ about 15 percent of all manufacturing workers in Syracuse. Thus, these relatively high-earnings industries could have a substantial effect on the fortunes of manufacturing workers and earnings in the Syracuse region. The pessimism about manufacturing employment prospects nationally are shared in Syracuse, but Syracuse does not appear to be suffering from manufacturing job losses in key major groups and industries to the same extent as the nation as a whole.

4. Service Sector Employment

Browning and Singelmann have usefully grouped services into four categories: distributive services, producer services, social services, and personal services.[5] In this chapter, their categorization is modified somewhat so that distributive services are disaggregated into transportation services and wholesale and retail services. Producer services include communications), banking, insurance, real estate, accounting, legal, engineering, and other business services. Social services include medical services, hospitals, education, welfare, nonprofit, postal, government, and other social services. Personal services include domestic, hotels, eating and drinking, repairs, laundry, barber and beauty shops, entertainment, and miscellaneous personal services.

Table 10–3 lists the annual average employment growth rates between 1979 and 1986 for these five service categories in the Syracuse metropolitan area. For the period as a whole, producer services and personal services had annual employment growth rates of 4.1 and 3.5 percent,

Table 10–3. Annual Employment Growth Rates for Service Industries by Group

	1979–1984	1984–1986	1979–1986
Transportation Services	0.2	6.2	1.9
Wholesale and Retail Services	0.3	5.5	1.7
Producer Services	4.0	4.5	4.1
Social Services	0.9	3.1	1.5
Personal Services	2.4	6.3	3.5
Total Services	1.6	4.5	2.4

Source: Computed by author using unpublished ES202 data provided by the New York State Department of Labor.

respectively, compared to 1.5 percent for social services, 1.7 percent for wholesale and retail services, and 1.9 percent for transportation services. The relatively sluggish employment growth in the last three service categories is due to slow growth in the 1979 to 1984 period. During the 1984 to 1986 period, the annual employment growth rate ranges from 3.1 percent in social services to 6.3 percent in personal services.

4.1 Employment Growth in Services

In what follows, the service sector is disaggregated into major groups. The employment trends for these major groups are examined, and the annual earnings in the growing service major groups are compared to the earnings in both the declining service major groups and the declining manufacturing major groups.

In table 10–4, major service groups are also put into one of five categories according to their employment growth rates between 1979 and 1986: (1) decline over the period 1979 to 1986; (2) decline during the 1979 to 1984 period, followed by growth for 1984 to 1986; (3) relatively little change during the 1979 to 1986 period; (4) continuous growth during the 1979 to 1986 period; and (5) growth from 1979 to 1984, followed by decline from 1984 to 1986. Seven major groups are in the continuous-decline category, but only four of these major groups have more than 500 employees. These four include: Communication, Membership Organizations, Administration of Human Resource Programs, and Administration of Economic Programs. Except for Communication and Membership Organizations, these major groups in this growth category do not have a significant presence in Syracuse and, as a whole, they account for only about 4 percent of total service employment in Syracuse.

There are 14 major service groups in the decline-followed-by-growth category. As a whole, the 14 industries in this category account for about 27 percent of service sector employment in the Syracuse metropolitan area. Three of these major groups are in transportation, and four are in wholesale and retail trade. Five of these seven industries had about 5,000 or more employees in 1986. Under personal services, only hotels and other lodging places in this growth category had a significant number of employees, and employment grew at a 9.1 percent annual rate between 1984 and 1986. Of the three social services in this category, only postal services with a 4.7 percent annual growth rate and social services with an 8.8 percent annual growth rate had significant employment gains between 1984 and 1986.

Table 10–4. Growth Patterns of Major Service Groups Categorized According to Annual Growth Rates

| | | Annual Employment Growth Rate | | | 1986 |
SIC	Major Group	1979–1984	1984–1986	1979–1986	Employment
Continuous Decline					
	Producer:				
48	Communication	−1.08	−5.49	−2.37	7,907
66	Combined Real Estate, Insurance, Etc.	−0.30	−8.03	−2.57	3,464
		D	D	D	D
	Social:				
86	Membership Organizations	−0.73	−2.49	−1.24	2,667
93	Public Finance, Tax, and Monetary Policy	D	D	D	D
94	Administration of Human Resource Programs	−3.43	−6.44	−4.30	597
96	Administration of Economic Programs	−2.94	−4.32	−3.34	1,179
97	National Security	D	D	D	D
Decline Followed by Growth		−1.25	4.52	0.36	55,585
	Transportation:				
42	Trucking and Warehousing	−0.43	6.67	1.55	4,352
44	Water Transportation	D	D	D	D
45	Transportation by Air	−0.68	9.05	2.00	987
	Wholesale and Retail				
50	Wholesale Trade–Durable Goods	−1.70	3.43	−0.26	12,514
51	Wholesale Trade–Nondurable Goods	−0.86	7.56	1.48	5,869
53	General Merchandise Stores	−0.34	2.82	0.55	5,914
55	Automotive Dealers and Service Stations	−0.85	7.58	1.49	5,054
	Personal:				
70	Hotels and Other Lodging Places	−1.46	9.09	1.45	2,692
78	Motion Pictures	D	D	D	D

88	Private Households Social:	D	D	D	D
43	Postal Services	−0.17	4.75	1.21	1,795
83	Social Services	−0.78	8.75	1.85	4,298
91	Federal Government	−2.22	0.04	−1.58	12,110
95	Administration of Environmental Quality and Housing Program	D	D	D	D
	Neither Growth Nor Decline				
	None				
	Continuous Growth	3.29	5.32	3.86	144,121
	Transportation:				
41	Local and Interurban Passenger Transit	3.37	3.00	3.26	1,202
47	Transportation Services	0.47	5.62	1.91	821
	Wholesale and Retail:				
52	Building Material and Garden Supplies	3.54	8.33	4.88	1,751
54	Food Stores	2.62	5.92	3.55	10,209
56	Apparel and Accessory Stores	0.65	5.98	2.15	2,835
57	Furniture and Home Furnishings Stores	0.58	8.22	2.71	2,052
59	Miscellaneous Retail	3.20	6.40	4.11	5,775
	Personal:				
58	Eating and Drinking Places	3.01	7.36	4.23	15,755
72	Personal Services	5.41	4.60	5.17	3,200
75	Auto Repair, Services and Garages	2.52	0.40	1.91	1,906
76	Miscellaneous Repair Services	5.12	1.36	4.03	753
79	Amusement and Recreation Services	2.67	1.84	2.43	2,230
84	Museums, Botanical and Zoological Gardens	D	D	D	D
	Producer:				
49	Electric, Gas, and Sanitary Services	6.35	7.97	6.81	6,459
60	Banking	2.85	3.34	2.99	4,906

Table 10–4 continued

SIC	Major Group	Annual Employment Growth Rate			1986 Employment
		1979–1984	1984–1986	1979–1986	
61	Credit Agencies Other Than Banks	2.80	7.51	4.12	682
62	Security, Commodity Brokers, and Services	D	D	D	D
63	Insurance Carriers	3.43	2.53	3.17	8,289
65	Real Estate	3.13	3.39	3.20	2,996
67	Holding and Other Investment Offices	D	D	D	D
73	Business Services	6.16	8.71	6.88	12,784
81	Legal Services	5.76	8.64	6.58	1,996
89	Miscellaneous Services	3.26	5.91	4.01	4,168
	Social:				
80	Health Services	4.84	4.94	4.87	21,808
82	Educational Services	0.84	3.48	1.58	30,875
92	State and Local Government	8.84	4.90	7.70	669
	Growth Followed by Decline	2.59	-1.28	1.47	1,720
	Producer:				
64	Insurance Agents, Brokers, and Services	2.59	-1.28	1.47	1,720
	Unable to Classify				
	Transportation:				
46	Pipelines, Except Natural Gas	D	D	D	D

Note: "D" indicates that disclosure rules prevent reporting information for the major group. The major group has fewer than 500 employees.

Source: Author's tabulations based on unpublished data provided by the New York State Department of Labor.

No major service groups fall into the neither-decline-nor-growth group, but 25 major service groups fall into the continuous-growth category. These 25 major groups accounted for 69 percent of the 1986 total employment in services, and employment for these 25 industries grew at an annual rate of 3.3 percent per annum between 1979 and 1986. Moreover, service groups had continuous employment growth in all five service groups — transportation, wholesale and retail trade, producer, personal, and social-services — indicating that the growth was broad-based.

In addition, the three major service groups that employ relatively more people in the Syracuse region compared to the United States — Electric, Gas, and Sanitary Services; Insurance Carriers; and Educational Services — fall into the continuous employment growth category. Together these three major service groups accounted for 21.6 percent of the 1986 total employment in the region's service sector. Health services accounted for another 10.3 percent of 1986 total employment in the service sector, and it also had continuous employment growth during the 1979 to 1986 period.

In terms of employment growth, the service sector performed well during the 1979 to 1986 period, creating 32,354 jobs while the manufacturing sector lost 7,075 jobs over the same period. Between 1984 and 1986, major groups employing 95 percent of the 1986 service work force had employment growth. Nonetheless, there may be industries within the major groups that experienced a significant decrease in employment. The only major industry in which employment growth departed significantly from that of its major group is elementary and secondary schools. Employment in this industry numbered 17,376 in 1986, and the industry had an employment decrease of 0.24 percent annually between 1979 and 1984, and then an increase of 3.2 percent annually between 1984 and 1986. Overall employment in this industry grew 0.8 percent annually between 1979 and 1986, compared to a 1.6 percent annual employment growth rate for the corresponding major group over the same period. Other so-called trend-breaker industries account for only a minor share of the employment in their major group, and they do not significantly alter the picture of employment growth in the service sector.

5. Earnings in Service Industries

While service employment had grown almost across the board for the period 1984 to 1986, the average annual earnings in the service sector were $17,392 in 1986, as reported in table 10–5, compared to average an-

Table 10–5. Major Service Group Earnings, Earnings as a Percent of Mean Service Earnings, and Share of Service Employment

SIC	*Major Group*	*1986 Annual Earnings*	*Percent of Average Annual Earnings*	*1986 Employment Share*
Continuous Decline		$22,281	128.11	3.99
	Producer:			
48	Communication	29,657	170.52	1.64
66	Combined Real Estate, Insurance, Etc.	D	D	D
	Social:			
86	Membership Organizations	10,607	60.99	1.26
93	Public Finance, Tax and Monetary Policy	D	D	D
94	Administration of Human Resource Programs	26,702	153.53	0.28
96	Administration of Economic Programs	24,780	142.48	0.56
97	National Security	D	D	D
Decline Followed by Growth		18,259	104.98	26.68
	Transportation:			
42	Trucking and Warehousing	23,167	133.21	2.06
44	Water Transportation	D	D	D
45	Transportation by Air	27,270	156.80	0.47
	Wholesale and Retail:			
50	Wholesale–Durable Goods	25,447	146.32	5.92
51	Wholesale–Nondurable Goods	19,623	112.83	2.78
53	General Merchandise Stores	8,544	49.13	2.80
55	Automotive Dealers and Service Stations	17,792	102.30	2.39
	Personal:			
70	Hotels and Other Lodging Places	9,299	53.47	1.27

Code	Industry			
78	Motion Pictures	D	D	
88	Private Households	D	D	
	Social:			
43	Postal Services	27,784	159.75	0.85
83	Social Services	11,155	64.14	2.03
91	Federal Government	15,713	90.35	5.73
95	Administration of Environmental Quality and Housing Progress	D	D	D
	Neither Growth Nor Decline			
	None			
	Continuous Growth	16,629	0.96	68.52
	Transportation:			
41	Local and Interurban Passenger Transit	15,599	89.69	0.57
47	Transportation Services	21,057	121.07	0.39
	Wholesale and Retail:			
52	Building Materials and Garden Supplies	16,059	92.34	0.83
54	Food Stores	10,723	61.66	4.83
56	Apparel and Accessory Stores	7,787	44.77	1.34
57	Furniture and Home Furnishings Stores	14,685	84.44	0.97
59	Miscellaneous Retail	10,728	61.68	2.73
	Personal:			
58	Eating and Drinking Places	6,893	39.63	7.46
72	Personal Services	10,771	61.93	1.51
75	Auto Repair, Services and Garages	15,575	89.55	0.90
76	Miscellaneous Repair Services	18,846	108.36	0.36
79	Amusement and Recreation Services	8,970	51.58	1.06
84	Museums, Botanical and Zoological Gardens	D	D	D
	Producer:			
49	Electric, Gas, and Sanitary Services	37,556	215.94	3.06

Table 10-5 continued

SIC	Major Group	1986 Annual Earnings	Percent of Average Annual Earnings	1986 Employment Share
60	Banking	15,658	90.03	2.32
61	Credit Agencies Other Than Banks	20,585	118.36	0.32
62	Security, Commodity Brokers, and Services	D	D	D
63	Insurance Carriers	22,001	126.50	3.92
65	Real Estate	14,736	84.73	1.42
67	Holding and Other Investment Offices	D	D	D
73	Business Services	13,829	79.51	6.05
81	Legal Services	19,878	114.30	0.94
89	Miscellaneous Services	23,377	134.41	1.97
	Social:			
80	Health Sesrvices	18,524	106.51	10.32
82	Educational Services	19,594	112.66	14.61
92	State and Local Government	28,533	164.06	0.32
	Growth Followed by Decline	20,993	120.71	0.81
	Producer:			
64	Insurance Agents, Brokers, and Services	20,993	120.71	0.81
	Unable To Classify			
	Transportation:			
46	Pipelines, Except Natural Gas	D	D	D
	Average for All Services[a]	17,392	100.00	100.00

[a] Average earnings are computed as average earnings in each major group weighted by its employment share.

Note: "D" indicates that disclosure rules prevent reporting information for the major group. The major group has fewer than 500 employees.

Source: Author's tabulation based on unpublished ES202 data provided by the New York State Department of Labor.

nual earnings in manufacturing of $28,547, reported in table 10–2. The question here is whether earnings in the growing service sector are high enough to replace the earnings in the declining manufacturing sector.

In the continuous-growth category, there are only three major service groups with a significant number of employees that have annual earnings at, or above, the average annual manufacturing earnings. These three include Electric, Gas, and Sanitary Services, with 1986 average annual earnings of $37,556; Communication, with 1986 average annual earnings of $29,657; and State and Local Governments, with 1986 average earnings of $28,533. In total, these three major groups accounted for about 5.0 percent of 1986 total service sector employment. It seems clear that growth in service sector jobs did not replace the earnings losses in the manufacturing sector.

For the decline-followed-by-growth major service groups, average annual earnings for all 14 major groups in this category are below the average annual earnings in manufacturing. To be more precise, the average annual earnings in the decline-followed-by-growth major service groups were $18,259, and the annual earnings in the continuous-growth category averaged $16,629. In the shrinking manufacturing sector, the continuous-decline major groups had average annual earnings of $31,395 in 1986, and major manufacturing groups in the growth-followed-by-decline category had average annual earnings of $30,613. By contrast, the major manufacturing groups that are in the continuous-growth category had annual earnings of $20,657, and the major manufacturing groups in the decline-followed-by-growth category had annual average earnings of $22,957.

Thus, in Syracuse, annual average earnings in the growing major service groups were about $13,000 lower than the annual average earnings in shrinking major manufacturing groups, and about $4,000 lower than the average annual earnings in the growing major manufacturing groups. Thus, earnings from service jobs will not replace the earnings from the lost manufacturing jobs. In fact, the lowest average earnings in 1986 were found in the continuous-growth service category. The major service groups that had employment decreases during the 1979 to 1986 period generally had higher than average service sector earnings. Moreover, even though the manufacturing jobs that were growing had average annual earnings that were about $7,000 lower than the average manufacturing job, earnings in the manufacturing jobs that were growing were still better than the earnings in the growing service sectors.

Table 10–6 reports nominal and real average annual earnings for the Syracuse metropolitan area in 1979 and 1986 for total employees, manufacturing employees, and service employees. In nominal terms, average

Table 10–6.   Nominal and Real Average Annual Earnings for Total,
Manufacturing, and Service Employees, 1979 and 1986:
Syracuse Metropolitan Area

	Nominal Average Earnings		Average Annual Growth Rate
	1979	*1986*	*1971–1986*
All Employees	$13,224	$20,014	6.1
Manufacturing	$17,833	$28,547	7.0
Services	$11,406	$17,391	6.2
	Real Average Earnings (1979 Dollars)		
All Employees	$13,224	$13,249	0.03
Manufacturing	$17,833	$18,898	0.8
Services	$11,406	$11,513	0.1

ᵃThe consumer price index grew 51.06 percent from 1979 to 1986. In these calculations
1979 is treated as the base year.

Source: Computed by author using unpublished ES202 data as provided by the New
York State Department of Labor.

earnings for total employees grew about 6.1 percent per annum between
1979 and 1986. Average earnings grew 7.0 percent per annum in manufacturing and 6.2 percent per annum in service.

Real earnings barely kept pace with inflation. Overall, real earnings
were only $25 higher in 1986 than in 1979. Average real earnings in the
manufacturing sector increased about $1,065 between 1979 and 1986, but
average real earnings in the service sector increased only $107 between
1979 and 1986.

In addition, the gap in average earnings between the manufacturing and
the service sector increased between 1979 and 1986. In 1979, average
earnings in the manufacturing sector were 56 percent higher than in the
service industry. By 1986, average manufacturing earnings were 64 percent higher than average earnings in the service sector.

6. Shift-Share Analysis

The analysis in the preceding sections does not address how the economy
of the Syracuse region is doing relative to the United States' economy.

Shift-share analysis is often used to measure regional economic performance relative to national trends.[6] The relevant components of the shift-share analysis for Syracuse's manufacturing and services major groups between 1979 to 1986 are reported in table 10–7. To facilitate comparisons with tables 10–2 and 10–3, the major groups have been classified according to the five growth categories.

Based on the national effect and the mix effect, the level of manufacturing employment growth in 1986 is expected at 55,525, compared to the actual level of 54,293. Thus, during the 1979 to 1986 period, Syracuse was somewhat less competitive in manufacturing than the nation as a whole, as Syracuse lost 1,232 (or 2.2 percent) more jobs in manufacturing than expected based on national trends in these major groups. For specific manufacturing major groups, Syracuse did especially well, as measured by the absolute size of the competitive effect, in Primary Metal Industries, but did poorly in Machinery, Except Electrical, and in Chemicals and Allied Products. When the competitive effect is measured in terms of the percentage of the expected employment, Lumber and Wood Products, Fabricated Metal Products, and Instruments and Related Products also had a strong competitive component. However, three manufacturing major groups had substantial negative competitive effects: namely, Machinery, Except Electrical; Transportation Equipment, Excluding Motor Vehicles; and Chemicals and Allied Products. The competitive effect showed only minor changes in other major manufacturing groups.

For the services sector as a whole, the competitive effect is positive, and 1,141 more service sector jobs than expected are created. However, relative to the size of the service sector, the magnitude of the competitive effect means that only 0.6 percent more service jobs than expected are created in Syracuse. For major groups, the competitive effect is substantially positive in Miscellaneous Retail Stores; Personal Services; Electric, Gas, and Sanitary Services; and Insurance Carriers, where between 11.1 percent and 38.5 percent more jobs than expected are created. Electric, Gas, and Sanitary Services at 38.5 percent more jobs than expected represents the strongest growing major group. However, in six other major service groups with more than 1,000 employees — namely, Communications, Membership Organizations, Wholesale Trade–Durable Goods, Hotels and Other Lodging Places, Social Services, and Insurance Agents and Carriers — between 11.9 and 21.3 percent less jobs than expected are created as measured by the size of the competitive effect relative to the expected employment level. For two other large employment major service groups, 5.6 percent more jobs than expected are created in health services, and 2.0 percent more jobs than expected are created in educational services.

Table 10–7. Shift-Share Tabulations for Syracuse, by Major Groups, 1979–1986

SIC	Major Manufacturing Groups	1986 Employment	National Effect	Mixed Effect	Expected 1986[a] Employment Based on National Industry Trends	Competitive Effect
Continuous Decline						
33	Primary Metal Industries (Durable)	4,277	5,699	−2,731	2,967	1,310
35	Machinery, Except Electrical (Durable)	8,175	12,669	−3,105	9,564	−1,389
37	Transportation Equip. Excluding Motor Vehicles (Durable)	4,845	6,625	−964	5,660	−815
28	Chemicals and Allied Products (Nondurable)	2,676	4,716	−822	3,894	−1,218
30	Rubber and Miscellaneous Plastic Products (Nondurable)	1,645	2,003	−207	1,797	−152
Decline Followed by Recovery						
24	Lumber and Wood Products (Durable)	836	907	−173	733	103
32	Stone, Clay, and Glass Products (Durable)	1,756	2,569	−688	1,882	−126
34	Fabricated Metal Products (Durable)	2,321	2,768	−696	2,072	249
39	Miscellaneous Manufacturing Industries (Durable)	927	1,170	−325	845	82

22	Textile Mill Products (Nondurable)	D	D	D	D	D
26	Paper and Allied Products (Nondurable)	1,961	2,460	– 355	2,105	– 144
Neither Growth nor Decline						
	None					
Continuous Growth						
38	Instruments and Related Products (Durable)	2,062	1,744	– 115	1,629	433
27	Printing and Publishing (Nondurable)	3,394	3,267	156	3,423	– 29
29	Petroleum and Coal Products (Nondurable)	D	D	D	D	D
Growth Followed by Decline						
25	Furniture and Fixtures (Durable)	D	D	D	D	D
36	Electric and Electronic Equipment (Durable)	12,005	12,817	– 1,206	11,612	393
20	Food and Kindred Products (Nondurable)	6,382	8,044	– 1,417	6,627	– 245
23	Apparel and Other Textile Products (Nondurable)	D	D	D	D	D
Unable To Classify						
31	Leather and Leather Products (Nondurable)	D	D	D	D	D
	Total Manufacturing	54,293	69,035	– 13,510	55,525	– 1,232

Table 10–7 continued

SIC	Major Service Groups	1986 Employment	National Effect	Mixed Effect	Expected 1986[a] Employment Based on National Industry Trends	Competitive Effect
Continuous Decline						
	Producer:					
48	Communications	3,464	4,676	−456	4,220	−756
	Social:					
86	Membership Organizations	2,667	3,274	−107	3,166	−499
Decline Followed by Growth						
	Transportation:					
42	Trucking and Warehousing	4,352	4,397	−360	4,038	314
44	Water Transportation	D	D	D	D	D
45	Transportation by Air	987	966	103	1,069	−82
	Wholesale and Retail:					
50	Wholesale Trade (Durable Goods)	12,514	14,335	−129	14,206	−1,692
51	Wholesale Trade (Nondurable Goods)	5,869	5,958	−95	5,863	6
53	General Merchandise Stores	5,914	6,402	−605	5,797	117
55	Automotive Dealers and Service Stations	5,054	5,126	−472	4,655	400
	Personal:					
70	Hotels and Other Lodging Places	2,692	2,738	493	3,232	−539
78	Motion Pictures	D	D	D	D	D
88	Private Households	D	D	D	D	D
	Social:					
83	Social Services	4,308	4,350	1,212	5,465	1,115

Continuous Growth

Transportation:

41	Local and Interurban Passenger Transit	1,202	1,080	−51	1,029	173
47	Transportation Services	821	809	321	1,130	−309

Wholesale and Retail:

52	Building Materials and Garden Equipment	1,751	1,411	−23	1,388	363
54	Food Stores	10,209	8,996	912	9,908	301
56	Apparel and Accessory Stores	2,835	2,748	5	2,753	82
57	Furniture and Homefurnishings Stores	2,052	1,915	186	2,101	−49
59	Miscellaneous Retail Stores	5,775	4,901	296	5,197	578

Personal:

58	Eating and Drinking Places	15,755	13,260	2,142	15,402	353
72	Personal Services	3,200	2,529	140	2,669	531
75	Auto Repair, Services, and Garages	1,906	1,879	273	2,151	−245
76	Miscellaneous Repair Services	753	642	11	654	99
79	Amusement and Recreation Services	2,230	2,120	106	2,227	3
84	Museums, Botanical, and Zoological Gardens	D	D	D	D	D

Table 10–7 continued

SIC	Major Service Groups	1986 Employment	National Effect	Mixed Effect	Expected 1986 Employment Based on National Industry Trends[a]	Competitive Effect
	Producer:					
49	Electric, Gas and Sanitary Services	6,459	4,582	81	4,663	1,796
60	Depository Institutions	4,906	4,490	185	4,675	231
61	Nondepository Institutions	682	578	178	757	−74
62	Security and Commodity Brokers	D	D	D	D	D
63	Insurance Carriers	8,289	7,493	−137	7,356	933
65	Real Estate	2,996	2,703	385	3,088	−92
67	Holding and Other Investment Companies	D	D	D	D	D
73	Business Services	12,784	9,024	4,347	13,371	−587
81	Legal Services	1,996	1,438	642	2,080	−84

89	Miscellaneous Services	4,168	3,562	739	4,301	−133
	Social:					
80	Health Services	21,808	17,587	3,054	20,641	1,167
82	Educational Services	30,875	31,114	−835	30,280	595
	Growth Followed by Decline					
	Producer:					
64	Insurance Agents, Brokers, and Services	1,720	1,747	312	2,059	−339
	Unable To Classify					
	Transportation:					
46	Pipelines, Except Natural Gas	D	D	D	D	D
	Total Services	194,176	179,916	13,114	193,031	1,141

[a]Expected 1986 employment is computed as the sum of the national and mixed effects.

Note: "D" indicates that disclosure rules prevent reporting information for the major group. The major group has fewer than 500 employees.

Source: Author's tabulations based on unpublished ES-202 data provided by the New York State Department of Labor and the U.S. Department of Labor, Bureau of Labor Statistics.

The results of the shift-share analysis suggest that major industry groups in the Syracuse economy do not mirror national trends. Over the 1979 to 1986 period, the region's manufacturing sector grew somewhat more slowly than expected based on national trends, while the service economy grew somewhat more rapidly than expected based on national trends. Two industries — Machinery, Except Electrical, and Chemicals and Allied Products — lead the decline in the expected number of manufacturing jobs, but higher than expected job creation in primary metal industries offset this decline somewhat. For services, Wholesale Trade–Durable Goods, and Social Services, had the largest absolute number of job losses relative to expected number of jobs, while substantially more jobs than expected were created in Electric, Gas, and Sanitary Services, and in Health Services. Thus, the region's economy did not closely follow national trends, especially in a few large major groups.

7. Conclusion

The most important conclusion from this analysis is that Syracuse is losing employment in relatively high-earnings jobs and gaining employment in low-earnings jobs. Moreover, this trend applies not only to the loss of the relatively high earnings manufacturing jobs and the gain in lower earnings service sector jobs but also to the relative shift between high-earnings and low-earnings jobs within manufacturing and within services.

At issue is why Syracuse has incurred losses of higher paying jobs. One answer lies in the fact, as evidenced in the shift-share analysis, that Syracuse employment trends follow to some extent the national economy, which has undergone a similar phenomenon. Product life-cycle theories can explain this trend. As the manufacturing of a product becomes more routinized, production can move overseas to sites with lower labor costs. On the other hand, Syracuse employment trends in several major groups deviate significantly from national trends. It appears that the relatively high earnings and wage levels in Syracuse, as well as the relatively unfavorable tax climate in New York during this period, have accelerated the movement of jobs from Syracuse in certain more highly paid major groups. There have also been several plant closings in Syracuse during the 1979 to 1986 period. For example, the Allied Chemical plant, which produced soda ash, faced a decline in the world demand for soda ash. Allied had two plants producing soda ash and closed the Syracuse plant, which was the older of the two plants by a considerable margin.

There are several bright spots in the Syracuse economy. General Electric has received a large defense contract and recently advertised seeking 400 more employees. In the service sector, we have had relatively strong employment growth from Niagara-Mohawk, a major utility company located here, and from the MONY corporation in the insurance area. We also have a large presence of educational institutions; hospitals are also a large employer.

However, given the relative concentration of services in only a few major groups, the outlook for the near future is for only modest growth. While MONY corporation and the hospital sector will likely continue growing, the utility company has recently had problems with the start-up of a nuclear power plant and new employment prospects at that firm are not nearly as bright as in the recent past. Moreover, education services are split between primary and secondary employment and college and university employees. Tight budgets for local governments make employment growth unlikely in primary and secondary education. At the college and university level, the number of high school graduates will continue to drop until 1993 and then gradually turn upward. During that period, colleges and universities will try to maintain their enrollments, but there are few schools that would seek to increase their number of employees. Thus, growth in Syracuse's service employment will probably be slower than in the past.

Unless something dramatic happens at the national level, such as a substantial depreciation of the U.S. dollar against other currencies, boosting our manufacturing exports, I expect growth in Syracuse to be sluggish to modest. In addition, most of the restructuring of Syracuse's businesses has already occurred, and I expect future Syracuse employment patterns to mirror national trends more closely than they have in the 1979 to 1986 time period.

Acknowledgments

Jay Mooney of the New York State Department of Labor made the ES202 data available to me, and generously contributed his time and expertise to helping me understand these data. Robert Carroll and Laura Wheeler of the Metropolitan Studies Program and the Department of Economics provided very capable research assistance.

Notes

1. For a discussion, see Harrison and Bluestone (1988).
2. See *Syracuse Herald-American Newspaper,* Sunday, January 31, 1988, for detailed information on these companies.

3. Throughout this chapter, we shall only discuss employment in SIC categories that have over 500 employees in them.

4. The earnings figures are high compared to national averages. The relatively high earnings are due to both higher-than-average wages and hours worked in Syracuse compared to the nation.

5. See Browning and Singelmann (1978).

6. For a good discussion of shift-share, see Brown (1969). The original shift-share analysis is found in Dunn (1960).

11 YOUNGSTOWN/WARREN, OHIO: A REFLECTION OF THE BOOM AND BUST OF THE STEEL INDUSTRY

Terry F. Buss and David Gemmel

The Youngstown/Warren area is located in northeast Ohio midway between Cleveland and Pittsburgh. The metropolitan area of 531,350 people includes the cities of Youngstown (population 105,000) in Mahoning County and Warren (population 53,000) in Trumbull County.

For nearly 50 years, the Youngstown/Warren area was a world center for basic steel production. At its peak in the 1950s, nearly 50,000 workers were employed in primary metals. The dominance of steel changed in 1977 with the permanent loss of 5,000 jobs at Youngstown Sheet and Tube Company, followed in turn by closings at Jones and Laughlin (1,400), U.S. Steel Corporation (3,500), and Republic Steel Corporation (3,000) (Buss and Redburn, 1983).

While steel declined, auto manufacturing grew with the development of the General Motors Lordstown Plant and Packard Electric, together employing 35,000 workers. Since 1986, Avanti, the custom car builder, and American Sunroof, a custom convertible car rebuilder, have each added more than 100 new jobs.

The transformation of the Youngstown/Warren economy with the decline of the steel industry precipitated major socioeconomic changes. The population in Mahoning County in 1980 was 289,487; the projected pop-

ulation in 1990 is 269,357. Youngstown's population has declined 9.4 percent from 115,510 in 1980 to 104,690 in 1986. Some suggest that the 1990
population for Youngstown will be less than 100,000. Trumbull County's
population was 241,570 in 1980 and is projected to be 229,570 in 1990.
Warren's population has declined 6.6 percent from 56,629 in 1980 to
52,900 in 1986. The region is becoming increasingly poorer (one in eight
receive welfare benefits), elderly (16 percent are 65 years of age or older),
and disabled, as young people and skilled or educated workers leave the
area (outmigration is twice that of inmigration).

According to the Ohio Bureau of Employment Services, the work force
totaled 181,151 workers in 1986, down 11.2 percent from its high of
203,983 in 1979. The decline was not uniform, however; in 1983, the work
force reached its lowest level at 169,392, a decline of 17.0 percent.

Changes in employment as a result of the restructuring of the local
industry and changes in the business cycle have been profound from 1979
to 1987.

1. Employment Changes in Manufacturing

Both durable and nondurable goods manufacturing experienced decline
(see table 11–1) between 1979 and 1987. Durable manufacturing employment stood at 73,561 in 1979 and continuously declined to 44,078 workers
in 1987, a loss of 40.1 percent or 29,483 workers. Nondurable goods manufacturing declined 30.7 percent from 5,939 workers in 1979 to 4,118
workers in 1987. Over 30,000 manufacturing jobs were lost between 1979
and 1987.

Many of the major groups were in continuous decline over the decade.
Primary Metals (SIC 33) (including blast furnaces, steel works, smelters,
foundries, and shaping mills) was the biggest employment loser, falling
from 35,650 workers in 1979 to 18,259 in 1987, a loss of 48.8 percent of
the primary metal sector and 55.7 percent of manufacturing losses overall. Fabricated Metals (SIC 34) (including metal cans, hand tools, metal
forging and stampings, engraving, and sheet metal) showed heavy losses
over the period, plummeting 53.5 percent from 9,725 to 4,524 workers,
respectively. Together, Primary and Fabricated Metals accounted for 72.4
percent of manufacturing loss in the decade. Importantly, both groups still
produce 47.3 percent of all manufacturing employment, indicating that the
metals industry is not dead.

Two other groups — Furniture and Fixtures (SIC 25) and Electronic
and Other Electrical Equipment (SIC 36) — also experienced continuous
decline. Furniture production employment fell from 1,839 to 869, or 52.8

Table 11-1. Durable and Nondurable Manufacturing Employment

SIC Classification	Levels 1979	Levels 1987	Change (1979–1987) Absolute	Percentage
Durable				
24 Lumber and Wood	529	397	−132	−25.0
25 Furniture and Fixtures	1,839	869	−970	−52.8
32 Stone, Clay, and Glass	2,233	1,331	−902	−40.4
33 Primary Metals	35,650	18,259	−17,391	−48.8
34 Fabricated Metals	9,725	4,524	−5,201	−53.5
35 Machinery	6,539	3,787	−2,752	−42.1
36 Electrical Machinery	3,381	2,303	−1,078	−31.9
37 Transportation	13,665	12,441	−1,224	−9.0
Total Durables	73,561	44,078	−29,483	−40.1
Nondurable				
20 Food Products	1,723	1,441	−282	−16.4
27 Printing	1,392	1,171	−221	−15.9
30 Rubber	1,335	1,347	12	0.9
Total Nondurable	5,939	4,118	−1,821	−30.7

Source: Ohio ES202 employment and payroll data.

percent over the decade. Electrical machinery declined from 3,381 workers to 2,303, or 31.9 percent. Both groups together account for 6.6 percent of all manufacturing.

The years 1983 to 1984 signalled the bottoming out of the back-to-back recessions of the late 1970s and early 1980s. Transportation Equipment (SIC 37), including motor vehicles and equipment declined until 1983 to 1984, and then began a long recovery. In 1979, employment stood at 13,665 workers, only to fall 39.7 percent to 8,240 workers in 1983. Emerging out of its slump, the group now contributes 12,441 workers to manufacturing, or 25.8 percent.

Other major groups turned down between 1983 and 1984, but did not recover substantially from the slump in the early 1980s. Printing and Publishing (SIC 27), Food and Kindred Products (SIC 20), Nonelectrical Machinery (SIC 35), and Stone, Clay, and Glass (SIC 32) experienced a leveling off of employment following the recession. Printing employment dropped from 1,392 to 1,171 workers; Food Production from 1,723 to 1,441 workers; Nonelectrical Machinery from 6,539 to 3,787; and Stone, Clay, and Glass from 2,233 to 1,331. These major groups contribute 16.0 percent of manufacturing employment.

One group, Rubber and Miscellaneous Plastics (SIC 30), including rubber and plastic hose, experienced a curious pattern of growth and decline from 1983 to 1987. Employment in 1987 at 1,335 workers was nearly identical to 1979 and 1983 levels.

2. Manufacturing Trend-Breakers

Nine industry classifications in four different major groups with greater than 500 employees exist in the Youngstown/Warren economy. Within the Stone, Clay, and Glass Products group (SIC 32), structural clay products (including bricks, clay tile, and wall tile), pottery and related products (including china, earthenware, and porcelain), and miscellaneous non-metallic mineral products (including abrasives, asbestos, gaskets, and minerals) each exceeded 500 employees in 1986. Although the trend from 1983 to the present for these three industry groups was consistent with the overall trend in stone, clay, and glass products, between 1979 and 1983 the three industries gained employment, while the overall manufacturing group lost employment. Employment trends of the three from 1983 to 1986 followed the trend of the stone, clay, and glass category: slow employment growth until 1984, and some loss either in 1985 or 1986.

Within the Primary Metals group (SIC 33), blast furnace and basic steel (including steel wire, sheet, and bar production and furnaces, steel works, and rolling mills) and nonferrous rolling and drawing (including aluminum and copper extruding, rolling and drawing, and production of sheets, plates, and foil) employed 3,215 and 851 workers in 1986, respectively. Basic steel employment declined from 4,020 to 3,678 workers between 1983 and 1984, while the major sectoral employment increased. Nonferrous rolling and drawing employment replicated the trend: the number of workers rose from 730 in 1983 to 834 in 1984.

The major sector, Fabricated Metal Products (SIC 34), and its industry group metal forging and stamping (including ferrous and nonferrous forging, metal stampings, and automotive stampings), followed the same pattern during the study period. The industry group Fabricated Structural Metal Products (SIC 344) (including metal doors and trim, boiler shops, sheet metal work, and ornamental work), however, failed to replicate the pattern of decline to 1983, recovery in 1984, and then decline in recent years. Instead decline occurred in 1983 and 1984, followed by gains in employment in both 1985 and 1986.

The major group Industrial Machinery and Equipment (SIC 35) from 1983 to 1985 increased from 3,726 to 3,994 workers, only to fall to 3,846 workers in 1986. Metalworking machinery (including machine tools, dies, industrial molds, power hand tools, and rolling mill machinery) fell from 2,118 to 2,030 employees in 1983 and 1984. In 1985, employment rose to 2,194 workers and fell again in 1986 to 2,059 workers. The industry group miscellaneous machinery except electric rose from 392 employees in 1983 to 605 in 1984. Then, employment went flat: in both 1985 and 1986, the number of workers remained at 601.

3. Manufacturing Earnings

Average annual manufacturing earnings have increased from $20,451 in 1979 to $27,597 in 1986, an increase of 34.9 percent (see table 11–2). Durable goods manufacturing increased 37.1 percent, and nondurable goods manufacturing increased 46.7 percent. The fastest-growing groups by earnings included food products, furniture, and electrical machinery man-

Table 11–2.   Average Annual Earnings in Manufacturing

SIC Classification		Levels		Percentage Change (1979–1986)
		1979	1986	
Durable				
24	Lumber and Wood	$10,772	$13,922	29.2
25	Furniture and Fixtures	12,221	19,093	56.2
32	Stone, Clay, and Glass	15,744	22,325	41.8
33	Primary Metals	21,452	29,852	39.2
35	Machinery	19,584	25,153	28.4
36	Electrical Machinery	15,505	23,939	54.4
37	Transportation Equip.	21,846	26,688	22.2
38	Instruments	11,474	14,206	23.8
39	Miscellaneous	13,591	18,309	34.7
	Total	16,113	22,093	37.1
Nondurable				
20	Food Products	12,426	21,363	71.9
27	Printing	14,653	21,574	47.2
28	Chemicals	18,893	24,505	29.7
	Total	15,324	22,481	46.7

Note: As a reference, the national Consumer Price Index during this time period increased 51 percent.
Source: Ohio ES202 employment payroll data.

ufacturers, which increased 71.9, 56.2, and 54.4 percent, respectively.
Conversely, the slowest groups included transportation equipment, 22.2
percent; miscellaneous manufacturing, 34.7 percent; and nonelectrical
machinery, 28.4 percent.

Major groups in continuous decline during the study period had average annual earnings of $17,030 in 1979 and $25,082 in 1986, yielding a
growth of 48.7 percent. Manufacturers experiencing growth had lower average annual earnings: $12,533 in 1979 and $16,258 in 1986, an increase of
29.3 percent. Manufacturers who experienced either a decline and recovery or a decline with subsequent stabilization had average annual earnings
of $15,123 in 1979 and $16,258 in 1986. Earnings increased 38.4 percent
over the period.

Ironically, the major groups having the highest earnings in 1986, primary metals and fabricated metals, accounted for over 70 percent of manufacturing job loss during the period. Two major groups with employment
growth, miscellaneous manufacturing and instruments, had some of the
lowest earnings.

4. Employment Changes in Services

Five kinds of service sector industries were identified: transportation,
wholesale and retail trade, producer, social, and personal (see table
11–3).

The transportation service sector included local and interurban transit,
trucking and warehousing, water and air transportation, pipelines, and

Table 11–3.   Nonmanufacturing Employment

		Levels		Change (1979–1987)	
SIC Classification		1979	1987	Absolute	Percentage
Transportation Services					
41	Local and Interurban	233	424	191	82.0
42	Trucking and Warehousing	4,408	2,922	− 1,486	− 33.7
45	Transportation by Air	164	262	98	59.8
	Total	4,805	3,608	− 1,197	− 24.9

Table 11–3 continued

SIC Classification	Levels		Change (1979–1987)	
	1979	1987	Absolute	Percentage
Wholesale and Retail Trade				
50 Durable Goods–Wholesale	5,950	5,896	− 54	− 0.9
51 Nondurable–Wholesale	2,423	3,345	922	38.1
52 Building Materials	1,603	1,725	122	7.6
53 General Merchandise	7,681	5,365	− 2,316	− 30.2
54 Food Stores	6,269	5,982	− 287	− 4.6
55 Automotive/Serv. Station	4,452	4,162	− 290	− 6.5
56 Apparel and Accessory	1,890	1,621	− 269	− 14.2
57 Furniture, Home Furn.	1,357	1,103	− 254	− 18.7
59 Miscellaneous Retail	4,045	4,957	912	22.5
Total	35,670	34,156	− 1,514	− 4.2
Producer Services				
63 Insurance Carriers	1,188	1,129	− 59	− 5.0
73 Business Services	3,531	6,348	2,817	79.8
64 Insurance Agents	651	731	80	12.3
61 Credit Agencies	1,260	1,509	249	19.8
49 Electric, Gas, Sanitary	1,348	1,466	118	8.8
65 Real Estate	1,191	1,523	332	27.9
81 Legal Services	559	742	183	32.7
60 Banking	2,396	2,779	383	16.0
48 Communication	1,826	1,534	− 292	− 16.0
89 Miscellaneous	1,014	1,174	160	15.8
Total	14,964	18,935	3,971	26.5
Social Services				
86 Membership Organizations	2,615	2,001	− 614	− 23.5
82 Educational Services	1,507	1,896	389	25.8
83 Social Services	2,011	2,355	344	17.1
80 Health Services	14,392	19,193	4,801	33.4
Total	20,525	25,445	4,920	24.0
Personal Services				
75 Auto Repair	1,333	1,662	329	24.7
70 Hotels and Other Lodging	1,175	940	− 235	− 20.0
76 Misc. Repair	606	606	0	0.0
72 Personal Services	2,448	2,452	4	0.2
48 Eating and Drinking	11,056	12,993	1,936	17.5
79 Amusement/Recreation	1,582	1,538	− 44	− 2.8
Total	18,200	20,191	1,991	10.9

Source: Ohio ES202 employment and payroll files.

transportation services. In 1979, over 4,800 workers were employed in this sector. Declining to 3,230 workers in 1983, the sector partially recovered to 3,608 employees in 1987.

Wholesale trade in durable and nondurable goods as well as retail trade in building materials, general merchandise, food, automotive, apparel and accessories, furniture and furnishings, and miscellaneous comprised the trade service sector. This service sector declined from 35,670 employees in 1979 to 31,112 in 1983, then recovered, employing 34,156 in 1987.

Health services, membership organizations, education, and social services, forming the social services sector, is the second-largest employer. Continuous growth — 23.8 percent — characterized this sector. In 1979, 20,525 workers were employed, a work force that eventually reached 25,445 in 1987.

Personal services (including museums, amusements, recreation, eating and drinking establishments, hotels, miscellaneous repair shops, motion pictures, private households, and personal services) showed decline to 1983 and then sustained growth. In 1979, 18,200 workers were employed in the sector, falling to 17,313 in 1983. Some 20,191 workers were employed in 1987, an increase of 10.9 percent since 1979.

Producer services, such as legal, banking, insurance, brokerage, business services as well as electric, gas, sanitary, and communication services, constituted another service sector. Although little change in the work force occurred among the 14,964 employed in 1979, 1983 marked the beginning of growth. In 1983, 15,017 workers were employed in this sector; in 1987, 18,935 workers were employed, producing a 26.5 percent increase.

Within transportation services employment, the major groups trucking and warehousing leveled off after 1983, with employment declining from 4,408 workers in 1979 to 2,581 in 1983 and remaining at 2,922 in 1987. The major groups Local and Interurban Passenger Transit (SIC 41) outperformed the overall sector by steadily gaining employment from 1979 to 1987, while the air transportation group employment seemed erratic.

As previously mentioned, trade employment initially declined, then recovered after 1983. Two major groups, General Merchandise and Food Stores (SICs 53 and 54), experienced continuous decline. In 1979, general merchandise (including department and variety stores) employed 7,681 workers; in 1987, the sector comprised 5,364 workers, a percentage loss of 30.2 percent. Food stores (including grocery, meat and fish, fruit, vegetable, dairy, bakeries, and confectionery stores) continuously declined, from 6,269 workers in 1979 to 5,982 workers in 1987, a drop of 4.6 percent. Modest recovery peaked in this sector, followed by even lower employment throughout the period.

Major groups experiencing growth during the study period included wholesale trade in nondurable goods (including paper, drugs, apparel, groceries, raw farm products, chemicals, petroleum, and alcohol) and miscellaneous retail (including drug, liquor, and other stores). Wholesale trade in nondurables employed 2,423 workers in 1979 and 3,345 in 1987, an increase of 38.1 percent. Miscellaneous retail employed 4,045 at the beginning of the period and 4,957 in 1987, an increase of 22.5 percent.

Remaining sectors manifested employment trends similar to the trade sector. Trade services employment — apparel and accessory stores; wholesale trade in durable goods stores; furniture, home furnishings, and equipment stores; automotive dealers and service stations; and building materials and garden supply stores — declined, then recovered.

Business services; insurance agents, brokers, and service; credit agencies other than banks; electric, gas, and sanitary services; real estate; legal services; and banking were producer services in which employment expanded.

Communication employment unraveled during the period. In 1979, 1,826 workers were employed in the group. Falling 16.0 percent, communications employed 1,534 workers in 1987.

Although erratic, insurance and miscellaneous services (including engineering, accounting, auditing, and scientific) declined, then made a comeback. Insurance fell from 1,188 in 1979 to 1,073 in 1984 before acquiring 56 workers by 1987. Miscellaneous services declined 17.2 percent, from 1,014 workers in 1979 to 839 in 1983. This major group then rebounded by 39.8 percent, employing 1,174 workers in 1987.

Several social services, as mentioned above, grew between 1979 and 1987. Employment growth was attributed to health services, educational services, and automotive repair. The social services sector itself actually declined between 1981 and 1982. In 1979, employment stood at 2,011 in the sector, increasing to 2,155 in 1981. In 1982, the number of workers fell 9.8 percent to 1,945 before recovering in subsequent years. In 1987, the sector held 2,355 employees.

Membership organizations (including business associations, unions, religious, professional, and political organizations) experienced uniform retrenchment during the period, falling 23.5 percent from 2,615 workers in 1979 to 2,001 in 1987.

The performance of personal services, which declined to 1983 and recovered, was matched by component major groups performance: hotel and other lodging places; personal services (including laundry, photography, beauty and barber shops, funeral services, and shoe repair); and miscellaneous repair services (including electrical, watch, jewelry, reupholstery, and furniture).

The overall trend did not parallel growth in eating and drinking establishment employment or the erratic trend in amusement and recreation employment. Although employment fluctuated early in the period, the eating and drinking major group grew 17.5 percent from 11,056 workers in 1979 to 12,993 in 1987. The amusement and recreation major group's employed increased from 1,582 workers in 1979 to 1,929 workers in 1982. Then, employment fell to 1,538 workers in 1987.

5. Service Trend-Breakers

Contrary to the overall trend for general merchandise, which was in continuous decline, variety stores experienced recovery after 1983. General merchandise employment fell 6.9 percent from 6,155 workers in 1983 to 5,728 in 1986. Variety stores employed 443 workers in 1983 and 548 in 1986, an increase of 23.7 percent.

Grocery stores, as compared to other food stores, seem to be performing well. While food-store employment fell from 6,122 workers in 1983 to 6,023 in 1986, a loss of 1.6 percent, grocery stores employed 4,152 in 1983 and 4,260 in 1986, an increase of 2.6 percent.

Gasoline service station employment failed to rebound after 1983, despite the fact that the major group, automotive dealers and service stations, had recovered. The overall sector rose from 3,631 workers in 1983 to 4,123 in 1986, a 13.5 percent increase. Service station employment fell slightly — 1.4 percent — from 970 workers in 1983 to 956 in 1986.

Laundry and cleaning garment services employed 864 in 1983 and 840 in 1986, a loss of 2.8 percent. The larger personal services sector gained employment: 2,249 workers in 1983 and 2,332 in 1986, an increase of 3.7 percent. The major group enjoyed recovery since 1983, while laundry and cleaning garment services employment continuously fell.

Employment in automotive repair, services, and garages grew 40.1 percent from 1,187 workers in 1983 to 1,662 in 1986. Auto repair shops exhibited flattened growth — 13.2 percent — from 491 workers in 1983 to 556 in 1986.

Although amusement and recreation services showed an erratic trend between 1979 and 1987, miscellaneous amusement and recreation services, such as amusement parks, showed continuous decline. The overall group boasted 1,582 employees in 1979 and 1,702 in 1983, an increase of 7.6 percent, while the miscellaneous industry group yielded a loss of 5.4 percent, from 875 to 828 during the same period.

Health services employment increased 22.2 percent from 1979 to 1983, from 14,392 workers to 17,589 workers. Between 1983 and 1986, an additional 1,370 employees, or 7.8 percent, were added to this group.

Physician offices employed 1,722 workers in 1979, 1,515 in 1983, and 1,571 in 1986, a 12.0 percent loss between 1979 and 1983 and a 3.7 percent gain between 1983 and 1986. Thus, physician office employment decreased rather than increased in the early period, and increased less than health-care employment in the latter period.

Dentist office employment between 1979 and 1983 fell 23.6 percent and increased 3.2 percent between 1983 and 1986. This trend replicates that for physician offices. Hospitals continuously lost ground during the period, employing 9,121 in 1979 and 8,172 in 1986, a loss of 10.4 percent. Health services employment showed a 31.7 percent increase over the same period.

Employment in nursing and personal care facilities accounted for the difference between the aforementioned trends. Nursing and personal care employment rose from 1,929 in 1979 to 3,002 in 1986, a 55.6 percent increase.

Although miscellaneous services employment decreased from 1,014 in 1979 to 840 in 1983, a loss of 17.2 percent, employment in engineering services during the same period rose 81.5 percent from 205 to 372 workers. Between 1983 and 1986, miscellaneous services and engineering services grew at 34.9 and 70.7 percent, respectively.

6. Service Earnings

Service earnings were examined in two different ways. First, major groups were placed into the previously mentioned five categories: transportation, trade, producer, social, and personal services. Service industry earnings were also categorized by their employment patterns: continuous decline, decline and recovery, or flat, stagnant, growth, and other.

Average annual earnings in all service sectors increased 37.3 percent from $10,595 in 1979 to $14,542 in 1986 (see table 11–4). Fastest growing major groups by earnings included security and commodity brokers and services, miscellaneous services, and motion pictures, which increased 220.5, 91.1, and 83.3 percent, respectively. The slowest service areas, combination real estate, law, insurance, and loan offices and food stores, actually had declining earnings of −11.1 and −0.18 percent, respectively. Eating and drinking establishments had earnings increases of 19.3 percent.

Services in continuous decline over the last eight years paid out aver-

Table 11–4. Average Annual Earnings in Services

		Levels		Percentage Change
SIC Classification		1979	1986	(1979–1986)
Trade				
55	Automotive Dealers	$11,230	$16,264	44.8
57	Furniture and Home Furn.	10,624	13,261	24.8
52	Building Materials	11,045	14,171	28.3
56	Apparel and Accessory Stores	6,244	9,378	50.2
53	General Merchandise Stores	7,107	10,039	41.3
59	Miscellaneous Retail	7,350	9,971	35.7
54	Food Stores	9,261	9,244	−0.2
	Total	8,980	12,062	34.3
Transportation				
41	Local and Interurban Pass.	7,468	10,000	33.9
42	Trucking and Warehousing	16,649	20,302	21.9
47	Transporation Services	19,230	24,021	24.9
	Total	15,231	18,107	18.9
Social Services				
82	Educational Services	7,787	10,645	36.7
80	Health Services	13,575	19,510	43.7
83	Social Services	6,794	11,134	63.9
86	Membership Services	6,439	8,532	32.5
	Total	8,649	12,455	44.0
Personal Services				
78	Motion Pictures	5,454	9,999	83.3
76	Miscellaneous Repair	11,720	15,062	28.5
75	Auto Repair	10,031	13,571	35.3
72	Personal Services	7,311	9,189	25.7
58	Eating and Drinking Places	4,416	5,270	19.3
70	Hotel and Other Lodgings	5,193	6,713	29.3
79	Amusement and Recreation	5,204	6,462	24.1
	Total	7,047	8,736	24.0
Producer Services				
64	Insurance Agents	14,258	20,648	44.8
73	Business Services	7,067	9,257	31.0
89	Miscellaneous	11,525	22,024	91.1
67	Holding/Investment Offices	13,903	21,195	52.4
66	Real Estate Brokers/Services	13,187	11,729	−11.1
49	Electric, Gas, Sanitary	18,736	29,878	59.5
81	Legal Services	15,706	23,573	50.1
48	Communication	16,898	26,023	54.0
63	Insurance Carriers	14,208	21,614	52.1

Table 11–4 continued

SIC Classification	Levels		Percentage Change (1979–1986)
	1979	1986	
60 Banking	8,760	13,170	50.3
65 Real Estate	8,608	11,778	36.8
62 Security, Commodity Brokers	16,279	52,172	220.5
61 Credit Agencies, Not Banks	10,759	14,457	34.4
Total	13,069	21,347	63.3

Source: Ohio ES202 employment and payroll files.

age annual earnings of $9,926 in 1979 and $13,459 in 1986, an increase of 35.6 percent. Service firms with employment growth had higher annual earnings: $10,771 in 1979 and $17,422 in 1986. Wages were 61.7 percent higher.

Services with employment decline and recovery or decline and stagnant trends had average annual earnings of $10,843 in 1979 and $14,440 in 1986, an increase of 33.2 percent.

Services experiencing employment growth had the highest average weekly earnings in 1986 and the greatest percentage increase during the study period. Those firms with continuous employment decline had the lowest average weekly earnings.

7. Location Quotients

Using Ohio Bureau of Employment Services data, location quotients, the ratio of an industry's share of Standard Metropolitan Statistical Area (SMSA) employment to the industry's share of national employment for 1979 and 1986 was calculated. The difference between the location quotients for the two years demonstrates the relative advantage of a given local sector over the national economy over time.

In 1979, Youngstown's economic advantages were concentrated in the manufacturing sector. The major group, primary metals, had a location quotient of 11.53. Other important groups, but ones much less significant than primary metals, included fabricated metals production and transportation equipment, at 2.20 and 2.60, respectively.

Local economic advantages remained the same in 1986. Primary metals, fabricated metals, and transportation equipment had location quotients of 13.91, 2.80, and 2.53, respectively.

The location quotients increased in primary metals (11.5 to 13.9) and fabricated metals (2.12 to 2.80) despite employment decreases in both groups. For transportation equipment, the location quotient remained constant, despite a loss of employment. Although the competitive advantage of such local, basic manufacturing industries as primary metals, fabricated metals, and transportation equipment may have improved, the employment generated by these activities has decreased substantially. Youngstown manufacturing firms, then, have become more competitive over the decade, but at the cost of jobs.

8. Shift-Share Analysis

Using shift-share analysis, Youngstown-Warren employment changes were compared with (1) national growth in a given major industrial group, (2) the region's "share" of employment, and (3) the regional growth for a major group, the "shift" to the SMSA.

Major groups where local growth, or shift, outdistanced growth attributed to national trends, or share, over the 1979 to 1984 period included other services: retail trade, banking and finance, security, and wholesale trade. During the 1984 to 1986 period, only transportation equipment and construction improved. Transportation gained 1,125 workers of which 771 (68.5 percent) were attributed to the region's shift and the remaining 354 workers were attributed to the national share. Construction gained 1,002 of which 563 (56 percent) were the shift and 439 were the share. Remaining industries, especially manufacturing, either experienced losses or showed few regional advantages in the analysis.

9. Service and Manufacturing Compared

The service sector generally failed to replace lost manufacturing jobs (see table 11–5). Manufacturing net job loss from 1979 to 1987 was −31,304 workers, or −39.3 percent, while services during the period showed net gains: 8,171 or 8.7 percent. Earnings grew in the service sector at 42.0 percent, which exceeded manufacturing growth at 34.9 percent. But manufacturing earnings ($27,597) substantially exceeded services ($16,851).

Table 11–5. Comparison of Manufacturing and Service Employment, 1979–1987

Sector	Employment Change		Weekly Earnings Percentage
	Absolute	Percentage	
Manufacturing	−31,304	−39.4	34.9
Services			
Transportation	−1,197	−24.9	18.9
Trade	−1,514	−4.2	34.3
Producer	3,971	26.5	63.3
Social	4,920	24.0	44.0
Personal	1,991	10.9	24.0
Growing Sectors			
Manufacturing	—	—	29.3
Services	13,542	29.9	61.7
Declining Sectors			
Manufacturing	24,640	−48.7	48.7
Services	−3,510	−19.1	35.6
Decline and Recovery Sectors			
Manufacturing	−5,855	−22.0	38.6
Services	−1,937	−6.7	33.2

Source: Ohio ES202 employment and payroll files.

Service sectors that were continually growing from 1979 to 1987 contributed 13,772 new jobs, a 29.9 percent increase. Earnings in this growth sector also grew 61.7 percent to $17,422. By contrast, manufacturing in continuous growth sectors had no net change in jobs and contributed somewhat less in earnings at $16,258 for a 29.3 percent growth.

Manufacturing jobs in continuously declining, and in declining with subsequent recovery, industries far exceeded those in the service industry. Continuously declining manufacturing had twice (− 48.7 percent) the rate of job loss as services (19.1 percent). In declining with subsequent recovery sectors manufacturing was nearly four times (− 22.0 percent) that of services (− 6.7 percent). Earnings told a different story: continuously declining manufacturing earnings grew at 48.7 percent compared to 35.6 percent in services; while decline-with-subsequent-recovery manufacturers and services grew at nearly the same rate — 38.6 percent and 33.4 percent, respectively.

9.1 Employment and Industrial Organization

ES202 data used in this analysis do not include information on industrial organization and employment change. However, data from Dun and Bradstreet reported in 1976 and 1982 do contain this information. Findings from our Dun and Bradstreet study (see Ledebur and Buss, 1986) include the following:

Small business dominates the Youngstown/Warren economy. Small independent establishments account for roughly three-fourths (78 percent) of all businesses in 1982. By contrast, the remaining one-fourth (22 percent) were dominated by branch plants or subsidiaries (12 percent) headquarters firms (8 percent) and large independents (2 percent).

Although small businesses substantially outnumber larger establishments, larger establishments account for three-fourths (78 percent) of all jobs created. Branch plants and subsidiaries produced 54 percent of the area's employment in 1982, followed in turn by large independents (13 percent) and headquarter companies (10 percent). Small business produced 22 percent of all new jobs.

Large establishments all declined in number from 1976 to 1982. Branch plants and subsidiaries were reduced by almost a third (28 percent) with large independents (8 percent) and headquarter firms (4 percent) losing somewhat less. Small independents, by contrast, grew by 2 percent over the period.

Job loss from 1976 to 1982 occurred primarily in branch plants and subsidiaries (26 percent) and headquarter firms (17 percent). Large independents showed considerable growth (15 percent). Small business declined by about 2 percent. Overall, unemployment resulting from deaths of firms outdistanced unemployment from work force contractions. Employment from births and expansions was about even. Sources of employment growth (births or expansions) and decline (deaths or contractions) varied across establishment type. For small businesses, employment from births exceeded expansion nearly two to one. Likewise, employment from closings outnumbered contraction. Overall, births and deaths, and expansions and contractions among small business employment cancel each other out. Among large independents, births and deaths cancelled each other out, but expansions more than made up the difference. Employment growth among headquarter firms either through births or expansions was exceeded by a rate twice that in deaths and contractions. Branches and subsidiaries lost most employment from deaths and much less from contractions, while births and expansions were negligible.

9.2 Economics of Decline

No single model of economic change accounts for Youngstown's decline and retarded recovery. The decline of the economy appears to have resulted from restructuring in the steel industry with its attendant plant closings and work force retrenchment, and from back-to-back recessions that affected businesses in almost every sector. At least five economic change theories are required to explain the decline of steel. Export base theory, which states that local economies thrive only when they are able to continue to export goods and services out of a region, suggests that when steel exports from Youngstown were eliminated by foreign competitors, Youngstown was unable to attract enough outside dollars to sustain itself, much less grow. Product cycle theory, which states that products are developed in a process beginning with innovation, followed by growth leading to standardization, reveals that once products from Youngstown became standardized, foreign competitors displaced Youngstown producers with cheaper products. Location theory, which states that certain areas by virtue of their proximity to markets have comparative advantages over other regions, reveals that the location of steel mills dependent on rail and truck transportation could not compete with mills located on major waterways, especially those near iron ore and coal fields. Structural change theory, which holds that industries eventually mature and then decline because they cannot compete with their production facilities, coupled with a lack of demand for products that have become obsolete, asserts that the antiquated production facilities in Youngstown, which had become too costly to replace, were not competitive in the market for steel. Recession also devastated steel as it did many other types of businesses.

Economic theory explains the decline of Youngstown's economy in part. But these theories do not explain why Youngstown has lagged far behind every other major Ohio city in its recovery efforts. New industries did not replace steel or other businesses lost in the recession, and businesses hard hit by recession did not fully recover. Other models must be called into play to explain Youngstown's lack of progress.

9.3 Politics of Decline

Although they explain its decline, economic models are inadequate in accounting for Youngstown's sluggish recovery. Politics, not economics, may provide the clue (Buss and Vaughan, 1987).

Political choices by community leaders over the years sealed Youngstown's and Warren's economic fate in the 1980s. First, around the turn of the century, steelmaking began to transform the region from a sleepy little town into an industrial giant. As it grew, steelmaking demanded more and more workers. Steelmakers wanting to dominate the market took control of politics. Steelworkers and their unions, interested in high earnings and job security, supported community control. The steel industry became so powerful that it successfully kept other large employers — primarily automakers — out of the region. This strategy paid off handsomely for the region, but only as long as steel was booming. But the price was high: the region failed to diversify.

Second, when steel began to decline in the 1970s, most of the executives with local connections retired or moved away. In their wake they left caretaker managers who looked to corporate absentee owners for direction. Caretaker managers had no stake in the community and took no interest in its economic woes. Little of the community power structure remained to address revitalization politics and economies in the 1980s.

Third, the predominance of steel in the region had another curious effect: because local labor could not meet demand, workers were recruited from elsewhere, primarily eastern/southern Europe and the rural South. These recruits lacked any entrepreneurial tradition, having worked mostly as laborers. While working in steel — the highest paying blue-collar job — workers had no incentive to start their own businesses. When steel died, few workers were able to fathom starting a business. *Small business development was therefore retarded for decades.*

Fourth, following the closing of Youngstown Sheet and Tube in 1977, the community organized to address the waves of mass layoffs. Without traditional community leaders in place, new groups took control. Church leaders, organized as the *Ecumenical Coalition,* seized the initiative and devised a plan to reopen the mills under a community-worker ownership scheme. This idea caught the imagination of outside political groups, primarily labor activists and industrial democracy advocates, who took up the cause apparently to promote worker ownership at the national level. The political battles, waged over the economics of reopening the mills and over worker ownership, lasted nearly three years. No steel mills were reopened under the scheme. The community lost its window of opportunity to mount a viable revitalization effort.

Fifth, while steel was king, Youngstown dominated regional politics. With the demise of steel, other communities began to assert themselves. During the 1970s and 1980s existing regional cleavages were exacerbated: Warren versus Youngstown, Trumbull versus Mahoning County, cities versus suburbs, townships versus urban areas, and local government versus state and federal government. The rise of economic development corporations, economic development agencies, and non-profit development interests owing allegiance to different municipalities, worsened the situation. The region, not large by most standards, was unable to build a consensus about revitalization. Consequently, while other communities moved ahead, this region continued to wage internecine warfare.

12 THE FUTURE OF THE MIDWEST ECONOMY: TWO SCENARIOS

Richard D. Bingham and Randall W. Eberts

The Midwest has undergone significant economic restructuring since the late 1970s. As we have seen in the preceding chapters, this restructuring has been uneven, depending to a large extent on the industrial composition of these regions. The Syracuse region, for example, being less dependent on the cyclical-sensitive durable goods industries than other regions, experienced less restructuring than a region like Milwaukee, which experienced permanent job losses in its metal-parts and machinery industries.

In spite of some pronounced differences in recent economic histories, it is possible to distill a few common elements from the experiences of these regions and to draw a composite picture of the causes and effects of the restructuring of the Midwest economy. The purpose of this chapter is to conjecture how the forces that shaped these regional economies over the last decade might carry these regions into the near future.

1. Causes and Effects of Restructuring

Many factors have contributed to this restructuring — complacency on the part of U.S. manufacturers, technological innovation, and changing patterns of sectoral demand are a few. These factors have been present in earlier periods without bringing forth the dramatic restructuring witnessed during the 1980s. One essential ingredient that was missing before the mid-1970s, but which emerged as a significant force during the 1980s, is the increase in international competition. The economic effects of increased international competition can be both positive and negative. While it opens up foreign markets to U.S. producers, it also opens up our own markets to foreign competitors. For the nation and our ten metropolitan areas, the increased competition came predominantly at the expense of domestic producers. Between 1976 and 1986, U.S. imports (in constant 1982 dollars) rose 81 percent, while exports rose only 38 percent. With the dramatic increase in imports, U.S. companies lost 4.5 percent of the domestic market over the last ten years. Consequently, U.S. companies increasingly have found themselves head-to-head with foreign competitors not only abroad but also at home.

Some of this loss in competitiveness of U.S. firms can be attributed to the high foreign exchange value of the U.S. dollar. From its trough in 1980 to its peak in early 1985, the trade-weighted value of the dollar rose an incredible 70.2 percent. This meant that American producers of international goods faced a 40 percent cost disadvantage in relation to foreign producers. U.S. producers found their competitive positions severely eroded as foreign goods became far cheaper for Americans to buy and American products became far more expensive for foreign consumers to purchase. Since 1985, the value of the dollar has fallen significantly. While the lower value of the dollar has contributed to a resurgence of manufacturing through increased exports, it still takes time to regain lost markets. As we will discuss later on, it also takes more than lower costs. It takes improved product quality and advanced technology.

1.1 The Discipline of Labor

Certain commonalities emerged from the various Midwestern economies analyzed in the previous chapters. A common thread running through most of these chapters was that of employment declines in high-earnings manufacturing sectors and employment gains in low-earnings manufacturing industries. Furthermore, the same pattern emerged in the service sector — jobs in low-earnings industries increased while jobs in high-earnings industries declined.

These trends clearly mark a structural transformation and, in our view, the recognition by many U.S. producers of increased international competition. American manufacturers have been forced to streamline, to cut back on excess employment, to reduce costs, not merely in the final product but in all of the component products that go into a final consumer durable good. In the case of the automobile industry, which figures so prominently in many of the regions studied in this book, the pressure to cut costs was not merely on Chrysler and Ford and General Motors but on all the suppliers, large and small, of the major auto manufacturers.

While management was scurrying to become more competitive with foreign producers, labor was scrambling to protect jobs that remained after the massive layoffs and plant closings precipitated by the 1980 to 1982 recession. As a result, management was able to extract substantial wage concessions from their labor forces. Even during the expansion after 1983, wage increases were very moderate and unit labor costs remained low. In fact, with the help of a weaker dollar in recent years, U.S. labor became cheaper relative to countries that previously had been considered to have gained a competitive edge against the United States because of their low labor costs. From 1982 to 1987, United States unit labor costs (labor compensation divided by output) measured in U.S. dollars fell at an average annual rate of 1.0 percent, while Japan's unit labor costs increased at an average annual rate of 10 percent (Erceg and Bernard, 1988).

1.2 Structural Shifts in Product Demand

Ann Markusen and Virginia Carlson maintain that there is a dramatic recomposition of production taking place in the United States and that the major beneficiaries are sectors that have a new competitive edge: military hardware, various high-tech sectors, mass culture, and business services. Thus, the major losers are sectors hit hardest by competition by other countries: consumer goods, consumer durables, and nonmilitary capital goods. They believe that the poor performance of the Midwest in the current period can be attributed to changing weapons production. As aircraft and other weapons become more sophisticated and complicated, ever larger components of their costs are guidance systems, communication equipment, scientific instruments, and the like. These components utilize very little output from the steel and machinery industries, which have traditionally been the backbone of Midwestern manufacturing.

The regional consequences of this change in military procurement is a decline in the demand for steel and machine tools from our industrial heartland. As of the late 1970s, confronted with rising imports, Midwestern manufacturers found themselves to be relatively inefficient and high-cost producers. In response to foreign competition, they often abandoned entire markets such as tractors, subcompact cars, consumer electronics; and many of the companies in this industry have diversified, sold out, merged, or substantially reorganized (U.S. Steel, now USX; International Harvester, now Navistar). These companies have lessened their commitment to traditional specialties. They have shut plants to trim capacity and lopped off large segments of their customer lists. The result has been a process of disintegration and severe adjustments on surrounding sectors and suppliers as well as on workers and their communities (Markusen and Carlson, 1989). Nowhere was this more evident than in the cases of Pittsburgh, Buffalo, Youngstown, Cleveland, and Milwaukee. Although the cost-cutting and reorganization of these basic industries have paid off to some extent, the mere fact that some of these industries have become more productive means that they employ fewer workers to produce the same output.

2. The Future of the Midwest Economy

The restructuring that has occurred to date has exhibited both commonalities and idiosyncratic differences. We can expect more of the same in the future. Given the fact that the Midwest is no longer held together by the sectoral "glue" of linked heavy industrial development, we can expect a new spatial or geographic realignment of the Midwest's industries. This restructuring is likely to create a new round of uneven economic development within the region and, potentially, a new series of winners and losers.

In order to illustrate how the future might evolve, we have developed two scenarios. Both scenarios are spun from the realization that at some point in the not-too-distant future, the massive foreign debt that the United States has accumulated throughout this current economic expansion must be paid back. Dornbusch, Krugman, and Park (1989) calculate that even if the current account deficit declines steadily to zero over the next five years, the debt will eventually amount to as much as 15 percent of gross national product (GNP) (p. 6).

They lay out a convincing argument that the United States will have to achieve a merchandise trade surplus within the next decade to begin to pay back this debt and that this surplus will almost certainly be achieved by a trade surplus in manufactured goods. In order to achieve this surplus, they estimate that the manufacturing sector would have to increase at an annual rate of almost twice that of GNP. If this is the case, then the United States is headed for a period of marked reindustrialization.

Two questions arise for the Midwest: (1) Will the perceived gain in manufacturing come primarily from gains in productivity and improvements in product quality or will it come from a significant reduction in worker wages? and (2) Will it take place in this region? Of course, we have no definitive answers to these questions. We offer two scenarios that we feel reflect the two polar positions. Obviously, the actual path followed by this region will lie somewhere in between.

The first scenario sees this region increasing its manufacturing base through gains in productivity, improvements in productivity, and advances in technology. The twist to this story is that the catalyst for these advances will come from foreign affiliates that locate and manufacture in this region next to domestic producers. In many respects, foreign firms are very similar to domestic firms: they invest in new plants and equipment, invest in new technology, add jobs to the region's economy, and pay taxes to local governments. At the same time, foreign firms, especially Japanese affiliates, do some things differently. They typically organize the workplace differently from their U.S. counterparts, they pursue a different corporate strategy, and they locate production facilities in areas that typically have not been traditional industrial centers. Thus, the first scenario sees a resurgence in manufacturing for the region as a whole, but a dramatic realignment of economic activity within these regions, as we will illustrate for the auto industry.

The second scenario is less optimistic. It envisions manufacturing growing not from productivity gains but from lower labor costs. Two causes of lower labor costs are possible. The high foreign debt will devalue the dollar and swing the exchange rate in favor of lower-priced exports, making U.S. labor costs lower relative to the rest of the world. At the same time, however, the price of imports will rise, reducing workers' standard of living. The second cause is simply the ability of management, through the threat of foreign competition, to extract wage concessions from workers. Both causes increase the cost competitiveness of Midwest manufacturers, but reduce workers' standard of living.

3. Foreign Influence: The Case of the Midwest Auto Industry

The first scenario is best illustrated by looking at the Midwest auto industry. Just as the history of the auto industry is instructive to our understanding of the restructuring of the region, so too is current behavior of the industry instructive to the future. It is the behavior of the big three American manufacturing — Chrysler, Ford, and General Motors — relative to Japanese auto makers in the United States that leads to this first scenario. The head-to-head competition between Japanese and American manufacturers in other industries could also be included in this scenario. However, we focus only on the auto industry and its suppliers because of their prominence in the regions that we cover in the book.

In order to make our point more dramatically, we intensify the competition between Japanese and domestic auto manufacturers by assuming that all of the Japanese auto manufacturing plants under construction in the United States come on line in 1991, as predicted. We further assume that 1990 or 1991 represents a downturn in the economy, a downturn that means less of a demand for automobiles at the same time that peak productive capacity is available in the United States. The question is: What will the Japanese and American manufacturers do?

Japanese manufacturers differ from their American counterparts in four important characteristics: (1) their overriding concern with market share; (2) their concern with long-term growth rather than short-term profits; (3) their concern with employment stability; and (4) the organization of the workplace. Japanese and American corporations differ in other ways as well — in size, in their relationship to trading companies, in work hours, and in a whole host of other characteristics. However, we deal with only the first four differences here.

3.1 Market Share

The Japanese corporations, or *kaisha,* are typically regarded as price cutters, willing to sacrifice short-term profits to satisfy their desire for long-term growth and increased market share. Western executives believe that this behavior is reckless, as the Japanese slash prices in bids for increased market. To the *kaisha,* the reach for market share is as much a matter of survival as it is a reach for opportunity. In the high-growth Japanese economy becoming a winner is extraordinarily important. Companies that establish and maintain the cycle of this continued growth have consistently emerged as strong, profitable, and respectable. For a company to become a winner it must increase its market share so that its volume of business will increase at a rate greater than that of its competitors.

3.2 Long-Term Growth

The concern with market share and with the overall growth of the corporation means that Japanese shareholders accept lower profits and dividends than American shareholders would typically accept. The average dividend paid by all major Japanese companies in the mid-1980s was equivalent to a return of about 1.8 percent of the average share price. Toyota's return of dividends over the past five years was only 1.3 percent compared to 7.1 percent for General Motors. Hitachi's return was only 1.7 percent against 4.7 percent for General Electric.

In a study reported by the Japanese government, the corporate objectives of about 500 major U.S. and Japanese companies were compared. Executives of U.S. companies ranked return on investment as the principal corporate objective. Share price increase was ranked second, and market share third. Japanese executives, on the other hand, ranked market share first, return on investment second, and ratio of new products third. There is a distinct cultural difference between the two groups of executives — the Japanese corporations are willing to sacrifice short-term profits for the overall long-term benefit of the firm, while U.S. corporations are not (Abegglen and Stalk, 1985, pp. 168–177).

3.3 Employment Stability

The Japanese system of career employment differs significantly from U.S. corporations. Typically employees are hired directly from school rather than from the open job market. Second, they are hired for their general characteristics rather than for particular skills; third, and most importantly, the employee is expected to remain with the company for a lifelong career. In turn, the employee expects that he or she will not be laid off or discharged. We might add that this system applies largely to men.

While this model does not exactly fit Japanese recruiting practices in the United States for U.S. auto plants, some characteristics are very similar. For example, the consequences of this pattern of employment means that a great deal of time must be taken in the selection of new employees, for a recruiting error is not easily corrected and has long and expensive consequences. This has been the pattern of Japanese hiring in the United States where workers spend more than a week being evaluated for assembly line positions. The leaders of the *kaisha* can and do speak of entry into the company as being born again into another family. Furthermore, like the family, there is a real socialization process that takes place following entry into the firm. Again, the Japanese are attempting to transfer these techniques to manufacturing plants in the United States.

Also, while lifetime employment per se is not a part of Japanese employment in the United States, elements of the concept are. The Japanese transplant NUMMI (New United Motors Manufacturing, Inc.) located in the old GM plant in Fremont, California, offers its workers the strongest job security of any United Auto Workers (UAW) plant anywhere in the United States (Florida, Kenney, and Mair, 1988, p. 6).

3.4 Workplace Organization

The Japanese system of auto production differs significantly from the American system. The typical American system revolves around an assembly line where workers concentrate on a very limited part of the production process (for example, installing windshields). The jobs are very specific — thus there are almost 100 job classifications. There is a strict separation between labor and management. Other characteristics of the American system include "industry-wide unions; adversarial labor-management relations; arm's length relation with suppliers; and vertically integrated, multi-divisional corporate organization" (Florida, Kenney, and Mair, 1988, p. 4).

The Japanese system is very different. The typical Japanese assembly plant has two to four job classifications; workers are organized into self-managing teams; they rotate among jobs and participate in decisions about how to improve manufacturing processes. In addition, Japanese auto manufacturers have very close relationships with their suppliers. It is not unusual to find a Japanese auto employee in a supplier's plant helping to solve problems or improve quality control.

4. Predicted Responses to Sluggish Auto Demand

If both Japanese and American auto manufacturers are true to form, sluggish auto sales, if indeed this occurs in the next several years, will result in very different strategies with potentially very different outcomes. Japanese corporations will undoubtedly use this period to improve the market share of their U.S.-produced vehicles. They are likely to view the downturn as unpleasant (and costly) but also as a window of opportunity to gain market share. This will be done by continuing to produce motor vehicles, albeit not at capacity, and selling below cost in order to stimulate sales.

The expected response of American manufacturers will be dramatically different. With a short-term concern for profits and without the overriding concern with market share, U.S. manufacturers will undoubtedly respond to the recession in the traditional manner — they will drastically curtail production and lay off work2rs. Some may even see the downturn as a convenient way to permanently downsize the automobile portions of their businesses and expand into other areas.

If this scenario occurs, there will be a fundamental shift in market production of automobiles in this country from traditional U.S. manufacturers — General Motors, Ford, and Chrysler Corporation — to a dominance by Japanese-owned or Japanese and American consortia. What we are hypothesizing is the development of a "new" auto industry and a substantial downsizing of the "old" auto industry.

Recent evidence suggests that this is already occurring. Newspaper articles have chronicled the opposing strategies of Japanese and American automakers. For instance, within a day before Mitsubishi announced its Cleveland expansion of new dealerships, Ford announced its first U.S. layoffs since 1983. Other U.S. automakers have followed a similar course. A *Wall Street Journal* article reported that Chrysler had cancelled plans in the first half of 1989 to recall 1,600 laid-off workers due to slow sales (White, 1989).

More recently, Chrysler Chairman Lee Iacocca announced in July 1989 that some 2,300 white-collar workers would lose their jobs before the new year. Iacocca was quite pessimistic:

> The car and truck business in the U.S. is undergoing a dramatic and permanent transformation that puts enormous pressures on all manufacturers to get their programs and costs in line. . . . This is not simply a reaction to the current sales environment [White and Stertz, 1989, p. A1].

The Japanese companies are already gaining market share. After several years of losing out to American auto manufacturers, the Japanese have bounded back. Japan now controls a record 24 percent of the U.S. market — up from 21 percent in 1988. And the Japanese owe much of their success to the fact that they are producing many of their cars here — thus, they are not subject to import quotas.

5. What Does the Future Hold?

What does this scenario hold for the various regional economies of the Midwest? We suggest that it means very different outcomes for the various metropolitan areas. Figure 12–1 shows the Midwest locations of the major automobile assembly plants and their first-tier suppliers. By first

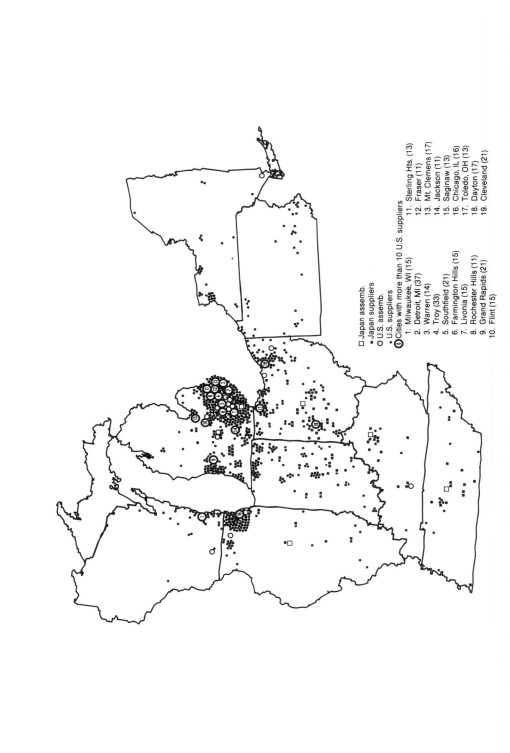

- □ Japan assemb.
- ▪ Japan suppliers
- ○ U.S. assemb.
- • U.S. suppliers
- ⊙ Cities with more than 10 U.S. suppliers

1. Milwaukee, WI (15)	11. Sterling Hts. (13)
2. Detroit, MI (37)	12. Fraser (11)
3. Warren (14)	13. Mt. Clemens (17)
4. Troy (33)	14. Jackson (11)
5. Southfield (21)	15. Saginaw (13)
6. Farmington Hills (15)	16. Chicago, IL (16)
7. Livonia (15)	17. Toledo, OH (13)
8. Rochester Hills (11)	18. Dayton (17)
9. Grand Rapids (21)	19. Cleveland (21)
10. Flint (15)	

tier, we mean those firms that supply their final products to the auto assembly plants.

The Japanese supply system is markedly different from the traditional U.S. system in that the Big Three auto makers have traditionally kept the bulk of their manufacturing in-house. GM, for example, produces about 70 percent of its own parts, while in Japan, suppliers account for about 70 percent of the component parts. In the figure, Big Three parts divisions are depicted as suppliers.

The Japanese supply system is also markedly different from the United States in that the Japanese develop stable arrangements with one or two suppliers as opposed to the typical American practice of multiple sourcing. Japanese suppliers, however, must locate fairly close to the assembly plants they supply because of the "just-in-time" inventory requirement.

There is one final note worthy of mention concerning Japanese suppliers. Most are also Japanese transplants (or consortia) and most hold to the Japanese management practices discussed earlier. (A Japanese auto firm, for example, will not even look at a job application from one of its suppliers' employees.)

There are six Japanese (or consortia) assembly plants in the region and 13 Big Three plants. There are 124 first-tier suppliers to the Japanese firms and 818 suppliers to the Big Three. Once the 158 Big Three parts division are added in, there are a total of 976 U.S. suppliers.

Figure 12–1 thus depicts the two networks between the auto manufacturers and their suppliers. These networks, or belts, form two ellipses. The old auto belt extends from the Milwaukee area through northern Illinois, Indiana, and Ohio; southern Michigan; and northwest New York. The new auto belt stretches from southwest Ontario and southeast Michigan south through Ohio, Kentucky, and Tennessee, and west to Indiana and Illinois. While there is some overlap, there is a distinctive "hinterland" nature to the new auto belt.

Under our scenario, the U.S. assembly plants of the Japanese auto firms will win a substantial increase in market share during the next business cycle. This means that suppliers and area services will also benefit.

Figure 12–1. Midwest locations of the major automobile assembly plants and their first-tier suppliers.

Note: The authors are indebted to Elm International, Inc., East Lansing, MI 48823, a market research and consulting firm specializing in the automotive industry, for providing data on the location of Japanese and U.S. parts suppliers.

Thus Dayton and other economies in the Japanese auto alley will emerge in the next few years stronger than before.

Detroit, Cleveland, Akron, Buffalo, and still, to some extent, the steel cities will not fare nearly so well. Given the dominance of U.S. auto manufacturers and their suppliers in these regions — the old auto industry — one can easily hypothesize a further industrial ratcheting down for the regions. Again, it will be a snowball effect similar to Pittsburgh in the 1980s. When you pull the bottom card out of a house of cards, they all come tumbling down.

U.S. manufacturers are likely to continue past practices. They will try to minimize losses by closing plants, cutting back on production, and laying off workers. Nor is it inconceivable that one or more will follow the lead of USX and diversify to the point that autos become a minor product. If the scenario plays itself out as expected, our old-auto centers will once again go through a wrenching restructuring, much like the steel centers experienced during the last decade. At the same time, the less traditional industrial centers, or the hinterlands, will emerge as the new industrial centers of the Midwest.

6. Increased Midwest Competitiveness by Cutting Labor Costs

The second scenario provides a much less optimistic picture of the Midwest economy and U.S. manufacturing in general. As mentioned earlier, there is little doubt that the United States must reverse its merchandise trade deficit within the next several years in order to begin to ease its foreign-debt burden. The first scenario that we presented accomplished this by increasing trade by being more productive and by producing more competitive products. This second scenario reaches the same end by simply lowering labor costs.

There are two key ingredients to reducing wages relative to foreign competitors. The first is depreciation of the dollar; the second is an actual reduction in manufacturing wages relative to our foreign competitors. We have seen the effects of both factors over the last several years. For example, labor compensation in the United States has increased 3.5 percent during the period 1982 to 1987, while labor compensation in Japan, measured on a U.S. dollar basis, has increased 15.2 percent. In fact, in 1987 U.S. labor experienced the lowest rate of increase of any of its major foreign competitors. The relatively slow growth in U.S. labor compensa-

tion between 1982 and 1987 has resulted primarily from the depreciation
of the dollar since 1985. Wages in the United States and Japan have been
growing at roughly the same pace during this time period, as measured in
their own currencies.

Reduction of labor compensation in the United States relative to our
foreign competitors has dire economic effects on the region, regardless of
how it is achieved. Chief among these is a reduction in the region's standard of living. Although a decrease in the value of the dollar reduces the
cost of our goods sold in foreign markets, which increases exports, it also
increases the price of imports. We rely heavily on foreign countries for
many of our consumer goods, including consumer electronics and components of many of the goods assembled domestically, and so these high
prices figure prominently in a household's budget. A decrease, or at least
a slowdown, in wage increases obviously reduces the purchasing power
of workers.

There is another element to relying on lower labor costs to stimulate
exports. By becoming a low-wage nation, the product mix of U.S. manufacturing and consequently Midwest manufacturing is skewed toward
products that have low value added. Instead of producing and selling
abroad products that embody sophisticated technologies and high-quality
workmanship, we will be producing goods that are labor-intensive and
little value added. The evidence presented in the preceding chapters that
the high-growth manufacturing sectors are the ones with the lowest wage
growth supports this view.

James Galbraith provides a somber assessment of wage-cutting
approach:

> We cannot maintain a comparative advantage in our older, consumer-oriented
> manufacturing industries at the present national living standards. If we are to
> become an ordinary industrial power, we will be forced to live on ordinary
> industrial wages. The industrial structure and patterns of employment and
> profitability that suited us well in the 1950s — when automobiles were (rela-
> tively) high-tech and Korea, Yugoslavia and Spain were still peasant back-
> waters devastated by recent wars — can be sustained in the 1990s only
> at the price of a growing, and ultimately destructive, reliance on products
> designed and built with other nations' means of production [1989,
> p. 25].

The second scenario has the Midwest producing its traditional goods
within the traditional manufacturing centers, but at wages that are more
in line with workers in newly developed countries.

7. Conclusion

We are pleased with the results of the efforts of the contributors to this book in assisting us to understand the economic restructuring of the American Midwest. The studies point out one thing with amazing clarity — the "region" is composed of a number of very different economies. Chicago is an international city and stands by itself. Syracuse reflects the national economy. Pittsburgh and Youngstown are still trying to recover from the collapse of the traditional steel industry in the United States. Detroit, Buffalo, Akron, Cleveland, and Milwaukee continue to struggle with the decline of their bread-and-butter industries — durable goods. And Dayton is basking in the sunlight of the "new" auto industry.

But so what? Why is it necessary to understand local economic regions and a geographic region such as the Midwest? Wilbur Thompson holds that ". . . a state is a federation of local economies." If this is true, then is not a geographic region the sum of its economies? The answer is no! The geographic region is identified by the interaction of its local economies.

Let us illustrate by returning briefly to our discussion of the auto industry. Assume that the Honda plant in Marysville, Ohio, gains an additional 2 percent market share. The plant and its suppliers thrive, and employment in the Dayton region increases by 3,000 jobs. At the same time the plant in Cleveland, Ohio, loses 2 percent market share, and the plant and its suppliers contract, resulting in the loss of 3,000 jobs in the Cleveland area. The overall change in Ohio is nil. Thus an additive model, which suggests that a geographic region is composed of the sum of the activity, is erroneous. It masks a massive interaction of sectors and regions and a resulting regional restructuring. A new auto industry is emerging in southern Ohio and an old auto industry is dying in northern Ohio. And yet judging by a statewide analysis of employment by SIC, the industry would appear to be stagnant. We thus contend that the only real way to understand the economy of geographic regions is by examining the economic activities of each region.

But what of the future? A belief that American management has become "leaner and meaner," more productive, and willing to take an aggressive stance toward foreign competitors leads one to have an optimistic view of the short-term economic future of the Midwest. On the other hand, a belief that American management is still a "complacent competitor" makes one quite pessimistic.

We have presented two extreme scenarios in the preceding pages. One suggests a significant restructuring of Midwest manufacturing, improving product quality, and adopting new technology. The other suggests that the region will simply revert to a low-value, low-skill manufacturing area, with lower wages and a lower standard of living.

What will decide the fate of the Midwest? Much of what happens to Midwest manufacturing will depend on whether U.S. companies are willing to change their attitudes toward research and development (R&D) and the planning horizon for the development and commercial implementation of new technologies. At present, corporations have a strong incentives, partially driven by the financial community's fixation with short-run returns, to give priority to short-run profit-maximizing strategies over long-run ones. As a result of this corporate viewpoint, research and development is considered more of a current expense than a long-run investment, reducing their commitment to develop products that embody new technologies and thus their products' superiority in the international marketplace.

Several proposals have been put forth over the ast several years to reform the tax structure in order to promote private industry's research and development efforts. It is uncertain at this time how successful proponents of these reforms will be in getting these measures passed through Congress and how successful the legislated incentives will be in inducing more privately funded research and development. What is certain is that the challenge facing U.S. manufacturing and the Midwest economy is to increase the quality and technological sophistication of the products they produce so that this region can maintain the relatively high standard of living it has enjoyed as America's industrial heartland.

Acknowledgments

The authors wish to thank Edward Hill, David Perry, and Donald Iannone for comments on an earlier version of this chapter.

REFERENCES

Abbegglen, James C. and George Stalk, Jr. *Kaisha, the Japanese Corporation.* New York: Basic Books, 1985.

Abernathy, William J., Kim B. Clark, and Alan M. Kantrow, *Industrial Renaissance.* New York: Basic Books, 1983.

Ahlbrandt, Roger S. and Clyde Weaver, "Public-Private Institutions and Advanced Technology Development in Southwestern Pennsylvania." *Journal of the American Planning Association* 53, 4 (1987):449–458.

Akron Beacon Journal. "Job Losses Slight in Local Tire Industry." January 9, 1989, C6.

—————. "Firestone Producing Akron Tires, City's Lost Love Gets New Chance." April 9, 1989, A1, A5.

Akron Department of Planning and Urban Renewal. "A Perspective on the International Center for Rubber and Chemicals." The City of Akron, November 1965.

Akron Ohio Historical Committee. *Centennial History of Akron, 1825–1925.* Akron, OH: The Summit County Historical Society, 1925.

Allen, David N. and Victor Levine. *Nurturing Advanced Technology Enterprises.* New York: Praeger, 1986.

Apgar, William C. and H. James Brown. *Microeconomics and Public Policy.* Glenview, IL: Scott, Foresman and Company, 1987.

Bell, Daniel. *The Coming of Post-Industrial Society: A Venture in Social Forecasting.* New York: Basic Books, 1973.

326 ECONOMIC RESTRUCTURING OF THE AMERICAN MIDWEST

Bensman, D. and R. Lynch. *Rusted Dreams*. New York: McGraw Hill, 1987.

Berry, Brian J.L., Susan W. Sanderson, Shelby Stewman, and Joel Tarr. "The Nation's Most Livable City: Pittsburgh's Transformation." In Gary Gappert (ed.), *The Future of Winter Cities*. Beverly Hills: Sage, 1987, pp. 173–197.

Bluestone, Barry and Bennett Harrison. *The Deindustrialization of America*. New York: Basic Books, 1982.

Bradbury, Katherine L. "The Shrinking Middle Class." *New England Economic Review*, (September/October 1986): 41–55.

Brown, H. James. "Shift-Share Projections of Regional Economic Growth." *Journal of Regional Science* 9, 1 (February 1969): 1–18.

Browning, Harley L. and Joachim Singlemann. "The Transformation of the U.S. Labor Force: The Interaction of Industry and Occupation." *Politics and Society* 8, 3–4 (1978): 481–509.

Buffalo News. "New York Leads Nation in Manufacturing Job Loss." May 28, 1987, C8.

Buss, Terry F. and F. Stevens Redburn. *Shutdown at Youngstown*. Albany: State University of New York Press, 1983.

Buss, Terry B. and Roger J. Vaughan. "Revitalizing the Mahoning Valley." *Environment and Planning C: Government and Policy* 5 (1987): 433–446.

Chinitz, Benjamin. "Contrasts in Agglomeration: New York and Pittsburgh." *American Economic Review* 50 (1961): 279–289.

Cohen, Stephen S. and John Zysman. *Manufacturing Matters*. New York: Basic Books, 1987.

Cole, Robert. *The American Automobile Industry: Rebirth or Requiem?* Ann Arbor: Center for Japanese Studies, The University of Michigan, 1984.

Cole, Sam, et al. "The Food Processing Industry in Western New York." SUNY-Buffalo Center for Regional Studies, August 1987.

Doolittle, Fred C. "Adjustments in Buffalo's Labor Market." *FRBNY Quarterly Review* 10, 4 (Winter 1985–86): 28–37.

Dornbusch, Rudiger, Paul Krugman, and Yung Chul Park. "Meeting World Challenges: U.S. Manufacturing in the 1990s." Eastman Kodak Company, Rochester, New York, 1989.

Dunn, Edgar S., Jr. "A Statistical and Analytical Technique for Regional Analysis." *Papers, Regional Science Association* 6 (1960): 97–112.

Dustin, Jack L., James L. Shanahan, and Peter E. Challis. "Polymer Technology, Innovation and Economic Development." Center for Urban Studies, The University of Akron, 1985.

Erceg, John J. and Theodore G. Bernard. "Productivity, Costs, and International Competitiveness." *Economic Commentary*, Federal Reserve Bank of Cleveland, (November 15, 1988.)

Esteban-Marquillas, J.M. "A Reinterpretation of Shift-Share Analysis." *Regional and Urban Economics* 2 (1972): 249–255.

Executive Office of the President, Office of Management and Budget. *Standard Industrial Classification Manual, 1987*. Washington, DC: U.S. Government Printing Office, 1987.

Federal Reserve Bank of Cleveland. "Common Bonds, Divergent Paths: An Economic Perspective of Four Cities." Cleveland, 1986.

Fitzgerald, Joan. "Class and Community Convergency Grassroots Movements: The Case of Tri-State Conference on Steel." Unpublished Ph.D. dissertation, The Pennsylvania State University, 1988.

Fitzgerald, Joan. "The Role of Community-Based Social Movements in Promoting Economic Restructuring in the U.S." Paper presented at the 29th annual meeting of the Association of Collegiate Schools of Planning, Los Angeles, 1988.

Flaim, P. and E. Sehgal. "Displaced Workers of 1979–1983: How Well Have They Fared?" *Monthly Labor Review* (June 1985): 3–16.

Florida, Richard, Martin Kenney, and Andrew Mair. "The Transplant Phenomenon: Japanese Auto Manufacturers in the United States." *Economic Development Commentary* 12 (Winter 1988): 3–9.

Flynn, Sharon A. "The Greater Cleveland Polymer Survey." Cleveland: The Greater Cleveland Growth Association, 1989.

Fuchs, Victor R. *The Growing Importance of the Service Industries*. Washington, DC: National Bureau of Economic Research, 1965.

Galbraith, James K. *Balancing Acts: Technology, Finance and the American Future*. New York: Basic Books, 1989.

Giese, Alenka S. and William A. Testa. "Can Industrial R&D Survive the Decline of Production Activity: A Case Study of the Chicago Area." *Economic Development Quarterly* 2 (November 1988): 326–338.

Glasmeier, Amy, Peter Hall, and Ann Markusen. "Can Anyone Have a Piece of the High Tech Pie?" *Berkeley Planning Journal* 1 (1986).

Goe, W. Richard. "Economic Transition and Population Decline: Implications of Migration Patterns for the Akron PMSA." *Ohio Economic Trends Review* (forthcoming).

Goldman, Mark. *High Hopes: The Rise and Decline of Buffalo*. Albany, NY: SUNY Press, 1983.

Great Lakes Commission. *The Great Lakes Economy: A Resource and Industry Profile of the Great Lakes States*. Chicago, IL: Federal Reserve Bank of Chicago, October 1985.

Gurwitz, Aaron S. and G. Thomas Kingsley. *The Cleveland Metropolitan Economy*. Santa Monica, CA: The Rand Corporation, 1982.

Hadeshian, Manoog and David Perry. "The Auto Industry in Western New York: An Impact Analysis." Buffalo: Center for Regional Studies, SUNY at Buffalo, 1988.

Harringston, James W. and John Lombardo. "Growth, Location, and Economic Role of Producer Services in Western New York." Department of Geography, SUNY at Buffalo, June 1987.

Harrison, B. "The Tendency Toward Instability and Inequality Underlying the Revival of New England." *Papers of the Regional Science Association* 50 (1982): 41–65.

Harrison, Bennett and Barry Bluestone. *The Great U-Turn: Corporate Restructuring and the Polarizing of America*. New York: Basic Books, 1988.

Heil, Shara L. "1989 Industrial Patterns Survey." Center for Urban Studies, The University of Akron, 1989.

————— and Elizabeth Dahl Voth. "1987 Industrial Patterns Survey." Center for Urban Studies, The University of Akron, 1987.

Hill, Edward W. and Thomas Bier. "Economic Restructuring: Earnings, Occupations and Housing Values in Cleveland." *Economic Development Quarterly* 3,2 (May 1989): 123–144.

Hoerr, John P. *And the Wolf Finally Came.* Pittsburgh: University of Pittsburgh Press, 1988.

Horrigan, Michael W. and Steven E. Haugen. "The Declining Middle Class Thesis: A Sensitivity Analysis." *Monthly Labor Review* 111,5 (May 1988): 3–13.

Howland, Marie. *Plant Closings and Worker Displacement: The Regional Issues.* Kalamazoo, MI: The W.E. Upjohn Institute of for Employment Research, 1988.

Iannone, Donald T. "Policy Implications of Foreign Business Recruitment Strategy: The Case of Japanese Automotive Company Investment in the United States." *Economic Development Review* 6,3 (Fall 1988): 25–39.

Jackson, James S. "Behind the Front Page: A Newsman Looks at Akron." Akron, OH: Summit County Historical Society, 1986.

Jacobs, Jane. *The Economy of Cities.* New York: Random House, 1970.

Jacobson, Louis. "Labor Mobility and Structural Change in Pittsburgh, 1977–1982." *Journal of the American Planning Association* 53,4 (1987): 438–448.

—————. "Structural Change in the Pennsylvania Economy." Unpublished manuscript, The W.E. Upjohn Institute for Employment Research, Kalamazoo, MI, December 12, 1988.

Kraushaar, Robert, et al. "Indicators of Maturity: An Examination of Large Manufacturing Establishments in Western New York." SUNY-Buffalo Center for Regional Studies, August 1987.

Kraushaar, Robert and Marshall M.A. Feldman. "Industrial Restructuring and the Limits of Industrial Data: Examples from Western New York." *Regional Studies* 23, 1 (1989): 49–62.

Kutscher, Robert E. "Structural Change of Employment in the United States." In Wray O. Candillus (ed.), *United States Service Industries Handbook.* New York: Praeger, 1988, pp. 23–44.

Lawrence, Robert Z. "Changes in U.S. Industrial Structure: The Role of Global Forces, Secular Trends, and Transitory Cycles." In *Industrial Change and Public Policy,* a symposium sponsored by The Federal Reserve Bank of Kansas City. Kansas City: Federal Reserve Bank of Kansas City, 1983, pp. 29–77.

Leahy, Peter and Gail Sommers. "The Composition of the Akron PMSA Labor Force." Center for Urban Studies, The University of Akron, 1988.

Ledebur, Larry C. and Terry F. Buss. *Industrial Development in the Mahoning Valley.* Youngstown, OH: Youngstown Area Chamber of Commerce, 1986.

Lurcott, Robert H. and Jane A. Downing. "A Public-Private Support System for Community-Based Organizations in Pittsburgh." *Journal of the American Planning Association* 53,4 (1987): 459–468.

Malecki, Edward J. "Industrial Location and Corporate Organization in High Tech Industries." *Economic Geography* (October 1985).

Markusen, Ann Roell. *Profit Cycles, Oligopoly and Regional Development.* Cambridge, MA: The MIT Press, 1985.

—————. "Neither Ore, nor Coal, nor Markets: A Policy-Oriented View of Steel Sites in the U.S." *Regional Studies* 20 (1986): 449–462.

—————, Peter Hall, and Amy Glasmeier. *High Tech America.* Boston: Allen and Unwin, 1986.

—————, and Karen McCurdy. "Chicago's Defense-Based High Technology: A Case Study of the 'Seedbeds of Innovation' Hypothesis." *Economic Development Quarterly* 3, 1 (February 1989): 15–31.

—————, and Virginia Carlson. "Losses in the Heartland." *Northeast Midwest Economic Review* 2 (May 1, 1989): 8–13.

Massey, Doreen. *Spatial Divisions of Labor: Social Structures and the Geography of Production.* New York: Methuen, 1984.

Mueller, H.G. "The Steel Industry." *The Annals of the American Academy of Political and Social Science* 460 (1982): 73–82.

—————. "The Changing Position in the International Steel Market." In M. Hochmuth and W. Davidson (eds.), *Revitalizing American Industry: Lessons from Our Competitors.* Cambridge, MA: Ballinger, 1984, pp. 213–262.

New York State, Department of Commerce. *Official Population Projections for New York State Counties: 1980–2010.* State Data Center, April 1985.

Noyelle, Thierry J. and Thomas M. Stanback, Jr. *The Economic Transformation of American Cities.* Totowa, NJ: Rowan & Allanheld, 1983.

Ohio Writers Project. *The Ohio Guide.* Washington, DC: Works Progress Administration, 1940.

Orth, Samuel P. *A History of Cleveland, Ohio.* Chicago: The S.J. Clarke Publishing Company, 1910.

Perry, David C. "The Politics of Dependency in Deindustrialized America: The Case of Buffalo, New York." In Michael Peter Smith and Joe R. Feagin (eds.), *The Capitalist City: Global Restructuring and Community Politics.* Oxford: Basil Blackwell, 1987, pp. 113–137.

Phillips, Robyn Swaim and Avis C. Vidal. "The Growth and Restructuring of Metropolitan Economies." *Journal of the American Planning Association* 49, 3 (Summer 1983): 1979.

Pound, Arthur. *Detroit: Dynamic City.* New York: Appleton-Century Company, 1940.

Reeves, Marilyn. "Issues in the Development of Tourism: Applications in Western New York." SUNY-Buffalo Center for Regional Studies, 1988.

Reich, Robert. *The Next American Frontier.* New York: Times Books, 1983.

Satterthwaite, Mark. "Location Patterns of High-Growth Firms: Considering the Role of Relevant Cost Factors." *Commentary* (Spring 1988): 7–11.

Sebastian, Pamela. "Buffalo N.Y.: Shows How Workers and Jobs Get Out of Alignment." *Wall Street Journal* 212,54 (September 16, 1988).

Shanahan, James L. "Economic Transition In the Akron Plus Region: Future

Prospects for Jobs and Population." Center for Urban Studies, The University of Akron, 1986.

———— and David Parry. "Polymer-Related Industry Growth for the Akron Plus Region: Assessing Job Prospects for the Future." Center for Urban Studies, The University of Akron, 1986.

Shapira, Phillip. "Recent Research on Manufacturing Sectors and the Trade Deficit." Presentation at the Department of Design and Planning, SUNY-Buffalo, Spring 1988.

Stanback, Thomas M., Jr. and Thierry J. Noyelle. *Cities in Transition: Changing Job Structures in Atlanta, Denver, Buffalo, Phoenix, Columbus (Ohio), Nashville, Charlotte.* Totowa, NJ: Allanheld, Osmun, 1982.

Stigler, George. "The Division of Labor is Limited by the Extent of the Market." *Journal of Political Economy* 59, 3 (June 1951).

Thompson, Wilbur. *A Preface to Urban Economics.* Baltimore: Johns Hopkins, 1965.

————. "Internal and External Factors in the Development of Urban Economies." In Harvey S. Perloff and Lowden Wingo (eds.), *Issues in Urban Economics.* Baltimore: Johns Hopkins, 1968, pp. 43–61.

Tiffany, P.A. *The Decline of American Steel.* New York: Oxford University Press, 1988.

U.S. Congress, Office of Technology Assessment. *Paying the Bill: Manufacturing and America's Trade Deficit.* Washington, DC: U.S. Government Printing Office, June 1988. OTA-ITE-390.

UAW-GM, Human Resources Center. *Local Paid Educational Leave Manual.* 1988.

Van Tassel, David D. and John J. Grabowski. *The Encyclopedia of Cleveland History.* Bloomington: Indiana University Press, 1987.

Voth, Elizabeth Dahl. "Economic Outlook for Service Firms in Akron/Canton." Center for Urban Studies, The University of Akron, 1985.

Waite, Charles A. "Service Sector: Its Importance and Prospects for the Future." In Wray O. Candilis (ed.), *United States Service Industries Handbook.* New York: Praeger, 1988, pp. 1–22.

Walker, Richard A. "Is There a Service Economy?" The Changing Capitalist Division of Labor." *Science & Technology* 49, 1 (Spring 1985: 42–83.

Wall Street Journal. "Goodyear to Build $80 Million Plant for Radial Tires." February, 24, 1977, 46.

————. "Union May Strike Big Four Tire Producers Next Week Over Wages and Job Security." April 16, 1976, 24.

————. "Rubber Workers Strike Enters sixth Week Amid Signs Pressure for Settlement Lags." May 27, 1976, 5.

————. "Nonunion Rubber Plants Help Lift Hopes of Averting Strike in Current Labor Talks." March 16, 1979, 42.

————. "General Tire To End Output at Akron, Ohio." March 2, 1982, 4.

————. "How Union, Tire Firms Cushioned Selves From Strike Impact, Prolonging Walkout." August 20, 1976, 26.

Warner, Paul D. "Alternative Strategies for Economic Development." *Urban Affairs Quarterly* 24, 3 (March 1989): 389–411.

White, Joseph B. "Chrysler Scraps Plans to Recall 1,600 Workers." *Wall Street Journal* (May 24, 1989b): A2.

———— and Bradley A. Stertz. "Auto Makers Drive into a Mess as Plants Expand and Sales Fall." *Wall Street Journal* (July 28, 1989): A1, A4.

Winger, Alan R. *The Ohio Economy: Past, Present and Future.* Cincinnati Federal Home Loan Bank, April 1989.

Wolman, Harold and Kenneth Voytek. "State Government as a Consultant for Local Economic Development." A paper presented at the annual meeting of the Southern Regional Science Association, Chapel Hill, North Carolina, April 29, 1989.

Wright State University and The Dayton Area Progress Council. *Community Factors Evaluation Project.* Dayton OH: Area Progress Council, October 1987.

AUTHOR
BIOGRAPHICAL SKETCHES

Akron

James L. Shanahan is director of The Center for Urban Studies and is professor of urban studies at the University of Akron. His economic research includes economic change in industrial-based urban areas, technology-based economic growth, and the restructuring of urban economics as service-based economics.

W. Richard Goe is with the Center for Economic Development at Carnegie Mellon University. His current research interests include economic restructuring and regional development.

Buffalo

Robert Kraushaar is director of the Bureau of Economic and Demographic Information of the New York State Department of Economic Development. Previously, he taught at the State University of New York (SUNY) at Buffalo. He is a senior research associate in the Center for Regional Studies at SUNY Buffalo.

David C. Perry is holder of the Albert A. Levine Chair of Urban Studies and Public Service at Cleveland State University. He is the author or editor of a variety of books and mongraphs on urban policy and social and economic change in the city.

Chicago

David R. Allardice is vice president and assistant director of research at the Federal Reserve Bank of Chicago, where he heads the bank's Urban-Regional Economics Section. He is also president of Illinois Economic Database, Inc., a not-for-profit corporation established to provide labor-market data. He has directed major economic development studies and has written articles for several publications.

Wim Wiewel is director, Center for Urban Economic Development, and assistant professor, School of Urban Planning and Policy, University of Illinois at Chicago. His articles have appeared in *Economic Development Quarterly, Administrative Science Quarterly,* and *The Journal of the American Planning Association.* He is currently editing a book with Pierre Clavel, *Economic Policy and Neighborhood Organization in Chicago, 1983–1987,* to be published by Rutgers University.

Wendy Wintermute is an economic development planner at the Center for Urban Economic Development, University of Illinois at Chicago. Her policy research interests focus on income, work, and economic development. She is also an instructor in community development and research at the University of Chicago, School of Social Service Administration. Her Ph.D. is in sociology and social work from the University of Michigan.

Cleveland

Edward W. Hill is assistant professor of Urban Studies and Public Administration at the Maxine Goodman Levin College of Urban Affairs, Cleveland State University. He is also an associate editor of the Economic Development Quarterly.

Dayton

John P. Blair, professor of economics, Wright State University, received his Ph.D. from West Virginia University. Prior to joining Wright State, he was a policy analyst in the Department of Housing and Urban Development. He has written numerous books and articles on urban economics, real estate, and public policy. Currently, he is working on a textbook titled *Urban and Regional Economics*.

Rudy Fichtenbaum, associate professor of economics, Wright State University, received his Ph.D. from the University of Missouri — Columbia. His current research interests are in the areas of labor economics research and regional development. He has published articles in the *Journal of Business and Economic Statistics, Eastern Economic Journal, Growth and Change*, and *Urban Affairs Quarterly*.

Detroit

Harold Wolman is professor of political science and research scholar, Center for Urban Studies, in the College of Urban Labor and Metropolitan Affairs at Wayne State University. Professor Wolman's previous positions include visiting professor in the Department of Politics at the University of Salford (England) and senior research associate at The Urban Institute in Washington, D.C. His research interests include urban policy and politics, public finance, housing policy, and economic development.

Kenneth P. Voytek is an economist with the Center for Local Economic Competitiveness, Michigan Department of Commerce; he was a research associate with The Urban Institute in Washington, D.C. His work has focused on issues relating to general policy analysis and evaluation, and on a variety of policy areas, including economic development and government service delivery.

Milwaukee

Sammis B. White is director of the Urban Research Center and an associate professor of urban planning at the University of Wisconsin — Milwaukee. Along with Richard Bingham he is a co-founder and co-editor of *Economic Development Quarterly*. White's main research interests lies in economic development, education, and housing.

James R. Paetsch is a program analyst for the Legislative Audit Bureau of the state of Wisconsin. Paetsch's research interests lie in local economic development and program evaluation.

Pittsburgh

Joan Fitzgerald is assistant professor of city and regional planning at Ohio State University. Her current research interests include local economic development practice and politics. She is currently conducting research on state efforts to assist the informal sector in Jamaica.

Syracuse

Michael Wasylenko is professor of economics and associate director of the Metropolitan Studies Program at the Maxwell School of Syracuse University. He has written numerous papers on economic development and on state and local fiscal issues. He recently co-directed a comprehensive tax study for the state of Nebraska.

Youngstown

David Gemmel is a research associate at the St. Elizabeth Hospital Medical Center in Youngstown, Ohio, and a doctoral candidate in political science at Kent State University. His current research interests include modeling the economic impact of hospitals on local economies.

Terry F. Buss is a professor of urban studies at the University of Akron, specializing in economic development, welfare policy, and health care. His latest books include *Hidden Unemployment: Public Policy for Discouraged Workers,* coauthored with Steve Redburn, and *On the Rebound: Helping Workers Cope with Plant Closings,* coauthored with Roger Vaughn. He is now at work on two books, one on urban policy and the other on welfare policy.

Co-Editors

Richard D. Bingham is professor of public administration and urban studdies and senior research scholar of the Urban Center, Cleveland State University. His latest books include *Evaluation in Practice: A Methodological Approach* (Longman, 1989) with Claire L. Felbinger and *The Homeless in Contemporary Society* (Sage, 1987) edited with Sammis B. White and Roy E. Green. He is co-editor of the journal *Economic Development Quarterly.*

Randall W. Eberts is assistant vice president and economist at the Federal Reserve Bank of Cleveland. He heads the research unit for applied microeconomics and regional economic analysis. Prior to joining the bank in 1986, he was an associate professor of economics at the University of Oregon. He has published numerous articles in academic journals on issues related to local public finance, labor unions, productivity, and regional economic development.